The Unconscious and the Id

A volume of Laplanche's *Problématiques*

by

Jean Laplanche

with

The Unconscious: A Psychoanalytic Study

by Jean Laplanche & Serge Leclaire

translated by

Luke Thurston with Lindsay Watson

REBUS PRESS

First edition 1999

Printed in Great Britain

Rebus Press
76 Haverstock Hill
LONDON
NW3 2BE

ISBN 1 900877 03 1

CONTENTS

A NOTE ON TEXTS

All references to Freud's writings are based on *The Standard Edition of the Complete Psychological Works of Sigmund Freud* (24 volumes), translated by James Strachey, published by Hogarth Press and the Institute of Psycho-Analysis (1961).

A Note on Problématiques

This volume is the fourth in the series published under the title *Problématiques* between 1980 and 1987. They are based on lectures delivered at the University of Paris between 1970 and 1979. The term 'problematic' as a noun is not widely used in English nor does it belong to traditional psychoanalytic terminology. It has had a certain currency in France in the work of Georges Canghuilhem and Gaston Bachelard in the History and Philosophy of Science[1]. The English language reader is most likely to be familiar with the term in the work of the Marxist philosopher, Louis Althusser, so influential in political and cultural theory in Britain from the late 1960's to the early 1980's.

Particular theoretical problems and the terms and concepts cannot be understood by themselves as free-standing entities. They belong to and derive their meaning from a conceptual system or field, a problematic, that is structured as much by absences and blindnesses, by what it excludes as by what it includes. The history of science is thus conceived not just as the accumulation of empirical discoveries but as the theoretical transformation of the underlying problematics. In Althusser's reading of Marx, it is associated with the notion of an 'epistemological break' , the moment when work on the internal contradictions of a problematic allows the exit from a pre-scientific or ideological problematic to a new problematic in which a properly scientific object of theoretical analysis is formulated.

In his systematic reading of Freud as it is presented in the five volumes of the *Problématiques,* Laplanche exemplifies a different understanding of the development of the psychoanalytic field. In his introduction to the first volume of the series Laplanche explicitly refuses Althusser's rationalist notion of an 'epistemological break' for its assumption of a linear—albeit discontinuous—progress of scientific thought.[2] He counterposes to Althusser's notion the Freudian concept of Nachträglichkeit, translated by Strachey in the *Standard Edition* as 'deferred action' but for which Laplanche suggests the new translation 'afterwardsness'.[3] As against the 'epistemological break' with its definitive dialectical rupture with the past, Laplanche invokes the temporality first formulated by Freud in his account of the action of hysterical trauma in which the first appearance of the symptom translates and reactivates an unintegrated and excessive element that has been inscribed in an earlier moment. So Laplanche interprets the movement of Freud's thought through the figure of the spiral rather than that of a linear progress, in which later concepts after the so-called turning point of 1920—such as the ego or the death drive—reprise certain earlier elements that have been lost or displaced from the psychoanalytic field. Associating the term 'problematic' with both 'history' and 'structure', he is concerned not just with the emergence and chronological development of individual concepts but with the structural transformations of the conceptual field in which they function.[4]

Laplanche thus formulates his own distinctive mode of reading and interpretation of Freud's work by 'putting Freud to work' in the reading of Freud. He invokes Freud's analysis of dreams and symptoms, in which the manifest text is segmented into certain components each with its chain of associations that leads to repeated knots, impasses, unconscious sequences and fantasies, as a guide to an interpretation of the detours, contradictory reversals and repetitions of Freudian methapsychology.[5]

Despite Freud's affiliation of psychoanalysis with the Copernican revolution as a break from the Ptolemaic model of a universe centred on 'man'—the human subject—to a de-centred, infinite universe, Laplanche demonstrates that 'if Freud is his own Copernicus, he is also his own Ptolemy'.[6] He traces Freud's continual oscillation between concepts and arguments that pose a radical decentering of the human psyche in relation to a primordial other (not the Lacanian Other but the parent or adult 'of personal prehistory' in Freud's phrase), on the one hand, and a continually resurgent movement of Ptolemaic recentering that either abandons those elements or draws them back into an endogenous model of psychic life. Laplanche has demonstrated that Freud's key concepts—the ego, narcissism, the unconscious, repression, the drive—are marked by an alternation between distinct and competing problematics in which an original, decentering 'Copernican break' is covered over by a recentering revision that initiates a certain 'going astray'[7] of the concept along structurally determined lines.

The originality of Laplanche is to grasp both movements of thought, both the breakthrough and the going astray, as governed by a theoretical necessity (*exigence*) that governs the field of Freud's thought and is determined by its object: the human psyche and its formation. These wanderings astray are magnetised and drawn by the human object of inquiry even when they lead to an impasse. The perpetual recentering in Freud's thought of an original other-centered breakthrough—essentially the formulation of the seduction theory and its constellated concepts in the years 1895-7—replicates the movement of just such a covering over and recentering in the human subject itself. The terms 'problematic' , 'going-astray' and 'exigency' belong together in Laplanche's symptomatic reading of the Freudian oeuvre. Their mutual implication can be summed up in Laplanche's parodic restatement of Haeckel's Law—'ontogenesis (the development of the human being) recapitulates phylogenesis (the development of the human species)'—of which Freud was so enamoured (often to such disastrous effect). 'Laplanche's Law' states that 'theoreticogenesis', the development of theory, reproduces ontogenesis, the narcissistic—Ptolemaic—recentering in the human subject of its foundational other-centredness.

John Fletcher
University of Warwick

[1] See the account in Dominique Lecourt, (1975) *Marxism and Epistemology*, London: New Left Books.

[2] Laplanche, J., (1980) *Problématiques I: L'angoisse*, Paris: Presses Universitaires de France p.14.

[3] See 'Notes on Afterwardsness' in *Essays on Otherness*, (1999) ed. John Fletcher, London: Routledge.

[4] 'Foreword' to Laplanche, J. and Pontalis, J.-B., *The Language of Psychoanalysis*, (1973) London: Hogarth p.xii. The English translation, however, in converting the French noun problématique in the English adjective 'a problematic area', loses the methodological specificity of the concept.

[5] Laplanche, J., 'Interpéter (avec) Freud' (1968), reprinted in *La révolution copernicienne inachevée*, (1992) Paris: Aubier.

[6] The Unfinished Copernican Revolution' in *Essays on Otherness* (1999) ed. John Fletcher, London: Routledge, p.60.

[7] Laplanche elevates the term fourvoiement —wandering or going astray —to the status of a methodological concept in the analysis of the Freudian oeuvre. cf. *Le fourvoiement biologisant de la sexualité chez Freud*, (1993) Paris: Synthélabo, pp.3-12.

Foreword to the French Edition

Since 1962, at the École Normale and at the Sorbonne, and since 1969 in the Department of the Clinical Human Sciences (Sorbonne-University Paris VII), I have pursued and opened to the public through my teaching a series of interpretations and problematisations, following certain major axes of psychoanalytic theory. The lectures I have given since 1970-71 have been collected[1] under the general title *Problématiques*. This originally spoken text has suffered no alterations, apart from those necessary for printed publication.

The themes of the successive years are linked according to no premeditated logic. The route was determined only by its content, and by my own personal development. It is only with hindsight that I was able to discern the possibility of re-grouping them in a certain number of volumes, without too much artifice.

The beginning of an annual course is usually inaugurated by a rather long methodological introduction. These introductions, printed in italics, mean that I do not have to re-rehearse those ideas here. They provide an account of a continuing reflection on the way I have proceeded, as well as on the legitimacy of pursuing such proceedings 'at the University'.

There is no doubt that the reader, according to his or her disposition and receptivity, will react to this publication in one of two ways. The classicism of the ideas, the frequent recourse to critical commentary, the returns and repetitions (governed by the fact that, each year, I was for the most part addressing a new audience) may mean that these texts are judged to be an extreme example of the much-maligned 'Freudian exegesis'. But maybe—if the reader can find in him or herself a certain amount of patience and benevolence, in order to fall in with me at my own pace, then he or she may become receptive to certain moments of deepening understanding or insight; to an attempt to approach theory whilst also taking account of analytic method; to a way of causing certain hinges to grate ear-piercingly; to a history of particular concepts. Through this method of rendering the doctrine problematic, yet also exploring its historical and clinical dimensions, the configuration of a new set of themes appears in outline.

I

REFERENCE TO THE UNCONSCIOUS

8 November 1977
Teaching Psychoanalysis at the University

Each year I offer you a sort of methodological preface, which I prefer to be brief, but which always requires, in the end, some elaboration. You will find the trace of this in the published version of these lectures.[1] *In particular, to be precise, you will find a thoroughgoing reflection on the sense of what* 'teaching psychoanalysis in the University' *can actually mean, according to each of its three components: Teaching, Psychoanalysis and University.*

Teaching: what can constitute a teaching worthy of the name? After all, it is not only psychoanalysis that deserves a teaching which is not a mere rehashing, a repetition. This is something already demanded at the level of the human sciences, and equally at that of their venerable mother, philosophy. That is to say, a teaching worthy of the name, wherever it is practised, in the human sciences and in philosophy (and from this point of view I make no distinction for the moment) can only be an integral part of a research programme. It may consist of the formal presentation of some current research which might be pursued partly in another field, or it may itself be the locus of its elaboration. The present teaching is where my own research crystallises—enriched as it is, obviously, by the daily experience of analysis.

'Teaching psychoanalysis'. *I have discussed at great length all the prejudices and accusations levelled at this formula in various milieus, but particularly in the analytic milieu; a prejudice which has found expression in an opposition which is not so new as is claimed, that of knowledge and truth. Psychoanalysis is supposed to be the locus of truth, while knowledge would only be the way of defending oneself, of congealing this truth. If the opposition is by no means new (it dates from very long ago: think of Socrates or the Socratics, of their methodological demand to know nothing in order to have access to a certain truth), it has certainly found a new vigour in respect to psychoanalysis and the precise demonstration of the defence mechanisms enabled by knowledge. It is nonetheless true that although all truth can certainly be congealed in knowledge, at the same time there can be no emergence of truth without the initial support of a certain knowledge. And I have had occasion to recall that the most recent thinker to have taken up this opposition—I am speaking of Lacan—has more than once emphasised that this formula becomes*

severely corrupted if it is used as an alibi in order to justify pure and simple ignorance. Nonetheless, to go and teach wherever the wind blows—the wind that blows one toward analytic societies, toward conferences, or indeed to a university . . . Well, I am not saying that psychoanalysis cannot be taught. The problem is to discover how such teaching can be deemed worthy in relation to its object, that object which for the moment we will qualify, very broadly, as 'the unconscious'. This is precisely the theme of our research this year.

But let me return to the formula 'teaching psychoanalysis in the University', in order briefly to examine its third component: 'in the University'. We could say that the objection to teaching psychoanalysis in this place can be broken down into two aspects: one individual and the other social (not to say political). Thus, with regard to individuals, teaching psychoanalysis at the University would by definition run up against the non-specialism of the audience, and—to put it more precisely, in the context of analysis—against the fact that it is not required of the audience that they should be analysts or (since to be an analyst is by definition to have been analysed) that they have been analysed. In any case, it is not a necessary condition and, I would add, thank Heavens for that! Thank Heavens that a certificate that you have been analysed is not required in order to hear analysis discussed at University, for this would quite simply be the end of analysis as an independent, non-normative, atopic process. Once analysis becomes the object of a certificate, once it offers rights—not as the result of its process, but as a purely formal sanction based on the fact that it took place—well, then it is something other than analysis.

However, there remains a more methodological, 'technical' problem, beyond the mere formalist objection. What is signified, what is implied by speaking about analysis to people 'not necessarily analysed'; by addressing a public not selected according to the criterion of a society of analysts, where in principle a teaching is given to people who, in one way or another, have a personal analysis in hand? Well, I have often wondered what this opposition could mean if it was rigidly maintained, with the kind of exclusiveness that analysts have often voiced (I am not speaking of Freud but of other analysts after him, and from every orientation); an exclusiveness which can take a thousand forms: the distinction between an exoteric and an esoteric teaching, an open and a closed seminar, introductory seminars and seminars reserved for trainees, etc. I believe such an attitude shows little faith in analysis and, as for the one who listens to this teaching, also in the receptivity, the reactivity of his or her unconscious. Analysis is localised in a place and a time, the place of the treatment and the time of its duration, even though it is precisely this limitation which raises questions: as everyone knows, analysis extends into self-analysis and, I would say, is already preceded by self-analysis.

But, from a more general point of view, what would analysis be if it did not refer to something accessible in everyone, and which precisely goes beyond the analytic treatment? There was something 'analytic', one must be sure, before analysis, and before Freud, as there was something of the unconscious or of transference. Unless we adopt an epistemological view here—of which the most eminent and eloquent representative is Michel Foucault—and which I personally consider unsustainable, in its historicist idealism. We are told, for example, without more ado, that man (and not a certain idea of man) was born in the eighteenth century and is dying in the twentieth, and that life (and not biology) did not exist before the eighteenth century. Furthermore, to return to our own territory, we are told that the unconscious signifies nothing before Freud, that one cannot speak of the existence of the unconscious before Freud. Without expanding on this question of history and humanity—and to speak, not of humanity, but of each one of us—there is in the same way something analytic beyond the more restricted site of analytic practice, and it is not just a whim of mine to formulate things in this way: you all belong—we all belong to those—'who have been, who are, who have yet to be (futuri)' in analysis, even if, in your lifetime, you never find yourself lying on a couch. To give up on teaching analysis to non-analysts, to those who are not necessarily analysts, like yourselves (even if by chance you were in fact all 'in analysis', you are not necessarily so in terms of your presence here), is to renounce inventing, or rather ceaselessly re-inventing, a mode of teaching which would be precisely permeable to the inspiration of analysis itself, permeable to the unconscious. It is a problem I shall soon have to take up again when I come to the point of explaining how it is that I moved on this year, from research and development concerning symbolisation or sublimation, to the theme I propose to deal with: that of the unconscious. Indeed, in symbolisation and in sublimation, a major question, which ultimately goes beyond all others, is to know whether there are symbolisations into which we could say that the unconscious passes, or sublimations which remain permeable to the unconscious.

I was saying that the repugnance against speaking of analysis in the University can take another form. This is not in relation to individuals (knowing whether or not they are analysts, therefore possible members of the audience, open to this discourse) but rather is a function of the University considered as an institution. It is an objection that is 'political', in the broadest sense of the term, and which could be formulated thus: in teaching psychoanalysis in the University, is one not participating in the institutionalisation *of psychoanalysis? What interests me in this objection is the problem of a politics of analysis (not the political problem in the general and habitual sense of the term, the civic sense); that is to say, in virtue of its ability to maintain itself in a certain atopia, in a certain non-institutionalised form, without however playing at esotericism, or the secret society—because, by the way, wouldn't the 'secret society' be another form of institution? Sometimes we speak as if the era of catacombs, the days of heading for the hills, were on the horizon for analysis. This possibility is after all entirely imaginable, in a civil society completely identified with its institutions, but in our current state such an outcome is unreal.*

Be that as it may, this 'political' relation of analysis and the University is ultimately, in my view, what is at stake in the play of forces. An institution—I mean the university institution—which is highly structured, highly socially integrated, narrowly defined regarding its objectives, would not leave room for an analytic teaching worthy of the name. Fortunately the University, at certain moments—and maybe a few years ago was one of these moments—in certain fields (to be precise, the badly defined, unprofitable field which is the 'human sciences') remains somewhat open to whatever the wind blows in. This is notably the case of this DEA,[2] *even that of the tertiary level, about which I would say, in order to completely discourage you, that if you look closely, their social usefulness is very doubtful and marginal. They won't be much use to you in the job market, unless you plead your case in a somewhat fraudulent manner, which in itself is not out of the question. But to take things literally, these are diplomas that confer the right to do research, and, possibly, are documents which can support an application for a teaching post. Well, this relation between forces which ensures that the University is open to the wind, and that the tertiary level is itself marginal, it is up to analysis to make the most of it, for as long as this relation lasts, even at the price of each analyst/teacher taking his or her bearings as regards the validity of participating in the work of the university—this in order not to lose his or her soul. Assuredly, no-one should take this apology for the non-finalised, for the non-profitable, as a stand in favour of 'anything goes'. That is not at all what I mean to say. Being open to the wind does not mean being arbitrary . . .*

The Thesis: A Contribution

So we have a 'DEA', a 'tertiary level degree', and very often when I receive a student I am asked, what are your requirements for a thesis, what is an academic project? Such and such a theme would interest me, but is it really 'academic'? And even, how many pages do I have to write for it to be a thesis? These questions, this anxiety, are quite understandable, and we have to try to respond. But I respond right away, firmly and without demagogy, that at this particular level I am sufficiently non-academic to not know what it means to be academic and to do an 'academic' project. Or even, to defend the 'good' universities (because as with anything else, there are good and bad ones), that I refuse the sort of assimilation that is beginning to appear here, of university, pedantry and purely formal requirements, even 'academicism'. After all, just as there are some universities that are full of pedantry and others that try not to be, there are also good and bad academicians. But when we speak of academicism it is not so much of the Académie Française that we are speaking, but of 'academies', these schools which teach drawing from the 'model' of the nude, and which are supposed to have reached a sort of formalism which is described precisely as academicism. Look in the Robert Dictionary, where you will find an exemplary sentence, summing up the entire culture of the Academy and even of the University: 'Some have accused Ingres of academicism, without understanding his profound originality.'

So what is a postgraduate thesis? After all, that is a legitimate question. More precisely, what is a research project leading to a thesis? And I can find only one term by which to designate what should be our demand in relation to such work: the term 'contribution'. For me, a doctoral thesis has to be a contribution, which allows us to define it in relation to certain other terms which are both closely-related and antithetical. One of these terms would doubtless be 'dissertation'. The dissertation is a genre which is not without its merits. Let us not throw the dissertation overboard. Perhaps you will be asked to produce a dissertation at the end of this year's teaching. It is an exercise which can bring out intelligence, talent . . . but it is by definition a genre that involves repetition and not contribution. At some time during your studies you will have been asked to produce a dissertation on 'The Theme of Love in Corneille' or 'The Cogito in Descartes and in Kant'. The 'Cogito in Descartes': it can be repeated, and it has been repeated thousands of times, for sure. And don't think for a moment that it's absent today. We may laugh about the 'Cogito in Descartes and in Kant', but will you laugh so much—indeed maybe there'll be someone among you who will laugh on the other side of his face—if I say that there is also 'the subject in Freud and Lacan'? That is the equivalent of 'the Cogito in Descartes and in Kant'! Or even, in a triangle of rather amusing combinations: 'body and language', 'language and institution', 'institution and body'. You can make tens of thousands of these.

The dissertation can sometimes open out into a contribution. Think of how Rousseau got himself known through two dissertations on topics proposed—precisely—by 'academies', and how Kant's first text to break with his dogmatic writings was the famous '1770 dissertation'. But in any case let us put these down as exceptions, and bear in mind the notion that the contribution is *not* a dissertation, that it does not amount to a rhetorical treatment of a theme which is currently fashionable and which hundreds of students may address without the debate budging by one millimetre. That is not a postgraduate thesis—at least, not as I understand it.

A further antithetical term, which I find more difficult to define, is what I would designate as *testimony*: the testimony of a particular route, of an experience, of a reading, and so on. Like the dissertation, the testimony should not be thrown overboard. Testimony alone is not negligible; its trajectory is indispensable. Indeed, how could any psychoanalyst, or clinician, deny it? And before psychoanalysts, we could think of someone like Hegel, for whom *truth* and *the history of the unveiling of truth* are ultimately one and the same thing. Effacing the trajectory would be a way of denying the testimony. There are ways of beginning, a methodology of research; there are preliminaries, a whole work of preparation; and then finally the scaffolding can be removed, and there is the fine edifice to be offered as it is.

Allow me to say that I don't share this conception. I know only too well that there are links between the beautiful edifice and the facade, between the facade and its secondary elaboration, which were masterfully brought to light by Freud when he clearly showed the relation between secondary elaboration and the effacement of the first process of elaboration. Thus, what I mean is not that one must efface the trajectory and deny any testimony—a contribution legitimately can and *should* make visible its trajectory—but it can be nothing but a testimony to that trajectory. Ultimately, I would say, if that was all it was, the thesis would not serve to communicate anything at all; it would be a clinical document which would need to be judged as such, its author becoming the object of an clinical evaluation, and not an interlocutor. It would be—sometimes it is—a purely narcissistic production, which would not open onto a communication. One hears quite often, and justifiably, of students who come to do a doctoral thesis with the principal aim of 'reading Freud'. That is completely legitimate—everyone should make his or her pathway through Freud, should produce, individually, his or her own Freud. But 'my Freud'—unless one is like Valéry and able to produce 'my Faust'—cannot be the subject of a thesis. Or again, to go to the other extreme, from the point of view not of textual documentation but of the clinic, 'my experience of the mental asylum' cannot be, as such, the subject of a thesis.

What do I mean, then, by 'contribution'? What I am driving at here is clearly that our field—that of analysis or psychopathology or, more broadly, that of the human sciences—has a certain *cumulative* aspect. We are not in a labyrinth, with each one of us tracing his own pathway in a purely individual, incommunicable fashion and nothing more. Such a pathway would be unique, would be by definition of no use to anyone else; no use to some other rat who, having been put into the same labyrinth, will trace a totally different pathway, although perhaps arriving at the same result.

It's not that I'm saying that we're not in a labyrinth; there is a fair amount of that in what we do, and each of us has to follow such a wholly individual pathway. However, the postulation of a 'contribution' and of 'accumulation' bring with them, in spite of everything, another dimension. Even if, above all else, there is repetition, individual things which cannot be capitalised on by others, this is not all there is.

What does it mean, for a thesis to be a contribution? It means, concretely, that this text—which will be 'defended', which will be the object of an 'examination' and a 'certificate' (such as 'Doctor of Philosophy')—must be a document, a possible source of reference for another researcher. That is to say, if in five years' time someone else wants to take up a particular point of clinical or theoretical psychopathology, or even of applied psychoanalysis or a particular author, one should be able to suggest this document as preliminary work. Go and look at the theses of the last few years and you will find in them research related to your subject, which it will be in your interest to take into account.

One is almost embarrassed to have to stress this cumulative aspect of intellectual production—which, for all its obviousness, is indispensable—as if people imagined that, in our field, one should be able to recreate from scratch everything, out of one's own head. It is, however, imperative to rely on the work and the results of other researchers, in relation not only to past work but also to contemporary projects. For your research, your thesis, to become a contribution, a possible reference for another researcher, quite a few things are already necessary, regarding its editing, its composition and its methodology; you need a plan, and must submit to certain minimal requirements of communication.

There is another way I can put this, which will be more blunt. A thesis has at least three readers, who are mercenary readers, paid by the State to read the thesis, pass judgement on it and discuss it. Let us accept this for a moment, even if there is something repellent in the idea that some remuneration or other puts me under the obligation of reading attentively some piece of writing which is precisely not going to communicate anything at all, and which does not engage me as interlocutor. We should accept, in the end, the presence of 'salaried readers': the three professors of the jury. Well, in order to make your thesis a contribution, you should aim it at a 'fourth' reader, or, which amounts to the same thing, the one among the three who would have taken some interest in reading this work even if he hadn't been constrained to do so because of his function within the University, due to his official role. This contribution may or may not be great; it is rarely brilliant—sometimes quite modest: a reference, a new connection, a bibliography—a new perspective, for sure; the discovery of a few interesting documents, clinical or otherwise; but let there be an element of this work worthy of being archived, and it—once in the archive—will not be covered over for ever with the dust of never-borrowed manuscripts!

So please aim at this fourth reader, aim at him through the content of your research, but also respect him as a reader—and that is where we come to some of the supposedly formal requirements. Carelessness of style, of presentation, the fact that a thesis in the worst case may be unreadable because of errors, because of poorly indexed bibliographies, inaccurate references—these are intolerable defects; not because of an obsessional and antiquated formalism, but because of the disdain for the reader they show, this reader to whom you are aiming to communicate something. If you are present at the defending of theses, you will sometimes hear from the mouth of one of the members of the panel reflections of this kind: on page 50 there is such and such an error, there is such and such an expression, did you not mean to say this word in place of that one? This number does not refer to the corresponding note, etc. This attention to detail may appear droll, and indeed it would be if the professor did not have some 'deeper' objections to formulate. But carelessness is cumulative . . . For my part, I do not consider myself a mercenary, and I consider that I am allowed to throw down a text in a fit of anger if it does not show a minimal degree of respect for the interlocutor, and thus a minimum of attention to the rules of communication and dialogue.

So here is the beginning of a methodological introduction to this DEA, and to these theoretical lectures, which in spite of everything are very individual, and are entitled 'Clinical Psychopathology and Psychoanalysis'. With the first of these lectures, I shall in some way introduce all three of them.[3] Each of the three lecturers conceives of things in his own way, but none claims, in any case, to bring you knowledge, nor even the foundations or the tools necessary for your own work. It is up to you to define the foundations, to forge your tools in whatever field you choose. Indeed, these theoretical lectures in the end have little to do with the transmission of fundamental elements. One should think of them rather as samples of various schools of thought, samples of research that someone or other really has in progress (and where could be a better place to communicate it than at this level, at doctoral level?)—a sample that may be stimulating, instructive, both in terms of its content, and by the testimony it bears to a way of proceeding and a methodology.

Breaking off and re-engaging

This year I have chosen a theme which I have described in a rather long title: not 'the unconscious', but *Reference to the Unconscious, its Putting to the Test in Practice and in Theory*. Here, again, I want to raise the question with you: why this subject? But let us ask ourselves first: how does one choose a subject? Perhaps some teachers do not ask themselves this; but after all, it is a question. Let us leave aside the subject of the 'programme'. As we have just seen, it is not a question of that; there is no programme in the DEA. There is no 'programme' of psychoanalysis, except in certain Institutes of psychoanalysis, at certain moments in their history, when in all truth it was a question of covering psychoanalysis by dividing up into squares the entire field of what could be known about it.

At one end of the spectrum of motives for making a choice, one may choose a subject because it is 'on the programme', because it will help people, because it's a fundamental concept—who knows? At the other extreme, in opposition to the programme, there might be what we could term 'desire', the most secret of motives: why this subject at this moment in one's life, in one's practice, in one's analysis, in one's self-analysis, why choose this at that particular moment? It is never just chance. All the same, I think it's quite difficult to reach this point of unveiling things; all one can do is not systematically mask things (which is already an achievement).

Between these two extremes, that of pre-ordained work and that of the most profound motives, I have tried more than once to define what I call a sort of intermediate layer, which is interesting in that it can serve as a guide to a certain interpretation of the work. In the reading of a work—in particular, let's say, that of Freud—we could locate these three levels: the level of rationality; then, at the other extreme, the level, ultimately, of Freud's own analysis, such as one can try to reconstitute it. (There has been more than one attempt to do so, both now and in the past, and I am not criticising this approach. I have in mind, particularly, Didier Anzieu's work [1986].) But then there is this intermediate level, which I designate as the *unavoidable*. Since I am using the example of Freud, I have had occasion to throw into relief this level of the unavoidable in relation to what is termed the 'turning point of 1920' and, more precisely, the reasons why Freud at this precise moment began to talk of the death drive.

We can easily distinguish the three levels here. One can go straight to the plane which is seen as the deepest. Indeed, people did not fail to say it to Freud—nor he to deny it in the most strident fashion—namely: 'you are speaking of the death drive because your beloved daughter has just died, because there has been the shock of the 1914 war', and so forth. It would be a question then of a 'traumatisation' very close in time; but as we know that trauma only takes on its value on the basis of what is 'already there', onto which it is inscribed, one could point to the specific details of Freud's much older relation to death—as did Max Schur in his work *Freud: Living and Dying* (1976)—upon which the theoretical changes of 1920 came to play.

In contrast to this attempt to analyse the most profound level, which certainly always entails risks, we have Freud's own rationalisations. And if there was ever someone who 'destroyed the scaffolding', it was he. He did this in the true sense, to the point of burning everything that could have served as a document allowing a history of his thought to be written. He carried out gigantic *autos-da-fé'* on his correspondence, his manuscripts, his notes, as if to burn the bridges in advance for the future analyst. If therefore one can speak, in relation to a work, of a façΔade, of rationalisation and of the destruction of evidence, the 'master' is the very first model of this type of 'work'. In any case, by remaining (as Freud often did in order to relate the history of his thought) at the most rational level, it can be demonstrated that the death drive was a necessary moment in the theory, since it was necessary to integrate new clinical findings, even if one had to reply to this objection: 'But why then, for all these years, have you refused to accept the destructive or aggressive drive which was proposed to you by Adler? He was offering you a helping hand for years, and you never gave up saying "no"; and here you are taking up this theory, claiming that it is not the same thing, that it is not the same aggressive drive'. (In fact, it is not the same; but that has to be demonstrated!)

Still on the subject of this turning-point of 1920, there is what I call the unavoidable dimension of thought itself. This is not the rationality of a development that can be delineated chronologically, in a temporality that would be a simple progression, an accumulation without any fault, without regression—in a word, a temporality of the progress of knowledge. Neither is it the timeless temporality of desire, of the unconscious, which we have to rediscover between the atemporality of repetition and the very particular temporality which relates to trauma. With our term *unavoidability* we could say that the temporality in question is of a type, this time, much more closely linked to a certain structure of experience and of thought. A temporality where one is allowed to introduce something like a dialectic. Thus, the whole meaning of what I have been able to say in interpreting the 'turning-point of 1920' has been to show how the death drive was the *renewal* of something that already existed, and that needed to be reaffirmed in another way because the entire equilibrium of Freudian thought had been displaced, and in particular because the whole dimension of narcissism and of the narcissistic Eros had appeared, and it was necessary to get sexuality 'cleared' in relation to this narcissistic Eros.

An unavoidability does not therefore exclude a breaking off, *if* it is a question of a dialectic. (I am taking the verb 'to break' [*rompre*] in all its senses, including that used in sword-fighting, in fencing.) People have asked me: 'Why did you break off from sublimation, the theme of your last lectures, it wasn't finished, it was interesting, you should have gone on!' As in fencing, I break off in order to re-engage. I hope to explain partly why and how next time. I break off still holding on to the thread, just as much with the antepenultimate session which touched on symbolisation and castration, as with the one before last, which concerned sublimation. Breaking off and re-engaging. It is clear that I have been led to re-examine something to which I am once again drawing your attention, which is, at least for other generations, the 'famous' Bonneval conference (1960) which has been consigned to a weighty tome published by Desclée de Brouwer with, among other texts, the introductory paper by Leclaire and myself: 'The Unconscious: a Psychoanalytic Study'.[4] Obviously, I am not intending to re-hash it this year, but to use it as a kind of reference which I shall be led to test, possibly to contest—'to put to the test', as my title would have it—'The Reference to the Unconscious, Putting it to the Test in Practice and in Theory'.

15 November 1977
Spirals since Bonneval

I refer you therefore to this momentous, weighty volume which contains a good number of contributions apart from that of Laplanche and Leclaire, and also some discussions of that text by Conrad Stein and André Green, as well as a complementary text by Leclaire in which he explores further the analysis of his 'dream of the unicorn'. In addition, you will find there a text by Lacan—I say 'in addition' because the text was entirely written after the conference.

Today, I will seek to reconnect the theme of the unconscious, which I approach with caution, to the movement of what I have been able to think and elaborate here in the course of the last few years. It may seem presumptuous to examine in this way the movement of one's own thought, to ascribe importance to one's own errors, one's repetitions or stumblings. But to suppose that such a movement interests you is, after all, to suppose that this DEA has a meaning, that academic research on a DEA in psychoanalysis can properly be situated as a 'composite' between what, last time, I termed a 'contribution' (that is to say, the cumulative aspect of certain offerings, not all of which sink without trace the moment they are presented), and the singular, unique character of the individual approach. Showing that a particular approach can be of a certain assistance to others in reflecting upon their own approach. Then there is the basic demand of lucidity which requires you to ask yourself what it is, effectively, that makes you, at a given moment—with no external necessity or programme—speak so much about castration, about sublimation or symbolisation, or—now—about the unconscious.

Last time, I tried to situate something between rationalisation and self-analysis, which I term the level of the 'unavoidable'. I sometimes use a spiral to provide a schema for this level. The spiral is a flat curve which describes concentric cycles starting out from a point termed a pole, cycles which become wider and wider. One could just as well speak of the helix, because what is often incorrectly called a spiral (a 'spiral' staircase) is in fact a curve in space, and no longer only in two dimensions; a curve, for example, which can be inscribed on a cylinder.

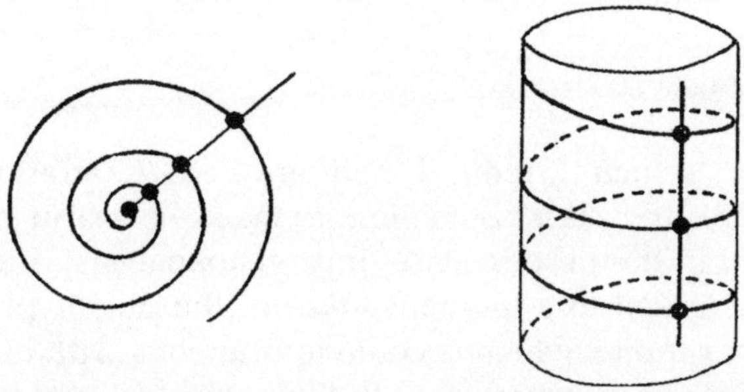

What is it that interests me in this spiral—or this helix? It is not only to know whether thought is in a state of expansion, or is purely and simply repetitive. This is not for me to judge, and often one deludes oneself, imagining that one is evolving and broadening the field, while in fact all one is doing is describing, at different levels, curves superimposed on one another. What is important to me in a particular curve, however, is the idea that if you draw a straight line that bisects the curve (the 'radial vector' of the spiral or the 'generating line' of the cylinder), you thus define points that are projected onto one another. What I want to imagine by this is that, finding myself directly above certain points, I am given a sort of bird's-eye view over one, two or n previous turns of the spiral. Does this mean that all thought is repetitive? Certainly. In the ideal case, let us hope that it is in a state of relative expansion, or at least that it unfolds on planes that, in spite of everything, are changing.

So what makes me go back to the vertical line of the unconscious? The question might seem superfluous, since when we speak of psychoanalysis, we are always speaking of the unconscious. Thus there should be no need for further explanation; it is our 'favourite' notion, our presupposition. We speak of the unconscious without generally asking ourselves the ultimate question about its existence and its foundations . . . and so much the better. This 'reference to the unconscious' is what we find particularly in the treatment, which can get by very nicely without an ontology or an epistemology—at least, without these being explicit. If, in spite of everything, it seemed to me necessary to re-open the question of this universal reference of analysis, this was part of the movement imposed by the two final turns of my spiral: the penultimate turn, devoted to castration and forms of symbolisation (the years 1973-1974 and 1974-1975); and the last turn, on sublimation (the years 1975-1976 and 1976-1977).

Spirals of Castration

The first course to which I refer, I had entitled 'Castration: its Precursors and its Destiny'. It is convenient to take our bearings from this title. Castration, in the proper sense, in psychoanalysis, is a complex, very precisely linked to a moment—that of the phallic phase—and to the Oedipus complex which is contemporaneous with it. (That is, if we refer to a Freudian perspective.) But however strict its temporal limits, the castration complex, this phallic complex (if we can call it that), is to be situated between, on the one hand, certain precursors, a genealogy, and on the other hand, an ultimate destiny—neurotic, cultural, or even (why not?) psychoanalytic. We can attempt to take the question term by term or, more precisely, two by two. In relating the castration complex to its precursors, I was trying to bring out a double genealogy: on the one hand, that of a representation; on the other, that of an affect, precisely the affect one calls anxiety.

I insist on the following: the distinction, concerning castration, between the register of affect and that of representation has nothing to do with some *artifice of presentation*. On the contrary, it is situated in the line of one of the primordial and fundamental discoveries of psychoanalysis: that in a psychical event there is an independent movement, an ever-present possibility of dissociation, between representational content and the accompanying lived emotion (both qualitative and quantitative). In contradiction to the observations of common sense and the descriptions of phenomenology, the experiences of being 'terrified' about, 'heart-broken' about, or 'over the moon' about something do not constitute indissociable totalities, modes of consciousness in which *noemis* and *noesis* necessarily correspond. The 'about' of these descriptions signifies only the most fragile, the most mobile of bonds, where its reality is concerned.[5] It is a questionable, perhaps deceptive bond, which is always sufficient justification for an analysis—as far as its essence is concerned.

The genealogy of the representation, in the case of castration, is essentially the misadventures of a fantasy, that of separation. It is in this sense that we are led to speak of pregenital 'castrations'—of an oral kind, for instance, with the repeated withdrawal of the breast, or, more generally, the moment of weaning; or even a so-called anal or, more broadly, excremental kind of castration; and lastly, a more archaic and also more enigmatic kind, the separation of birth. This is more enigmatic since it is a 'castration' not experienced as such by the subject, and which cannot initially be thematised by the child, but by the mother. This sequence could be given a meaning which would ultimately be highly genetic, very linear, or even—viewed from the perspective of developmental stages—as a sort of apprenticeship, the progressive mastery of separation, leading up to the final stage of the castration complex. In other words, the assumption of sex as something which it is possible to separate, founding the male/female distinction.

To this view, which one could still term constructivist, we should oppose a perspective I would call more dialectical and which, precisely, brings in the hypothesis of the unconscious. What I mean here is that the primordial, pregenital kinds of 'castration' are not, to make use of an image, the stones of a building which, once the building is finished, could still be individually recognised. They are, at the very most, the building's foundations or, better still, they resemble those blocks of cement or stone sometimes thrown into the sea for the building of a jetty. These 'castrations', then, are swallowed up, caught in a relation of repression *vis-à-vis* the subsequent configuration. In particular, they are repressed in relation to the phallic castration complex. Maybe, even (and this is a question we shall have to address) what we have here is an instance of primordial, originary repression.

The question, then, would be the following, starting from these precursors of the representation or complex of castration: can the fate of these archaic representations which come before the castration complex, give us *a more concrete idea of what constitutes the depths of the unconscious*? A sequence of stages is thus a sequence of repressions, and also a sequence of symbolisations—that is to say, of repetitions in another language, of something said in a previous language. In speaking of 'another language' I am not, for my part, especially speaking a 'Lacanian' language. In the first place, I am speaking a Freudian language, since it was Freud himself who spoke to us, precisely, of the language of a particular stage, and notably, in his paper on 'Negation' (1925), of the language of the oral drive. The theme of separation would then be taken up again, expressed in a 'language' (a 'dialect', as Freud called it at other times), in a complex of 'representations' (to use a term less marked by linguistics) which is different each time. As an illustration of this idea of inscriptions which take up each repeatedly, you could take the famous letter 52 of 6th December 1896 (one of the most important in the collection of letters to Fliess) which bridges the gap between the 'Project for a Scientific Psychology' of 1895 and the metapsychology which will form chapter VII of *The Interpretation of Dreams* (1900). Here are a few significant passages:[6]

> As you know, I am working on the assumption that our psychic mechanism has come into being by a process of stratification [a term which *could* evoke the model of a constructivism, with a first stage, a second, etc.]: the material present in the form of memory-traces being subjected from time to time to a *rearrangement* in accordance with fresh circumstances . . . [so here we leave behind construction and sedimentation of inert layers: there are rearrangements]. Thus what is essentially new about my theory is the thesis that memory is present not once but several times over, that it is laid down in various kinds of indications . . . I do not know how many of these registrations there are—at least three, probably more. (Masson 1985: 207)

You see how important all of this is. Freud emphasises the specific and innovative dimensions of his theory. Memory is present not just once but several times, and this will be echoed by an insistently-recurring question, whether there are several inscriptions of the same thing in different places. If this were the case, we would have a truly realist, topographical conception of the unconscious. These 'various species of indications' certainly make us think of systems of expression which are organised differently, and that is what we are told in what follows, without the word 'language' being pronounced. Each of these registers is disposed according to a certain type of association, each differing from the others. And then there is the more geneticist view, which truly prefigures the notion of developmental stages:

> I should like to emphasise the fact that the successive registrations represent the psychic achievement of successive epochs of

> life. At the boundary between two such epochs a translation of the psychic material must take place. (Masson 1985: 208)

We might think that this notion of translation could be a good model for repression, in that what is translated remains as the repressed of the new translation. Well, that is not at all what is said, which introduces a new enigma . . .

> I explain the peculiarities of the psychoneuroses by supposing that this translation has not taken place in the case of some of the material, which has certain consequences . . . [And further on:] A failure of translation—this is what is known clinically as 'repression'. The motive for it is always a release of unpleasure that would be generated by a translation; it is as though this unpleasure provokes a disturbance of thought that does not permit the work of translation . . . Within one and the same psychic phase, and among registrations of the same kind, a normal defense makes itself felt owing to a generation of unpleasure. But *pathological* defense occurs only against a memory trace from an earlier phase that has not yet been translated. (Masson 1985: 208-9)

You can see that we have here a sort of model of the passage from one phase to the next, a model which could be called that of 'symbolisation', or even of 'metaphorisation', to return to the term I used in the 1960 report. But with the very particular idea that a perfect symbolisation would leave no residue, that a perfect translation would be possible. This, in one sense, reminds us of something which is discussed at length in the Bonneval paper: namely, Politzer's hypothesis according to which the language of dreams is not an *inadequate*, but simply an *unconventional* expression of desire (cf. Politzer 1994). So much so that between conventional expression—which would correspond to our everyday language—and this non-conventional, purely individual expression—this idiolect of dream-images—between these two versions, there would be no remainder. Each, by rights, could be translated into the other, or rather, as Politzer said (we have laid stress on this 'or rather'), it is not even a question of the translation of one language into another: the same 'signifying intention' is at one point translated into one language and, at another, for various reasons, into a different one.

In Freud, things are rather different. Repression signifies a certain failure of symbolisation . . . which, however, leaves open, by rights, the possibility of a symbolisation without failure. This would thus confront us here, *a contrario*, with the kind of ideal (probably impossible to attain) to be found in the problematic of sublimation or even that of the treatment, if it aims at a sort of recovery 'without remainder' of unconscious desires. Whatever the case may be, this genealogy—of successive schematic pictures of fantasies in which absence and separation are given concrete expression—will lead us to re-examine, and perhaps better exemplify or diversify, this schema of 'metaphor' which Leclaire and I had tried, via a certain formalism which seemed mathematical, to describe.

The other genealogical line of the castration complex is the genealogy of anxiety. This leads us again to insist on the central problem of affect and representation. The distinction between them in Freud appears as the point of departure of his thought, since it is on the experience of a certain independence of affect in relation to representation that the *Studies on Hysteria* are played out and, likewise, all the early developments on obsessional neurosis. An affect can be misplaced ('falsely connected') in relation to the representation which would logically be its intentional correlative: this observation is the true foundation of the first notion of analytic treatment.

In Lacanianism, unfortunately, this dissociation leads to the rejection of one of the two terms, and to an absolute priority being accorded to representation, to the primacy of the 'signifier', adopting the term used by Lacan. You do not need to read many Lacanian texts to be convinced that the Freudian distinction between affect and representation has become—in Lacanianism—a real rejection, sometimes scornful, of the affective and of lived experience, which moreover, are usually *affected* by signs of irony or inverted commas.

If we return to Freud, we observe that the emphasis is exactly the opposite. What is essential for the individual, both in life and in the treatment, is the destiny of affect. But the problem becomes more complicated, further questions arise. To say that the destiny of affect is essential does not amount to saying that affect can be manipulated. The whole transition from the so-called cathartic method—a method which consists precisely in 'bringing out' affect—to the analytic method begins with the discovery that, ultimately, it is not by seeking to play on affect that one will best intervene in the destiny of the affect. This discovery still remains valid today, at a time when so-called neo-cathartic therapies are flourishing.

Freudianism has nothing of the scorn for affect shown by our Lacanians. You only have to refer to a text such as 'The Claims of Psycho-Analysis to Scientific Interest' (1913a) to find cited as one of the major discoveries of psychoanalysis the importance of affect in psychic life. But the point of transition, which effectively led Lacanianism to be interested in privileging the 'signifier', is that the means by which one can modify the economy of affect consists of representations, of fantasies.

With the problem of castration, we confront an affect which is quite particular and is at the same time absolutely primordial—the affect of all affects. It can be termed the lowest common denominator of all the others, the lowest in the sense of most blind and least specific: I mean *anxiety*. Thus, the genealogy of fantasies I was talking about a minute ago, regarding pregenital 'castrations', is punctuated, in counterpoint, by a genealogy of anxieties. In this sense, anxiety often appears as anxiety *about something*, as 'intentional', and so as ultimately close to fear.[7] With this idea of anxiety as anxiety-about-something, we rediscover the phenomenological interlocutor, he whom I baptised 'Politzer'—because, if Politzer were not an adherent of the phenomenological school, his inspiration was nonetheless very close to it.

Now, we can see that this intentionality of affect is misleading, because behind any particular object we can always discern the outline of another. Again, beyond the relative independence of affect and representation, we even observe that affect, in the form of anxiety, can appear absolutely free, and without representation, and that this is even its true character *vis-à-vis* other affects. Anxiety is perhaps only 'soldered' (that is Freud's term) artificially to one or another anxious representation—for example, in phobic representations: the spider, the thunderstorm, and so on. According to Freud, this soldering is not originary, but comes later, and more or less contingently. First there is anxiety, and *then* anxiety-about. Sometimes anxiety passes from one symbol to another; sometimes it appears in a pure form ('free') in crises, at a moment we might describe as desymbolisation.

Well, if we bring these two lines together, the genealogy of fantasies and the sequence of anxieties, from anxieties about separation or the most primitive fragmentation, up to anxiety about castration and even anxieties described as secondary (social anxiety, anxiety before the super-ego, etc.), then the problem of symbolisation, which leads me directly to the question of the unconscious, presents itself in a double form. Symbolisation is assuredly the symbolisation of representations, since it is a question of substituting one idea for another, the second thus becoming the symbol of the first. However, in a sense that is perhaps far more primordial, symbolisation appears as something which bears directly on the affect; that is to say, it would not originally be a substitution of representations but, in the first place, a binding, the soldering of anxiety so as to master it.

Whence the danger of what Freud called *unbinding*, that is to say, the *releasing* (in Freudian language it is the same thing) of an affect: an affect of anxiety, of desire, or of pain—which is ultimately, in a certain sense, one and the same affect. Here, once again, we come across a problem that is primordial in relation to the unconscious, to the extent that it furnishes the title of one of the chapters in Freud's work bearing that name—I mean the situation of affect in relation to the unconscious. It seems to me that this question of affect in relation to the unconscious should be posed in two different ways: there is, first of all, a formulation I would describe as classical, in that it comes from Freud—namely, the question: are there unconscious affects? Now, Freud's argument here is highly curious. As we know, in the numerous discussions in which he engages, in order to defend the notion of the unconscious, he regularly turns up his nose at the usual philosophical objection—the so-called 'consciousness' objection—according to which there is a contradiction between the terms 'psyche' and 'unconscious'. Here, Freud aims not to respond to the philosophers, but to disqualify them in so far as they oppose facts with words. Maybe there is a contradiction in terms, he argues, but that doesn't matter because it does not prevent the unconscious from existing; there most certainly is something which has psychical characteristics and which is at the same time unconscious. It is the philosopher who should adapt his theory—and firstly his words—to the way things are.

Now this objection which, when it is a question of defending the unconscious psyche, he considers to be of a purely formal, verbal order, he uses again concerning affect, but treats it with a different kind of respect. When, in particular, Freud speaks of the unconscious feeling of guilt, this is how he puts it: a feeling is something that one senses, one feels, something necessarily linked, as if in its essence, to consciousness. The sense of guilt is consciousness of guilt, to the point where the German uses the two terms as equivalent: *Schuldgefuhl* and *Schuldbewusstsein*. What can it mean, then, to speak of an 'unconscious sense of guilt', or even an 'unconscious consciousness of guilt'? So really we see here that Freud is strangely aware, when it is a question of affect, of this *contradictio in terminis*, while he is not at all when it is a matter of unconscious fantasies or representations. We will certainly have to re-examine this problem—and will do so by concentrating on the affect of all affects, anxiety, in order to show how it requires the introduction of the second topography,—in other words, the introduction of the agency of the ego as that which is 'affected' by affect. The question will arise in a new form: is there a portion of the ego that is unconscious, and what could that really mean?

I mentioned that there was a second possible sense of this question of affect, a way of posing the question beyond the classic problem of its topographical position: conscious, preconscious or unconscious. To be brief, I will say that, in this new perspective, it is the very presence of affect, its very surging forth, which provides the major argument, the essential evidence in favour of an unconscious reality, that reality which precisely *affects* me. In affect, there is something 'affected'—which is the ego—and something which 'affects', which is the unconscious reality, or what we can try to perceive of it *via* the affective phenomenon.

This unconscious reality is, in spite of everything, rendered bodiless if we speak, with Freud, purely and simply of 'representations'. We have learned, notably with Melanie Klein, that unconscious representations are objects which are internal, introjected. But when we say 'with Melanie Klein', we could also say, 'already with Freud'. To see why, you only have to refer to the text that could be termed (perhaps rather provocatively for those who despise affect) an essay in 'affective psychology', the title of which is 'Mourning and Melancholia'. There we can verify that the affect of melancholia is wholly linked not to a representation, but to the active presence of an introjected object, an object that I have come to describe as an *object-source*, because I see it as—at the same time—the source of the drive. Clearly, this object-source will have to be examined in its close relation to the unconscious.

Having dealt with the precursors, let us move swiftly on to the castration complex itself. I will only take it up again in order to schematise the major question which it poses from the point of view of the unconscious. The castration complex, as I have insisted—and this is how it appears in Freud's work—is firstly and above all a theory, in the literal sense of the term, an 'infantile sexual theory'. It is a symbolisation at once narrow, rigid and eminently inclusive, since it extends to the whole world, or at least the human world. It is a theory apparently without ambivalence, which Freud attributes to the child at a major stage in its development. This so-called 'phallic' phase is about 'having or not having', having the phallus or not having it. I will not dwell on what I have been able to develop concerning this topic—for example, the problem that arises again and again of knowing what it is that, based on a perception (or a so-called 'perception') of the anatomical difference between the little boy and the little girl, together with a threat (actually made or not, more or less remote), suddenly crystallises into a theory. The problem here concerns whether a supplementary element is needed as a catalyst, or whether simply: perception + threat = theory.

However that may be, here we are with this theory—in what I have termed, to demonstrate clearly its resolutely rationalist nature, 'phallic logic'. It is a logic of absolute contradiction, in which 'minus times minus equals plus', in which no third term, no combination or compromise, is possible. If you are not phallic, you are castrated, if you are not castrated you are phallic. It is here that the famous 'phallocentrism' of Freud takes root and thrives. He certainly never resolves the problem of the transition (a hypothetical one, endlessly put off until a later date) from the 'phallic-castrated' opposition—in which only one of the two terms is '*marked*'—to the 'masculine-feminine' bipolarity. Let us add that this difficulty, unresolved by Freud, is again accentuated by the Lacanians, at least to the extent that they make of the assumption of castration the horizon, and ultimately the aim, of psychoanalysis. To 'assume castration': one often finds this formula penned by numerous Lacanians (is it to be found in Lacan?). Obviously there is a relation here which could be termed philosophical, even religious; we can easily see the link between castration and finitude: accepting our 'castration' is to assume unfinishedness or, as some say, a gap, to not allow ourselves to be lured by the narcissistic illusion of omnipotence.

However that may be, and even if Freud stumbles up against a possible beyond of the 'phallic' position, we cannot do otherwise than confront it, this logic of 'yes' and 'no', with what Freud never ceased to affirm about the characteristics of the unconscious: that it includes neither negation, different degrees of affirmation, nor doubt; that the most contradictory psychic impulses coexist there and thus, necessarily, that it includes the phallic and the castrated, without *one coming to exclude the other*. Again, how are we to avoid confronting this phallic logic, leading to a logic of negation, with Freud's text on 'Negation' (1925) (*Die Verneinung*), where the symbol of negation appears precisely as a characteristic of the conscious level. How, then, is castration present in the unconscious? And is it even present there at all? Does the unconscious not seize hold of castration, making its 'either/or' into a 'both . . . and': both phallic and castrated?

The third point, finally, which I envisaged through the term 'destiny' (of castration), I have approached above all under the heading 'symbolisations'. Is there an 'afterwards' of castration? There ought to have been an 'afterwards', an enigmatic one, of the pair 'masculinity-femininity'. In any case, there is the destiny of neurosis—for example, that of phobia, which presents us with a symbolisation itself relatively univocal, but which does not really move beyond phallic logic. We could say that phobia tames anxiety, but only for it to re-emerge at another point, which does not sound like a truly successful symbolisation, escaping the logic of castration. On the other hand, we have attempted a line of research into rites of passage and initiation, in order to take our bearings from symbolisations which may be more all-encompassing, more ambiguous, ambivalent, bisexual maybe, with a more slender residue of neurosis than in the phobic symptom. The opposition between the symptom (the phobic symptom) and the ritual, the initiation rite (circumcision) is only schematic, since there are phobias that can appear, retrospectively, as structuring moments, and some rituals are more neuroticising than others, as some writers have shown rather clearly in relation to Jewish circumcision. The problem, in any case, is as follows: what can happen beyond the castration complex? Or more exactly, what can *pass* from the unconscious? What would constitute a successful symbolisation? This is a major problem for the treatment, even if its success appears as an ideal which is impossible to attain. It is a problem, in any case, which I have posed in a new way over the last two years, in relation to sublimation in these two explorations: 'Situating Sublimation' and 'The Derivation of Sublimation'.

29 November 1977
Sublimation and the Originary

'Situating Sublimation' took up the problem of the relation between the sexual and the non-sexual, since it is precisely a process described as the re-investment[8] of the non-sexual by a sexual energy which serves as the definition of this enigmatic concept. That led me, two years ago, to re-define the problem known as that of leaning-on [*étayage*] and thus, in the process, to re-open a question: that of the relation between this moment which we can call originary, even if it is in part mythical, and a no less fundamental moment designated by Freud as primal repression. Primal repression is posited as the constitution of an initial unconscious, necessary to account for the fact that there is always, in any so-called secondary repression, an attraction exerted by something already there (as you see, we are deliberately situating ourselves in the midst of a realist and spatial metaphor).

Now, on their side, leaning-on and seduction also seek to account for the constitution of the first fantasies, and in particular of that which I think is essential to them—what I call the source-object of the drive, the internal source-object. Is this moment of leaning-on a repression? Is it a moment preliminary to a repression? In this obscure domain of origins and genesis, is there not room for a type of constitution of a first fantasy which would not yet be exactly repressed, nor yet exactly unconscious, and which would be destined, in a secondary moment, for repression? We may also wonder how to situate this constitution of a first fantasy in relation to the schema—which we shall have to come back to—of the process of symbolisation.

Certainly, leaning-on and seduction are accompanied by a symbolisation of the phenomena of self-preservation. However, at the same time they amount to a breaking-off, the constitution of a new domain, so that it is difficult to say, without further elaboration, that the sexual object purely and simply symbolises the non-sexual. This takes me back to last year, when, having situated the emergence and the breaking-off which causes the sexual to be grafted onto the non-sexual, we had then to consider the relation the other way around, the passage from the sexual into the non-sexual and the possible existence of this process of sublimation. This is a process very difficult to grasp if we want to maintain its specificity in relation to the neurotic symptom and repression. Indeed, whilst Freud unceasingly reaffirms the possibility of this particular destiny of the drive, each elaboration of it brings out the difficulty in separating sublimation from repression—and this is as evident in the study on Leonardo as it is in the text on 'The Acquisition and Control of Fire' (1932), in which Prometheus, the hero of sublimation, is likewise presented as a champion of repression. It was this sort of impasse which from that point led me to wonder if it might not be appropriate to explore the 'derivation' of sublimation. Perhaps this could mean that it was possible to shift the concept slightly and to ask if psychoanalysis, through its intervention in treatment, and through its *cultural* intervention, does not create the prospect—if not the definite possibility—of a better communication between conscious and unconscious, the ideal of an elaboration which would be closer to the unconscious than that which elsewhere Freud called sublimation—a communication, in any case, which would not forget its sexual sources even in activities termed non-sexual.

The unconscious: corpse or revenant?

I find here a clear connection with the problem raised by Freud in his 1915 text, 'The Unconscious', in the last chapter entitled: *'Die Agnoszierung des Unbewussten'*, or 'Assessment of the Unconscious', as it is translated by Strachey.[9] But *Agnoszieren* is a most uncommon word, of Latin rather than German origin (*'agnoscere'*). The dictionary I consulted mentions that, on the one hand, it is an especially Austrian term and that, on the other, it is employed particularly for the identification of a corpse—for example, at the morgue.

'Identifying a corpse'. Let us say that this phrase tallies well with the distinct lack of optimism in Freud's final chapter regarding the famous movement between unconscious and preconscious that we are seeking. To be light-hearted for a moment, we could say that in these last lines we confront an alternative that offers little comfort. On the one hand, the unconscious is in the position of a *corpse* which must be identified, with on one side the thing, the 'thing-representation', and on the other the word, the two of these together constituting the identification; but there's no sign of the living person—the corpse 'plus' its identification can never give us the unconscious 'in person', as it were. Or else, the other possibility, if the unconscious is not a corpse, it is a *revenant*. This is the psychotic alternative, in which the unconscious certainly *returns* in person but, as one might say, as if to haunt the conscious. Remarkably, Freud concludes this little book with the famous passage in which he brings together schizophrenia and philosophy.

This problem, obviously an essential problem for psychoanalysis, never ceased to preoccupy Freud, and it cannot be restricted to these its most pessimistic figures, the 'corpse' and the 'revenant'. The problem 'returns', I would say, throughout the work, just as much in its beginnings—with, from the outset, the notion of an almost ecmnesic coming-to-consciousness, a veritable resurgence—as in later notions, such as 'working through'; or again, at certain moments, that of 'construction', which is in a sense a step backwards, a failure, since to resign oneself to the reconstruction of the past is to admit that it is very difficult, if not impossible, to summon up the unconscious 'in person'. It returns yet again in terms such as 'repetition', which postulates a sort of rock against which it repeatedly collides; the rock will be stumbled against, but in the end it will never be shaken, even if sometimes it is completely exposed.

I will abandon these metaphors in order to mention—in the text to which we are referring, 'The Unconscious'—a passage from the paper (given at the same Bonneval conference) by Diatkine and Lebovici, in which they oppose two views of psychoanalysis, one which can be qualified specifically as Jungian, in which sexuality and the unconscious are gradually replaced by the notion of destiny, a destiny which would be there to be *fulfilled* (you can easily hear echoes here of a more modern line of thinking where it is a question not of fulfilling but of 'assuming', for example, 'one's desire', 'one's castration', and so on). The other view, which these authors present as the truly Freudian line, would consist in liberating the individual from the archaic constraints which weigh him down. Lebovici and Diatkine refer in particular to Pasche, in his refusal of any 'gnostic' reformulation of Freudianism.

However, things are not so simple, even if we limit ourselves just to Freud. Freudianism is certainly not something that could be termed a gnosis, nor obviously is it a Dionysianism of the unconscious, and you only have to read the correspondence between Freud and Groddeck to realise this. Groddeck remains one of our reference points concerning this problem of the unconscious, giving us bearings that are all the more important for being so long obscured. Until his works started to be published again, Groddeck's thought was limited—for psychoanalysts—to that little phrase in *The Ego and the Id* with which Freud indicates he has borrowed the notion of the 'id' [*ça*] from Groddeck.

Now, the Groddeck-pole remains most important, fundamental, in an obvious sense as a pole of repulsion for Freud, but one which, since it never ceased to be present and active, shifted the entire balance of his thought. To be sure, then, Freudianism is not a Dionysianism *à la* Groddeck. Nor does it purely and simply, as Diatkine and Lebovici would have it (at least at the time of the conference), aim at mastery and rationality, even if formulations supporting such a view are not lacking, if you wished to fish them out from Freud's work. I have in mind one of the first formulations, in *Studies on Hysteria* (1895), where psychoanalysis is presented to us as what has allowed the transformation of neurotic misery into the acceptance of real unhappiness—thus, indeed, a work of realism. Or again, in the analysis of little Hans, where the aim of the analysis would be to replace unconscious repression with a judgement of condemnation. Here is the exact formula: 'Analysis replaces the process of repression, which is an automatic and excessive one, by a temperate and purposeful control on the part of the highest agencies of the mind' (Freud 1909: 145). A text of this kind, fortunately, finds its counterpoint in other places where Freud explicitly links the condemnatory judgement with repression, for which, ultimately, it could only be the substitute at an intellectual level.

And then, still within the field of our enquiry, is the question: how does the unconscious 'move'? We have the famous formulation, *Wo Es war soll Ich werden*, which I attempted to situate last year in a fairly precise way, in the following sense: 'Where it was, there shall I become.' Here, in the very way one translates, one is led to take into account the ambiguity of the formula, with its two possible interpretative paths, both of which are present—very explicitly—in Freud's text. Firstly, there is the metaphor of the drying up of the id, the id being compared to the sea around Holland which is converted into polder through continuous work. However, a few words further on, we come across a diametrically opposed reference: alongside technique, there is mysticism as a means of making the 'higher' and the 'lower' psychical agencies communicate. The introduction of the mystical is, to put it mildly, unusual in Freud; we cannot fail to recognise the influence of Groddeck, but this was an influence against which Freud never ceased to defend himself, this qualification of his 'It' as 'mystical'.

So we propose, as our theme for reflection: *'The Reference to the Unconscious: Its Putting to the Test in Practice and Theory'*. A title always has its intentions, and in this case they are clear enough. Firstly, with 'Reference to the Unconscious', I wanted, at the outset, to find a formulation more neutral than 'the unconscious' pure and simple, so as better to leave open the epistemological, even the ontological problem. In psychoanalysis, how do we refer to the unconscious? Is it a question of a dimension, as is sometimes said? Is it even, as some claim, a purely operative postulation? Or is it more than a reference? Is it something that has the solidity of an existence or, at least, not being a thing, a domain of being? The idea of 'reference' thus leaves open to re-examination the hypothesis of the realism of the unconscious. As to its being put to the test, I indicated a double confrontation. However, on reflection, I would say it is actually three-fold, comprising practice, theory and also culture.

References in theory and in practice

'Putting it to the test in theory'. This is doubtless one of the essential points for reflection, and one to which Freud returned incessantly, even in his treatments, to take up a certain scientific position in a domain which he himself had discovered, precisely, the discovery of the unconscious. So 'putting it to the test in theory': what does this domain of the unconscious mean? What status can we give it? How can we conceive of it, how can we in particular define its processes and outline its contours? 'Putting it to the test in practice': well, that means primarily the practice of the treatment itself, the analytic situation. Today, we can raise questions about what we might term the collective significance of this reference, whereas there was no such collective dimension at the beginning—to the extent that Freud was led to 'indoctrinate' his patients. Re-read the 'Rat Man' case, and you will see how, step by step, like a 'teacher', Freud reveals to his patient the three major features which exist between every analysand and analyst as a sort of preliminary axiom. There is an unconscious towards which one aims, even if it is not spoken about as such, even if it is not theorised, in the way Freud did more openly.

Is this reference to something other[10] an illusory element, a lure? Already the lure goes further than a simple illusion, since it is what moves someone along, what guides someone, ultimately as a prey, along a path, clearly in order to trap them. Is it a pure instance of alienation, of 'reification' as some claim, this search for a knowledge, which may extend to the excavation of a scene? At this point I would like to refer you to issue 15 of the *Nouvelle Revue de Psychanalyse*, which centres on precisely the theme of memory or memories, and in particular to a quite extraordinary text by the analyst Guntrip. He is a contemporary analyst, trained in ego psychology, who did the rounds of Kris, Hartmann, Loewenstein, Winnicott, etc., and who, to his last days—since he is continuing his self-analysis right up to the last minute, right up to the age of 68—is still in pursuit of an infantile scene, which was told to him, but which he has never been able to remember, and for him the goal of research is ultimately to rediscover this scene through his analyses with Fairbairn and Winnicott, and subsequently through his self-analysis. Anzieu, Pontalis and Rosolato give us most pertinent commentaries on this text, from which we isolate this major point: here we have an experienced analyst who, naively, trusts in a dream, in the *manifest content* of a dream, to tell him that he has at last truly rediscovered the lost memory—as if he has forgotten everything Freud said about the dream . . . It is an exciting text, in that it testifies to the realism of the unconscious—others will say the illusion of the unconscious—which persists throughout the entire development—and what a development—of analytic theory. Freud has thus put something in place there which cannot easily be removed.

This reference to the unconscious, to pursue our discussion of the treatment, is what is put to the test in so-called technical problems, and in particular in the famous alternative, which is far from resolved, between the analysis of content, of fantasy, through a sort of direct tracking of the unconscious, and the analysis of resistances. The opposition is constantly renewed, by turns denounced and restored to favour; denounced in the sense that if the fantasy never presents itself in a pure form, or in only an illusory ecmnesis, it is necessary—this is the essential point, and without it there would not be any analytic process—to chart a course, to do some work, and in particular, as they say, to overcome resistances. From there, we are pulled in the direction of so-called 'ego psychology': working on the ego, working on the resistances, to which Freud applied the term 'working through'. Obviously there is a great temptation to move to a practice of apprenticeship (or 'dis-apprenticeship' if it is a question of the ego's 'bad habits').

The opposition between the repressed and the resistances is assuredly to be denounced for its abruptness. It is not so much that resistance is purely and simply the other side of the repressed, a notion that has in its favour only the appearance of truth. Resistance is not a pure and simple mechanism, a habitual and stereotypical mode in the functioning of the ego; but neither is it simply stuck on to what it is a defence against, any more than the symptom or the reaction formation is purely and simply the negative of what it comes to cover. Freud was quite categorical in his formulation that repression and the return of the repressed are *not* one and the same thing. So if we have to refuse an excessively clear-cut opposition between the analysis of fantasy and the analysis of resistances, it is thus not according to a simple 'optic' which would see, in resistance, the simple negative of the repressed, so that one would carry out the same work in working on resistance and working directly on the repressed. What we must realise is that resistance itself functions like the unconscious. This so-called mechanism, what are termed its mechanisms, whether that of isolation, reaction-formation, conversion, etc., are certainly modes of functioning of the ego, but which are led to react according to the modalities of unconscious functioning—that is to say, fundamentally, the irrationality of displacement, condensation and symbolisation. This is what Freud formulated very early on, in the 'Project for a Scientific Psychology' (Freud 1950), where he tries to explain that 'pathological' defence, as opposed to 'normal' defence, depends precisely on the fact that the ego is led to function in the same way as that against which it functions; not to be a 'carbon copy' of that against which it functions, but to function in the same way. Freud shows here, in an extremely 'anthropomorphic' fashion, that the ego is positioned (in the sense that, in war, defences are 'positioned'). It is attacked on the side it least expects, and it is because it is taken from behind that it is unable to put into operation those normal mechanisms proper to its rationality. It is thus forced to function according to the cataclysmic mode of intemperate and excessive discharge.

The unconscious in culture

Earlier I announced the existence of a third terrain on which we might put the unconscious to the test: what could be called the cultural site. It is that which I emphasised last year, in relation to sublimation, and which just now I was trying to make clear. The position of psychoanalytic problems (for example the problem of sublimation: namely, what is a charge of unconscious energy in an activity that has a social value?) cannot be abstracted from an element which must be termed historical. In other words, the appearance of psychoanalysis itself as a cultural phenomenon must be taken into account. It is a problem which can thus be considered cultural, and which is confined, in more than one sense, to ethics (the ethics of psychoanalysis which embraces the ethics of treatment, but which is broader).

The question, the most general one, I would formulate in these terms: is there such a thing as 'psychoanalytic man'? What is psychoanalytic man? What is man afterwards, having been submitted to, having traversed, etc., psychoanalysis? Is he the man of the unconscious? Is he even the man of the It, as Groddeck would have had us believe? What kind of presence of self to itself is brought about or at least broached in psychoanalysis? Does psychoanalysis announce a new mode of this presence, and in what sense could we also say that this presence to oneself is mediated, perhaps necessarily, by the other (this time I am speaking of the other person and not of the other thing, without, however, affecting this 'other' with a capital or a small initial letter).

Right now I am taking you—and indeed myself—on a sort of return, into what Bion called *second thoughts* (which he even made the title of one of his books). Second thoughts. That is to say, taking a trajectory *again*, reflecting on what one has already said, bringing to focus, working-through. In these second thoughts, in this return, I would like to refer you to the 1960 article by Laplanche and Leclaire.[11] In this 'report', there are first of all two parties who are very clearly delimited. The text was drafted by Leclaire and myself, but in an alternating way, so that chapters III and V were written by Leclaire, and chapters I, II and IV by myself.

Chapters III and V are the clinical illustration—based on the case, which has since become famous, of Philippe, the 'unicorn man'—of what we had tried to formulate from a theoretical point of view, inspired by Freudian metapsychology. I will first say a few words about Leclaire's development because he, too, has re-worked more than once what he proposed there. First of all, his elaboration in the volume itself is taken up, not without some pertinence, by Conrad Stein (Colloque de Bonneval 1966: 131-143). If you read Stein's text, you will see that he pushes further, and in a more precise fashion, the delineation of what repression is in this case, not without raising a question which remains fundamental and which is here perfectly circumscribed: that of knowing whether, ultimately, what we call unconscious is not always the outer defences of the unconscious. In other words, that we will never grasp the thing itself, the unconscious fantasy 'in person'.

Leclaire's pathway

Leclaire then returns to this analysis, which he really takes to heart, in his second intervention; a response rewritten some years later,[12] and which goes a good bit further (precisely provoked by Conrad Stein's intervention) to define something as close as possible—or closer, at any rate—to the unconscious fantasy. What I am alluding to here is the sequence of phonemes that Leclaire wrote, in the case of Phillippe: 'poor d'jeli'. Would I say that in this way he was allying himself more closely with Lacan, in seeking to define a 'linguistic' content of the fantasy? It is not entirely clear, notably because the expression 'as close as possible to the unconscious' signifies—as Stein himself had said, and

Freud too, already, in a certain way—that one is not there. What Leclaire, later on, was to name 'the letter'—taking up a word with a familiar face[13]—would be, more and more, in his later texts (in *Démasquer le réel* he again takes up this dream and the position of 'poor d'jeli', the unconscious fantasy) a sort of *analogon* of the unconscious; not the unconscious in person but what he terms, in a lengthy discussion of it, 'the representation of a representative'.[14] In this formula, deliberately inverting Lacan's, the *representation* of the representative is precisely the phonematic sequence; but this is still only a sort of projection of something—the representative of the drive—which itself is obviously not linguistic, and which *the letter comes to obscure rather than to reveal.* Thus, Leclaire's route defines itself in a sort of navigation, never allowing the Lacanian river-bank to vanish from sight, but keeping its distance, and very often distinguishing itself from it, often quite considerably.

At this point, in order to place this text of 1960 within its context, I would remind you that it was situated in an ambience which could only make it appear an expression of 'Lacanian' thought. Presented by Lacan's pupils, it had to be an expression of Lacanianism—and Lacan, preoccupied above all with his 'political' impact, did not dispute this, at least not at that time, and for good reason. Now, in fact, while in its method it makes use of certain Lacanian contributions, this work is to be sharply distinguished from that of Lacan, and to be located in a deepening of Freudian theses. The introductory note which I added summarises quite clearly the essentials of what was intended, across the lapidary formulation of the 'unconscious structured like a language'. This formulation, taken up by Leclaire and myself, had above all the effect of marking—through the terms *'like'* and *'a'*—the differences between the unconscious and language, our language made of words.

I am going to have to follow fairly closely the principal detours of this text. Certainly not because I consider it untouchable or sacred—but because if we go through it too quickly we will miss out on its force, and will no longer have anything for our 'spiralling thoughts' (or *second thoughts*) to hook on to.

Realism or Signifying Intention

A first chapter is entitled: 'Three pathways towards the realism of the unconscious'. You can see that the cards are dealt straightaway, since it is a question of realism, of the scandal which lies in affirming the unconscious as a reality and not, as one might say with a quite positivist prudence, as a scientific concept, a law or a simple reference. The position sets itself up as deliberately provocative in relation to a very interesting critique of realism, formulated by Politzer. Whence the first of these three pathways: *meaning and letter: an examination of Politzer's critique.*

Politzer is perhaps, in 1977, not a terribly evocative name. Let us situate him as a Marxist philosopher and, from that point of view, very classical or even dogmatic (you can refer to what is entitled his 'Principles of Philosophy', which is really primary school stuff—the A.B.C. of the Marxist Vulgate—for this was, I presume, one of Politzer's tasks in the Communist Party, where he was supposed to propound Marxism in the party schools). What is interesting is his own movement in relation to psychoanalysis. He began this work in 1928, with *A Critique of the Foundations of Psychology*. In fact, two volumes had been planned, one devoted to psychoanalysis, the other (volume II), on the *Gestalt*, never saw the light of day. Politzer's project, at that time, was to found what he called a 'concrete psychology' on the basis of these two paradigms, psychoanalysis and *Gestalttheorie*, on the condition of ridding each of them of whatever remained of metaphysical, reified and 'idealist' claptrap.

6 December 1977

The first volume of *A Critique of the Foundations of Psychology* ends as follows:

> Psychoanalysis is, precisely, nothing but a beginning, and now that light has been shed upon its true essence, we must pursue our research by taking up a new perspective. On the other hand, behaviourism and *Gestalttheorie* need to be completely revised, too, so we can say that from the point of view of technique, everything remains to be done . . . But one thing is certain, that there is no going back. Psychology will never be able to return to realism and abstraction: the problem is now posed on a completely new terrain. And it will never be able to return, either to physiological psychology, or to introspective psychology; two obstacles bar its way: behaviourism and psychoanalysis. In a

> word, and whatever may be the imprecision of our formulae and the disagreeable resonance of this kind of formula: *metapsychology* has had its day, and the history of psychology is beginning. (Politzer 1994: 262)

Beyond, then, a very radical critique of—on the one hand—all experimental psychology, and—on the other—all introspective psychology, a way is sought, via psychoanalysis, to inaugurate a concrete psychology. It is only the conceptual apparatus of Freudian metapsychology that is to be swept away: the psychoanalytic discovery, the treatment, remains the model of a 'concrete' approach. In fact, however, Politzer was to undergo a change as a result of his political allegiances, or at least in parallel to them. Firstly in the *Revue de la psychologie concrète*, which he dominated, and then definitively, in 1939, he announced the end of psychoanalysis and decided that nothing of Freudianism could be saved. This happy inspiration derived from a moment in 1928, a moment which I linked to phenomenology. It is not that Politzer explicitly espouses that doctrine, but it appeared to me that in this desire to rediscover, behind the so-called 'machinery of metapsychology', an intentionality, a signifying intention, including how this signifying intention is opaque to itself, there is certainly a phenomenological inspiration at work. (It is the same as can be found in three texts in the same volume on 'The Unconscious', those of De Waehlens, Lanteri Laura, and Ricoeur—cf. Colloque de Bonneval 1966.)

In the name of concrete psychology, then, it is a question of disengaging from psychoanalysis a 'first person psychology', whose essential schema is drama—in particular the Oedipal drama. From this perspective, it is thus a question of getting rid of such metapsychological concepts as the ego, the super-ego, repression, etc.—and even the unconscious—which are considered of a mechanistic type. The aim is to foreground the properly dramatic, inter-human aspects of analysis: the Oedipus as scenario rather than complex. This drama, this dynamic knot of significations, is in a relation of immanence to the contents which express it, not a relation of conflict or dialectic, and still less in a mechanistic relation. Drama entails protagonists who are people, whereas metapsychology presents abstractions which it 'realises', which it makes into 'things', by endowing them with capital letters: the Unconscious, the Conscious, the system Perception-Consciousness, or later: the Ego, the Super-Ego, etc. Metapsychology thus abandons subjectivity—what is dubbed the 'first person' relation—and substitutes for it with a mechanical process, taking place between abstract 'third person' entities.

I formulated my response to Politzer as follows. The unity of a signifying intentionality is not necessarily linked to the grammatical first person; it is possible to conceive of a signifying intention in the second or third person. To be precise, that which appears to us in the 'formations of the unconscious' (dreams, slips of the tongue, bungled actions, etc.) is certainly the unity of a discourse or of a desire. It is something which speaks; as Lacan said, 'it speaks'. However, it speaks—effectively—in the third person, in a person not assuming its discourse as an 'I'.

Today, I consider this response imperfect, in a double sense. Firstly, this reflection on the unconscious was very closely linked to Freud's first topography and particularly to the 1915 version. This was conditioned by a sort of necessity, since Freud's major text on the unconscious dates from 1915, and is preliminary to the second topography, which would go further in a direction that seemed to accentuate the Freudian paradox—by positing an intrapsychical mechanism in which—simultaneously—characters appear.

The truth of the machinery

Whereas in the first topography the opposition Conscious—Unconscious—Preconscious was an opposition of systems, the 'systems' of the second topography, called 'agencies' this time—the ego, id, super-ego, ego-ideal, etc.—are conceived of as real 'characters' in the drama. Freud has often been reproached for representing censorship as a little internal man, a guardian or door-keeper situated inside our head, whose task would be to screen the visitors wishing to pass from one room to another. There, word for word, we have a metaphor which is pursued in certain texts, notably in the *Introductory Lectures* (1917). Freud does not in any way counter this objection; on the contrary, he takes this metaphor on board even more openly in the second topography. Certainly, here there is a machinery, here there are internal characters. The machinery is itself a drama introjected into the interior of the person, a transposition of interpersonal relations to the intrapersonal. The ego is treated sadistically by the super-ego; the ego, under the orders of the super-ego, defends itself against the id, and so on. In Freud's perspective, this is to be envisaged not merely as a mechanistic relation of agencies, but as a sort of debate taking place inside the subject. We have therefore to go beyond the 1915 paper in order to encompass, to turn around, the objection of abstraction and realism. Indeed, in psychoanalysis we deal with combat between characters, inside the subject, which is certainly real or realist.

But I think we have to go even further—and this is where my text was completely inadequate. We have to find room in the unconscious—and for now let us say, in psychoanalytic psychology, in metapsychology—not only for internal characters, but for internal things. In psychoanalysis, there is a *truth of reification*, a truth which is very precisely linked to that dimension which Freud discovered only very partially, and did not make visible, something he did not take as the centre his thinking. This is a genuine element of the unconscious which, in modern psychoanalysis, appears absolutely essential. I am referring to the part-object.

Of course, Freud encountered the part-object right the way through his experience, from the moment when, in a moment of intuitive genius at the beginning of the *Studies on Hysteria* (1895), he speaks of the 'internal foreign body'. This *internal foreign body* is nothing other than the part-object, whether 'good' or 'bad', as Melanie Klein was to put it. The id, ultimately, is to be interpreted in terms of introjected things, in terms of objects. However, these are objects which do not possess the inertia of things, but at the same time act as stimulators, as sources of excitation.

You can see that by thus turning around the accusation of abstraction, we are at the same time facing up to what Politzer called the realist objection. In the end, these are simply two sides of the same objection since, according to the latter, Freudianism would be constituted on 'realised' abstractions, on 'realised' significations, or, if we wish to take up a metaphor from Rabelais, on a language that is petrified or frozen and where words have become objects which can be thrown in your face.

There is certainly a seductive aspect to this critique, which seeks to return to the subject—in the strongest sense of this term, to the active, speaking, inter-human subject—its fluidity, ridding it, so to speak, of the belief (that Freud helped so much to consolidate) that it has within it things which it does not know about, which it needs to discover. Think, also, of that other metaphor, recurring constantly in Freudianism, that of archaeology: digging through the soil in order to discover, almost intact, whole fragments which are unknown to us, but which are somehow called to signify something, even if they no longer mean anything to anyone.

It should be emphasised that the intellectual tradition in which this critique of Freudian abstraction and realism is located in no way died out with Politzer. It is implicit when one speaks, for instance, of 'the illusion of interiority', or again 'the construction of the analytic space', and hence the construction of the unconscious, which implies that the unconscious is not 'down below' like a thing which one could simply go and fetch. This point of view cannot be dispensed with so easily. That, indeed, is what I made clear in my paper, by giving Politzer such an important place as the most distinguished exemplar of this way of conceiving the psychoanalytic discovery, transposing it into an intentional perspective, something which belongs to phenomenology.

The 'wish to signify' leaves no room for conflict

I will once again discuss a significant passage from Politzer:

> In short, we are faced with two hypotheses. One, the Freudian hypothesis, considers the dream as a veritable transposition of an original text that the dream distorts [this therefore is the realist hypothesis, according to which the dream only translates an unconscious text which pre-exists it in reality]; for the other, on the contrary, the dream is the result of the operation of an individual dialectic. The essential difference between these two conceptions arises from the fact that in the first, the dream is something which is derivative, and that in the second, it is the primary phenomenon and is self-sufficient. In the latter case, the dream does not have, strictly speaking, two contents: a latent and a manifest one. It can only have a manifest content, in fact, if we try to interpret it in terms of conventional dialectics [the 'manifest content', the narrative of the dream in our everyday language, cannot be considered a 'content' unless one restricts oneself to it]. Now it is just these dialectics [the conventional ones, this everyday language, this manner of taking the dream at face value] that are powerless in the case of dreams: the dream is not their product since it can be explained only by a personal dialectic. The dream, therefore, has only one content, the one Freud calls the latent content. But the dream has this content immediately, and not *after being disguised* [and it is this which is

> emphasised]. (Laplanche & Leclaire 1972: 123 n3/p.285-6, below)[15]

Politzer's theory is that there is only one signifying intention, an intention which should not be reified into an original text. There is one and the same 'wish to signify' which, depending on the case, may materialise in so-called conventional language—the one we use to communicate—or instead in a 'dialectic', a purely individual, personal language, which would be the idiom of the dream. We can thereby see how Politzer is led to reject the notion of a disguise, which would imply the existence of a primary expression, then a secondary expression, and, between the two—as in an imperfect or censored translation—lacunae, absences, and all the operations of deception.

Now this, let's say, 'phenomenological' conception of the formations of the unconscious, leads—and this is my principal objection—to the erasure of an essential dimension of the Freudian discovery of the unconscious. Put quite simply this is *the* Freudian discovery in the neuroses, in concrete analyses; the bringing to light of psychical conflict, and of the compromises into which the latter is finally translated, whether a particular symptom or any of the 'formations of the unconscious'. To restore due honour to this notion of conflict is to demonstrate proof of a Freudian orthodoxy from which it seems to be impossible to deviate. The notion of defensive conflict is one of the pivots of analysis, an axis which it is impossible for us to abandon, even if we may call into question plenty of other Freudian concepts. As an aside on the subject of Lacan (since this report might have appeared to conform to Lacanian ideas), if you refer to the index of German and French terms that accompanies Lacan's *Écrits*, you will find that the term *defence* simply does not appear there.

Conflict and defence are concepts which have no place within Politzer's conception, nor indeed in any attempt to reduce the psychoanalytic discovery to a schema of a phenomenological kind. The very notion of conflict, the way in which a conflict is translated into a symptom—this sort of pact where everyone makes concessions in the most realist sense of the term, where the unconscious finds the possibility of expressing itself, yet at the same time where elements of defence and of the ego infiltrate themselves—all this implies that there is only *one scene* shared by the characters in the conflict. There is no conflict between a signifying intention (if this is not already lodged in a text, if it is still only intentionality) and the way in which it is realised. The notion of conflict obliges us to conceive of agencies which are already situated in the same field, and it also presupposes that the forces which are to join together take a concrete, material form.

Politzer clarifies his point of view through several comparisons. The unconscious, he says, has no more reality than a law of physics—for example: the law constructed by scientists to account for the fall of a body: *e*='gt^2 The unconscious should not be 'realised' any more than the rules immanent to a game of tennis; the only reality is the game of tennis, and the rules, for an observer, can be reconstructed in the same way as the law of physics was constructed to account for the fall of bodies.

Well—I said—if one conceived of the unconscious as simply constructed in the same way as a law of physics, no physicist would entertain the idea of a conflict *between* the law *'(GT^2)* and the particular fall of a body. There is simply a particular instance of this law in the fall of a specific body, and the very idea of a conflict between the two is inconceivable. This would lead us to support the scandalous type of materiality which belongs to the unconscious, a materiality to which Freud refers with the term *Vorstellung*, 'representation'. When he speaks to us of unconscious representations they are not schemas, they are not laws, they are beings, which he traces as such. Likewise, when Lacan speaks of the 'signifier', he takes this term in its most material sense. Even if the question of knowing what kind of signifiers these are remains open, for it is entirely legitimate to consider that there might be signifiers other than verbal ones, even if a whole current, among Lacan's followers, has reduced the notion of the signifier to verbal language. However, what is at stake here is not that alternative—verbal or non-verbal—but the problem of a materiality, of the concrete, tangible existence of what Politzer, for his part, wanted to reduce to a sort of immanent law.

Focusing on the two modes of listening

This brings me to the second development of this first chapter, in which my theme was *the two modes of listening, the gaps in conscious discourse, and the notion of formations of the unconscious*. I emphasised the fact that the unconscious reveals itself to us, in analyses, not in an homogeneous way 'beneath' what is given as manifest. The unconscious is not inscribed, as if on a second stave, to be discovered continuously, following manifest acts or words. Instead it is always something revealed at particular points, which one could describe as the greatest load-bearing points. This is evident specifically in the notion of 'formations' of the unconscious, or in the image of lacunae. These formations—let us imagine a slip of the tongue which inserts itself into a conversation or a lecture—break into a text which elsewhere offers a certain coherence. If the unconscious is not present everywhere with the same density, if it is not there like a parallel text which would be the unconscious signification of what I am in the process of saying, but instead emerges in some failure of my discourse, then this means it can neither be heard nor decoded (as I put it in the text) 'simultaneously'. This expression is obviously a reference to the practice of simultaneous translation, where interpreters, enclosed in a booth, with headphones on, are able to convert a discourse into another language immediately. The model is scarcely a caricature, but reflects an attitude which is more widespread than might appear, and which is particularly evident, not in psychoanalytic technique, but in what we might call the practice of wild psychoanalysis, which is much more prevalent now than it was in Freud's time, in society . . . even in analytic societies.

With the notion of unconscious formation, on the contrary, one is oriented, once again, towards the affirmation of a reality, the scandalous and paradoxical affirmation of a realism. The unconscious, epistemologically speaking, is not a 'functional' notion. The analyst, in his or her research, is a 'naïve realist'. One could perhaps compare this return to the most primary realism with what appears to have happened in the development of the notion of energy in physics. For a long time energy was considered a purely functional concept, like an X carried from one equation to another, but whose ultimate nature was not to be interrogated. Remarkably, physics has now arrived at a kind of realism (will it remain there?) since energy—to the extent that it is equivalent to matter, where quanta of energy can be detected materially—has become a sort of material reality. This was deeply shocking news for physicists used to thinking of their science simply as a 'well-made language', as Poincaré used to put it. To reach the point of detecting energy at particular points, to speak of particles of energy, is clearly a scientific attitude which might seem to us as mad as that of Reich, when he claimed to have observed orgones—that is to say, 'particles of orgasm'!

Nevertheless, regarding the radical opposition I claimed to uphold between two mode of listening in analysis itself, in analytic technique—a continuous listening or simultaneous translation, and a listening which is more particularly attentive to load-bearing points, nodal points, or, on the contrary, to points free of any 'load' in the discourse of the analysand—I would today be less peremptory. I would be less categorical in precisely the following sense. One notices, if one wishes to transpose the notion of unconscious formation into analytic treatment, that it is perhaps the session as a whole which should be viewed as a large formation of the unconscious. A formation of the unconscious brought about by a situation which is completely new, completely original, in which the discourse spoken is necessarily produced in the milieu of the transference. On that basis, the idea that *in the analytic session* attention should be not evenly-balanced but selective, seems to me far more questionable. The nodal point, the load-bearing point, is effectively the session as a whole. So much so that, regarding the analytic attitude during the session, I do not think it appropriate to maintain an absolute opposition, and to put forward a choice. There are in fact two *moments* of listening: that which Freud called 'evenly-suspended'—which implies that nothing is privileged—and, on the other hand, starting from this evenly-suspended listening, a focussing-in on certain points which seem more appropriate for interpretation.

The inadequacy of the criterion 'consciousness'

I ended this first chapter under the title of 'The Unconscious and the Problem of Consciousness' by analysing very closely the process through which Freud takes us, across different conceptions of the unconscious, to the properly psychoanalytic sense of the term. This is a sense which, I emphasise here, is essentially topographical or systematic. What is the meaning of this allusion to the 'problem of consciousness', if not that the very term *unconscious* (Freud does not deny this, at least at the beginning of each of his developments) refers us back to consciousness, even *defining* the unconscious in relation to it, as that which in the psychical domain is not submitted to consciousness.

This definition of the unconscious takes us back to what Freud called the unconscious 'in the descriptive sense', which is to say: everything that is not present at a given moment in the field of my consciousness. This unconscious, Freud tells us, is much more vast than the unconscious in the properly psychoanalytic sense of the term, since it comprises everything which, at that precise moment, forms part of a sort of unrealised stock, whether that be memories, pieces of knowledge, opinions, perceptual sketches, etc. With Freud, this reminder leads us very quickly to distinguish, at the heart of this unconscious described solely in terms of the criterion of consciousness (this un-conscious) a part that is in principle easily accessible to consciousness (which Freud, in his first topography, calls the system Preconscious-Conscious, or simply the Preconscious) but also an unconscious which is now actively excluded, repressed, which is not accessible to consciousness in principle, and which cannot be reached except with the aid of an extremely slow and complex procedure which is, precisely, the analytic method. This unconscious is a domain which perhaps (and here we have a fundamental question) will always retain depths that will never be brought into consciousness, but at most will be reconstructed.

You can see that in this subdivision of the unconscious in the descriptive sense, we actually connect a part of this unconscious to consciousness, in speaking of the system Preconscious-Unconscious, and then we are led to distinguish another system, another psychical 'place' (that is why we are here speaking in the 'topographical' sense) which is in opposition to the former, to the system Preconscious, in the sense that it is actively repressed. If the opposition Preconscious-Unconscious is an opposition of systems, one could even conclude that the reference to the phenomenon of consciousness—a reference which, in the descriptive sense, would seem to be essential, because to speak of the unconscious one must certainly 'know' what consciousness is—becomes, for this new opposition, secondary or even illusory. In what sense? Well, there may be, for example, sudden resurgences of the unconscious. We might think of the re-emergence of a forgotten memory in the first treatments related in the *Studies on Hysteria* (1895); or of what reappeared under hypnosis, or again, through artificial means such as those of 'narco-analysis'. This sudden re-emergence into the light of consciousness of an element manifestly belonging to the unconscious in no sense indicates that a particular element, a particular traumatic memory, has now passed into the Preconscious system. An unconscious element, in the topographical, systematic sense of the term, can become conscious from a phenomenological point of view while continuing to participate in the Unconscious system. It was thus not in relation to consciousness, but as system, as configuration, as a structure in relation to another structure that I opposed here (with Freud) the Unconscious to the Preconscious system. So 'making conscious', in the psychoanalytic sense of the term (not ecmnesic resurgence, the reappearance, without connections, of a forgotten memory or a fantasy that had apparently disappeared), is never truly effective, and is not truly a transformation until this element is re-woven, worked through (*durcharbeitet*), as we say, in the Preconscious system.

. . . and the inadequacy of the purely 'topographical' opposition

So there you have the mainspring of this paragraph on 'the unconscious and the problem of consciousness'. But there remains the fact that if we oppose the Unconscious and the Preconscious as two systems, having the same status of reality—as distinct but similar—then nothing has been said on the major consideration that these two systems are at the same time profoundly different, in the sense that they obey different laws of functioning. We need to think of two systems which are at once on the same level of reality—allowing us to understand what is both a compromise and already a conflict between them—but at the same time we have to conceive of them as subject to different processes.

I mentioned a moment ago the experience, which is not unusual, of a memory emerging 'fully armed' from the Unconscious, isolated, like a block out of place. Topographically, such a memory continues to form part of the Unconscious system. But we can go further along this path and refer to psychosis, where it is not just an isolated element but entire sections (for some, even the whole unconscious) which, in the end, would be completely out in broad daylight. Now, it is certainly paradoxical, from a purely descriptive perspective, to speak of an unconscious 'out in broad daylight', of a conscious Unconscious (*sit venia verbo* . . .). However, just as the descriptive path leads to an impasse, so a purely *topographical* opposition of the two systems cannot be adequate. If the Unconscious were merely *another* system in relation to the Preconscious, but of the same order, you can see that we would be led back to something that appeared at a certain moment in the history of psychiatry—during the years 1890-1900, to be precise, concerning what at the time were called 'double personalities', 'alternating personalities', so dear to Janet. The idea was that a certain hysteric, all of a sudden, and sometimes according to a certain daily rhythm, was first Miss A, and then Mrs B. Janet's idea was that we are not right to consider one of these personalities to be more unconscious than the other; there were simply two groups, two sets of affects and representations, of which at any time now one and now the other might be in the position of being hidden, or of coming to the surface. Well, any hypothesis which would not give sufficient space to the laws of functioning proper to each system would end up in this paradox of conceiving the unconscious as simply, let us say, another person. At the same time this prevents us from accounting for that other paradox (this time a very real one) that, in phenomena such as psychosis, we really and truly have a discourse that functions like the unconscious and which at the same time shows forth in broad daylight.

13 December 1977

We have now passed, then, from a descriptive unconscious, defined in relation to consciousness by its non-conscious quality, to the unconscious as system, as an organisation of representations or, to accept Hegel's term, to a 'consciousness', another 'consciousness'. This takes us so far that Freud himself sometimes uses this argument of the 'other consciousness' to prove, or at the very least to justify, the hypothesis of the unconscious. Just as we infer in our neighbour, he tells us, the presence of acts signifying the existence of a psychical domain, so we can conclude that *in ourselves* there is a psychical *other*: '[A]ll the acts and manifestations which I notice in myself and do not know how to link up with the rest of my mental life must be judged as if they belonged to someone else' (Freud 1915a: 169). If we add that this 'other person', this 'other consciousness', is itself sometimes prone to emerge into consciousness, we would end up with the following paradox. Whereas at an initial moment of Freud's reflection, the unconscious was an especially dark and profound zone, of non-consciousness, at a second moment it would be another set, distinguishable term by term from our official personality. This, clearly, cannot be maintained, and would take us back to the *naïveté* of 'alternating personalities'.

The 'functional' approach

This leads us to the conclusion that we need a third approach, after the purely descriptive and the purely topographical, which we could call the functional approach (or the economic, it hardly matters), the essential point being to characterise the unconscious not only numerically as another, but as qualitatively different in relation to the preconscious system. What can be used to characterise it? Its contents, its connections or its mode of functioning? Maybe these different aspects are linked, and we are going to see that a certain type of contents (I am thinking in particular of visual contents, to which Freud ascribes such importance) imposes a certain type of connection or of functioning. But we could also imagine the inverse: what characterises the unconscious would be first and foremost its mode of functioning, and its laws could be imposed on any content whatsoever. This is what is called the 'primary process', a certain mode of circulation—let us say, for the moment, of meaning—among these representations. The primary process seeks precisely, Freud tells us in numerous passages, the identity of perception, and in this sense it would be more adapted to signifiers sprung directly from perception, that is to say, to images, to figurative representations.

Representability

By this route, I reach an important element of the dream, upon which we will pause for a moment. It is that which Freud dubs 'considerations of representability' (*Rucksicht auf Darstellbarkeit: Rucksicht* = 'taking into consideration of', and *Darstellbarkeit* = 'the possibility of being presented in figurative form'). The dream thus takes into consideration the possibility of representing in figurative form what it is saying, of presenting its language in a figurative form. In order to take this problem into account properly, it is necessary to remind ourselves of a certain number of elementary notions, without wishing to go through the whole theory of dreams. In particular, that the dream sets off from the dream thoughts, and among these, 'the day's residues' (you will see why this has such importance) form the vast majority. The material which the dream works on consists of thoughts from the previous day (taking this term in its broadest sense). These thoughts might have been desires—but not necessarily—possibly sexual—but not necessarily. There may be a whole series of other contents, everything that goes on in daily life: perceptions, events, rationalisations, fears, projects, calculations, or—again—uncompleted tasks or thoughts, to which Freud attaches very great importance. (This is where we might introduce the idea Lagache wanted to propose as the very basis of repetition, the *Zeigarnik* effect, which is to say, the necessity of completing unfinished tasks. Freud alludes very clearly to this notion: it is the treatment of the day's residues that embodies this attempt to complete or continue all the thoughts we stir up in a conscious or preconscious manner in our everyday life.)

I will deliberately remain, then, at the level of the most important part of the dream thoughts, the day's residues, and you will see how this could have led to a certain conception of the dream which is rather curious—at any rate, rather contrary to the spirit of the dream as the means by which to approach the unconscious. What, then, starting from these daytime thoughts, constitutes 'consideration of representability'? It bears upon concepts, on the one hand, and relations, on the other. In both cases, it is a question of transforming those elements of thought which are not imaged elements—but most often linguistic ones, as is, for the most part, our daytime thought—in such a way that they can be represented in the dream. You can refer to two chapters of *The Interpretation of Dreams,* the one on symbolisation and representability, and the other on the figuration of logical relations. First of all, concepts, the 'verbal representations' to use the Freudian expression, are seen to be substituted by images, either by means of conventional symbols or through a more or less individual symbolism. Examples include replacing an 'important person' with someone who is placed 'high up' spatially, perched on top of a column, and—equally—by making use of a certain number of verbal displacements for this substitution of images (the use of synonyms, etc.), verbal slippages end up at a term which facilitates figuration.

On the other hand, concerning the figuration of logical relations, Freud spends a great deal of time on the different modes of relation, the different conjunctions, to show the extent to which these relations or conjunctions are able to 'move', how they can move over into a figuration which employs only images and a spatio-temporal juxtaposition. Thus, for example, causality in thought will be represented in the dream by a succession (obviously, according to the old adage: *Post hoc ergo propter hoc,* which is to say that the dreamer deconstructs the notion of causality, just as a Hume was able to analyse thought himself).[16] This consideration of representability goes so far that the words in the dream, Freud tells us, are not in principle taken for what they say, for their linguistic value. In principle, Freud claims, a word or phrase is present in the dream only when it has been pronounced the day before. What does that mean? It means, precisely, that the dream does not think with words; these phrases pronounced during the waking period are not taken for what they say, but solely as an imaged sign of the situation in which they were pronounced. Imagine a phrase which might be found in a dream, for example: 'It's a rule of three'. Before looking for the signification in the rule of three, and possibly even in the Oedipus, before seeking a rational process or the prolongation of a mathematical reasoning you may have begun during the day, you need to ask yourself where and when this phrase itself or the elements of the phrase (rule-of-three) were pronounced. As a general rule these phrases are representatives of the daytime situation in which they appeared, and not linguistic representatives of their 'meaning'.

The words of the dream, to sum up, are representations of things or thing-representations, and not word-representations. We have to realise that this consideration of representability—this process which ends up making thoughts representable—is not an extrinsic process, something that would be like the final touch applied to the elaboration of the dream. Thus we need to compare and oppose the 'considerations of representability' to 'secondary revision', which, in an interesting parallelism, Freud also occasionally calls *'Rucksicht auf Verständlichkeit'*, that is to say, 'considerations of intelligibility'. Secondary revision, for its part, is indeed considered to be the final touch to the dish, so as to serve up a finished product which can be put in a narrative form. After the phase in which the dream is dreamt, there is obviously the recounting of the dream, and thus secondary revision is truly a second process. Consideration of representability, for its part, is in no way secondary; it is consubstantial with the dream, and Freud links it very precisely to that fundamental process of the dream he calls regression.

You will recall that Freud distinguishes, in *The Interpretation of Dreams* (1900), between three sorts of regression, which are not always easy to tell apart: topographical regression, formal regression and temporal regression. Distinctions between topographical regression and formal regression, ultimately, can only be made by entering into the Freudian machinery, that is to say, into a sort of machine for producing dreams, with perception at one end and motion at the other (Freud 1900: 536-49). Topographical regression would consist, Freud tells us, in a reverse trajectory, forcing back, precisely, some of this machine's energy towards its perceptual end. This evidently refers to a rather outdated conception of hallucination and perception.

Formal regression

However that may be, topographical regression, then, is the regression of thought towards perception. 'Formal regression' (and here we can see where we are more easily) is the return, Freud tells us, 'to more primitive modes of expression', modes that are less evolved. If you take the end of the 1915 text 'The Unconscious', for instance, which describes schizophrenic language as a way of treating word-representations, according to the primary process, as thing-representations, then you will find here a very precise illustration of what Freud calls 'formal regression'. The same goes for what I recalled a moment ago, the 'regression' to a figurative language, returning from developed logical relations to connections between representations capable of transformation into a 'rebus'.

A passage concerning the relation of manifest to latent content shows clearly this process of formal regression:

> The dream-thoughts and dream-content are presented to us like two versions of the same subject matter in two different languages. Or, more properly, the dream-content [that is, the manifest content] seems like a transcript of the dream-thoughts into another mode of expression, whose characters and syntactic laws it is our business to discover by comparing the original to the translation. The dream-thoughts are immediately comprehensible, as soon as we have learnt them. (Freud 1900: 277)

If we pursue this path, provisionally leaving the nature of the dream-thoughts indeterminate, and conceding that the vast majority of these are thoughts which have nothing mysterious about them, we can see that the unconscious treatment of the dream (since the dream is supposed to give us the best possible image of the way the unconscious functions) works according to laws of functioning which are archaic from the formal point of view, linked to a mode of representation which itself is archaic, figural, or, to adopt a term used by Piera Aulagnier, 'pictographic' representation. There would thus be two ways of treating the same content (I am now commenting on the passage quoted): one treatment would be simpler, more primitive and more reduced in its syntax (a syntax with fewer variables and axioms at its disposal). This would be, precisely, the regressive treatment in the dream. The other would be a more developed treatment, more discriminating, more distanced from the image and the thing, less adhesive and aiming, as Freud puts it, no longer at identity of perception but at identity of thought. Here, then, we have an outline of what Freud calls the primary and secondary process; however, through this notion of formal regression, we reach a rather baffling formulation. To the question: 'what is the unconscious such as it appears to us in the functioning of dreams?', the response could be: 'the unconscious is precisely a mode of functioning and (why not?) *is nothing but a regressive mode of functioning* without any specific content'.

Could the 'id' be empty?

This temptation to say that there is nothing *in* the unconscious, that the unconscious is just a kind of process without content, can be found in a very old image—one of Lacan's—according to which 'the purse of the id is empty'. In Freud himself, particularly when he became annoyed at the rather mystical search by his neophyte disciples for 'unconscious contents', one sometimes gets the impression that he approaches such a conception which, in a new way, would abolish any realist unconscious. We have, notably, a fairly late paper (1923b) entitled 'Remarks on the Theory and Practice of Dream-Interpretation':

> It is only too easy to forget that a dream is as a rule merely a thought like any other, made possible by a relaxation of the censorship and by unconscious reinforcement, and distorted by the operation of the censorship and by unconscious revision. (Freud 1923b: 112)

Here we find a kind of quadrille of four terms: censorship, on the one hand, which relaxes and distorts, and the unconscious, which reinforces and elaborates. If we were to take *only* two of these four terms—relaxing censorship and the elaborating unconscious—we would reach precisely what I am trying to convey: the possibility of an interpretation that would be, after all, very similar to all those which deny the reality of the unconscious. Let us recall the way that Politzer himself gathers together his understanding of the dream—since it is essentially on the dream that Politzer, too, is working. In the end, there are not two texts, one of which would be the translation of the other, but two expressions, one conventional and the other more personal, of the same signifying intention, of the same thought. Thus, in the dream of 'Irma's Injection', in which Freud reveals this thought: 'I wish for an error of diagnosis', the same wish, ultimately a preconscious one, is expressed either with precision in the 'conventional' phrase 'I wish for an error of diagnosis' or in the dream's mode of expression, a language created in an absolutely individual fashion. Politzer's kind of interpretation obviously does not give enough space to the problem of the image. However, I am thinking also of what Henri Ey set up as a theory of the dream, from a perspective which—for its part—also denies the effective, actual, and dynamic existence of the unconscious, in order to take account only of hierarchical modes of expression. Well, this idea that when censorship 'relaxes', the unconscious is going to be able to 'elaborate', would be nothing other (if we retain just these two factors) than a Jacksonian or neo-Jacksonian kind of solution. With the psyche considered as a hierarchy of functions and structures, the unconscious, for Henri Ey, is 'contained' by the conscious, playing on the resources of the word 'contained'. On the one hand, the unconscious is nowhere else than in consciousness; it is certainly there, immanent and non-transcendent. But on the other hand, the unconscious is contained by the conscious, in the sense that the regressive mode of expression is, as it were, kept on a leash by a more developed expressive mode. The dream, in a theory of this kind, appears as a destructuration, a *loosening*, determined by the psycho-physiological conditions of sleep, giving rise to the appearance not of new contents but solely a primary mode of functioning, the sole subject-matter of which is the same material as our daytime thoughts. Thus, *the dream would be nothing but the dream-work*, which could equally well be called destructuration or structuration. The unconscious, if we move towards this interpretation of the unconscious mode of functioning, would be characterised only by a type of functioning, and the dream would be nothing but the submission of everyday material to this other type of functioning.

I mentioned a minute ago Freud's irritation at an excessive mysticism of the 'depths'. We could add, this time with a dash of malice, that we could even draw on arguments from Freud's analyses in *The Interpretation of Dreams* (1900) to support such a position. These analyses are always partial, truncated, and very far from going to the last word of the story, of the analysis, right up to the individual element, that of Freud's desire, in particular his sexual and infantile desire. Obviously, Freud assumed the mantle of discretion, not to go any further—even if he sometimes gives away elements which have been used by others.[17] Most of the time, he relates his own dreams back to daytime thoughts, to relatively anodyne desires, which do not yet go into the depths. Freud thus conceals himself behind discretion, and also hides behind a scientific alibi, by only presenting these dream-analyses in a fragmentary fashion, the same dream being taken up several times over, each time used as material for a precise demonstration of a particular, isolated point of the theory. But, from then on, perhaps one could claim that it is no accident Freud did not go any further, and that perhaps, after all, further on there is nothing to find . . . ?

So we have arrived, let us recall, at a series of three terms. We move from the descriptive unconscious to the unconscious as system, and from the systematic unconscious to the unconscious as process. However, it must be clear that none of these aspects is able to get rid of the one that precedes it, and it is not a question of erasing each time what had been said on the first level. The unconscious as process is (as we shall see) linked to contents and not only to a mode of functioning; and these very contents themselves, which take us back to the unconscious as a system of representations, are in relation to the fact that the unconscious remains, at least in the majority of cases, separated, inaccessible to consciousness.

I would like at this point to bring in another passage from the same 1923 paper, which shows clearly that, while the dream can be interpreted at a level which is *almost* sufficient without the hypothesis of the unconscious as system, and solely with the hypothesis of the unconscious as process, yet, at the same time, Freud never limited himself in that way.

Dreams from above, dreams from below

> It is possible to distinguish between dreams from above and dreams from below, provided that the distinction is not made too sharply. Dreams from below are those which are provoked by the strength of an unconscious (repressed) wish which has found a means of being represented [which has made a representative for itself] in some of the day's residues. They may be regarded as inroads of the repressed into waking life [dreams 'from below' thus correspond to the most commonly-accepted conception in psychoanalysis]. Dreams from above correspond to thoughts or intentions of the day before which have contrived during the night to obtain reinforcement from repressed material that is debarred from the ego. When this is so, analysis as a rule disregards this unconscious ally and succeeds in inserting the latent dream-thoughts into the texture of waking thought. [This interpretation re-emphasises the diurnal text, it integrates it into the

> figure, into the Gestalt (*in das Gefuge*) of waking thought]. This distinction calls for no modification in the theory of dreams. (Freud 1923b: 111)

The idea in this passage, then, is that certain interpretations of dreams (and perhaps even the majority of dreams which come up in an analysis) can do perfectly well without recourse to the deepest unconscious desire; an adequate interpretation can be given at the level of the day's residues. This is what Freud was to do, for example, regarding a dream of Descartes', brought to him by Maxime Leroy, about which he gave a few indications for a possible interpretation, while apologising for practising wild interpretation without having the dreamer's associations. I can treat this dream, he would have said, as a dream from above, and try to see what it signifies in the framework of Cartesian thought. You can see, then, that for these dreams an 'immanentist' kind of explanation (whether we call it Politzerian or neo-Jacksonian) would appear to be able to suffice, whether one considers—with some justification—the dream to be a particular, specific, individual expression of a thought also able to flow into the mould of common language, or whether it is viewed purely and simply as a degradation of common thought caused by the disorganisation of sleep. Well, even for these 'dreams from above', Freud tells us, there is unconscious reinforcement, which we disregard only for methodological reasons: 'Analysis, as a general rule, disregards this unconscious support.' This will bring us to the question of the nature of this reinforcement by the repressed, by unconscious desire.

20 December 1977

We had got up to the dream. In what sense is it the 'royal road to the unconscious'? The dream is not the unconscious, but rather what we call a formation of the unconscious, and one would be very wrong (we all get caught out from time to time) to believe that the dream, like psychosis, shows the unconscious 'in broad daylight.' Let us recall our three senses of the unconscious: the descriptive unconscious, the systematic unconscious and the unconscious as process. Well, in the descriptive sense, the dream is not unconscious, but a form of consciousness. The systematic unconscious? As far as the nature of the contents goes, there are certainly some dreams where properly unconscious contents are barely visible, nor even interpretable. The dream contents, even if latent, are mainly of preconscious origin. As far as the unconscious as process is concerned, it is certainly what takes centre stage in the dream—that is to say, the subjection of some material, ultimately anything at all, to very particular formal conditions, something which can be termed, precisely, 'formal regression'. Processes which we have to emphasise once again, and which Freud describes with the terms condensation, displacement, symbolisation and representation.

In the 1923 paper we have considered, concerning 'dreams from above and dreams from below', Freud puts forward this distinction to qualify two types of dream. However, at the same time, every dream consists of elements from both above and below, so that every dream can be characterised as coming simultaneously from above and from below, according to a sort of gradient or 'complementary series', a series completely based on the spatial imagery always present in Freud, 'above' being the conscious and 'below' the unconscious. I was recently re-reading a paper by Octave Mannoni on the dream and transference, in which he claimed that the formula 'depth psychology' never appears in Freud's writing. This is totally incorrect. The image of the unconscious as being 'in the depths' can be found everywhere, including the 1915 paper devoted to the unconscious, where it appears co-extensive with the 'topographical' hypothesis (Freud 1915a: 168). The elements from above, to return to that opposition, are particularly evident in the course of treatment, to the point where the patients in Freud's analyses can lean on this fact in order to prolong discussion interminably, and prove that these contents, since they are woven from the day's residues, are suggested by the analyst or aimed at him. But at the same time, let us affirm that every dream comprises at least an unconscious reinforcement, if not an unconscious origin. (Someone who sought to push to its limit this distinction between origin and mere reinforcement would be mischievous! It is rather a quantitative difference, a question of proportion.)

What, then, is reinforcement by the repressed or by unconscious desire? The argument of this 1923 text is exciting, in its step by step progress. It places itself very close to clinical experience, and to the debate in which the patient appears as 'the sceptic' (*der Skeptiker*). He is sceptical for a good reason, because he is resistant to exposing his unconscious. However, he is also sceptical from the perspective of the very theory of dreams. Well, this text goes by a very indirect route, not getting straight to the point. It follows the course of the actual discussion, the hesitations caused by tracing the objections of the patient. It is in response to these objections which arise in the treatment that Freud gets to the bottom of the problem. His argument is, in the most profound sense, a *dialectic* with the patient.

The kernel of psychical reality

The question, ultimately, is this: is there something at the bottom of the dream which comprises an absolute reality, something like a hard kernel or, in other terms, something not caught up in the dialogue, not solely a part of the analytic dialogue? What is this ultimate unconscious element? For Freud, it is that over which the analyst has no influence, or which at any rate he is unable to make appear, let alone shape it in any way. Let me take up the following question: Can the dream be influenced by the analyst? As far as the manifest content goes, the answer is yes. It is obvious that many dreams, as far as the manifest content is concerned, have a relation to the analyst. Remarks, elements which relate to him, appear in the most obvious way even in the recounting of the dream. Can the analyst influence the latent content? Well, yes, and actually for the greater part. To the extent that the latent content is composed of preconscious thoughts, it is very widely influenced by the mere existence of the analytic relation, and this is outside any additional element of deliberate influence, of intentional suggestion.

What, then, does the analyst not have influence over? Here is one stage in the argument : 'On the mechanism of dream-formation itself, on the dream-work in the strict sense of the word, one never exercises any influence: of that one may be quite sure' (Freud 1923b: 114). I say that this is a stage in the argument, because if we stop there, we once again see a conception taking shape according to which the part 'from above' would provide the contents (the dream having no content other than our waking thoughts), and the part 'from below'—precisely that over which we can have no influence—does not correspond to any material, but simply to a mode of functioning, to a way of dealing with these contents—that is to say, to the dream-work. Whatever comes 'from below', from the unconscious, one might also say, is 'energy', but the only way of defining this is its mode of circulation.

If we call a halt here provisionally, in the complex dialectic we are pursuing with this text of Freud's, the unconscious would not be a 'content', but a 'force', and the dream would be nothing but the treatment of preconscious thoughts in the mode of unconscious functioning. I wondered if this solution, which in another perspective the phenomenologists would embrace willingly, and which allows us precisely to free ourselves of the fearsome hypothesis of unconscious *contents*, of unconscious *objects*—if this is not a possible consequence of Lacan's formula: 'The unconscious is structured like a language'. This is a hypothesis which can be upheld, and which we will have to examine. However, from the point at which the unconscious is no longer seen as anything but its *mode of structuring*, at which the unconscious is precisely nothing but its mode of functioning, without reference to any particular content—from that moment on, indeed, the 'purse of the id' is well and truly empty . . .

Let us return to the movement of the discussion, to that dialectic in which Freud offers the first guarantee of the objectivity of the analytic discovery. There is indeed something which is not influenced by us—that is, the mechanism of dream- formation. But this is only present for a moment, a milestone which will have to be grasped firmly, but which must then be left behind. We have further to go, in the direction of unconscious contents:

> . . . every true dream [note this curious term, 'true dream', which implies that there could be dreams which are not true . . .] contains indications of the repressed wishful impulses to which it owes the possibility of its formation. (Freud 1923b: 114)

Further on in the text, we see what it is in which these movements of repressed desire consist. It is, once again, a question of the discovery of the infantile, of memories, maybe of infantile fantasies. If it is a question of fantasies, then this entails the prospect of the argument beginning again. But in the end what is essential for Freud, in the dream, the proof of its fundamentally unconscious source, comes from the rediscovery of *infantile* material which can gradually be pieced together like a puzzle. It is at the moment when the last piece of the puzzle is put in place that one notices that everything which exists there is intricately connected, since no piece is missing and one has been able to reconstruct the image in the puzzle completely. Throughout this text, an important part of this hypothetical discussion with the analysand consists in putting exactly back in place the 'agreeable' dream' (dreamed to give the analyst pleasure) and the 'confirmatory' dream (that is, the one which apparently comes to confirm an interpretation or construction of the analyst). Now, the confirmatory dream may, later on, show itself to be an 'agreeable' dream, and the only proof that it is not arises when it entails new, unheard-of material:

> . . . I recall a discussion which I was led into with a patient whose exceptionally ambivalent attitude was expressed in the most intense compulsive doubt. He did not dispute my interpretations of his dreams and was very much struck by their agreement with the hypotheses which I put forward. But he asked whether these corroborative dreams might not be an expression of his compliance towards me. I pointed out that the dreams had also brought up a quantity of details of which I could have had no suspicion and that his behaviour in the treatment apart from this had not been precisely characterised by compliance. Whereupon he switched over to another theory and asked whether his narcissistic wish to be cured might not have caused him to produce these dreams, since, after all, I had held out to him a prospect of recovery if he were able to accept my constructions. I could only reply that I had not yet come across any such mechanism of dream-formation. But a decision was reached by another road. (Freud 1923b: 116)

Before we go on, we should emphasise that this is the conclusion of an entire discussion bearing on what is new in the dream, on the unforeseen, on whatever arises which certainly confirms what the analyst has said, but in an unexpected way, providing unsuspected historical details. So here is the 'decision':

> He recollected some dreams which he had had before starting analysis and indeed before he had known anything about it [a lucky man, who was able, at that time, to have never heard of analysis!]; and the analysis of these dreams, which were free from all suspicion of suggestion, led to the same interpretations as the later ones. It is true that his obsession for contradiction once more found a way out in the idea that the earlier dreams had been less clear than those that occurred during the treatment; but I was satisfied with their similarity. [And to conclude:] I think that in general it is a good plan occasionally to bear in mind the fact that people were in the habit of dreaming before there was such a thing as psycho-analysis. (Freud 1923b: 117)

The dream is not communication

Thus, the confirmation comes at the same time as a very important affirmation for Freud: the dream is not initially absorbed into the treatment, it is not part of a dialogue, any more than the symptom or the parapraxis. Therefore, neither is the dream primarily and above all the 'dream narrative'. There is a kernel which is removed from communication, and it is this kernel which proves to us, when we come across it, notably in dreams which are not dreamt to be analysed nor even to be recounted, the existence of an unconscious reality.

To finish my commentary, grafted on to the first chapter of our 1960 report, I would like to say a few more words about representability, that is to say the necessity for the dream to transpose its thoughts into modes of expression which can be put forth in visual images. Here, we recall, there are two regressions which go together: what Freud calls topographical regression, in accordance with his schema of the psychical apparatus (to think in images is to regress towards the perceptual end of a psychical apparatus conceived as leading from perception to motility) and, on the other hand, a regression said to be formal, the one with which we are beginning to familiarise ourselves, the return to a mode of functioning which differs from waking thought. In other words, what we are learning to call the 'primary process'.

So—what is the relation between these two regressions? Is there, between them, any priority or subordination? One might, for instance, assume that it is formal regression which necessitates topographical, perceptual regression. This would be because the dream has to function according to very particular modalities; it is led to find contents compatible with this mode of functioning—that is to say, images. Well, if Freud does not choose between topographical regression and formal regression in this sense (the determination of the perceptual aspect of the dream by the type of process which unfolds in it), neither does he come out in favour of an inverse determination. The dream process would be of the 'primary' type because it regulates the unfolding of images, not allowing a more developed mode of connection. Ultimately, one has the impression that the debate is decided by the *third* type of regression—that is to say, temporal regression, as a determining influence. Let us turn, for example, to a passage in *The Interpretation of Dreams*:

> The transformation of thoughts into visual images may be in part the result of the *attraction* which memories couched in visual form and eager for revival bring to bear upon thoughts cut off from consciousness and struggling to find expression. On this view a dream might be described as *a substitute for an infantile scene modified by being transferred on to a recent experience*. The infantile scene is unable to bring about its own revival and has to be content with reappearing as a dream. (Freud 1900: 546)

Here, it is certainly temporal regression, the infantile scene, which is at the origin of all the regression in the dream, through its attraction, through its extraordinary power of wanting to be *represented* over again, a scene which was necessarily something *represented* but not—in essence—something thought. It is thus temporal regression, that terrible thrusting-force of the infantile scene, dubbed the 'primal scene', which explains representability.

All this, to show how contrary it would be to Freud's thought, and—I think -contrary to the very dynamic of analysis and of the analytic dialogue (such as it is described, notably, in these pages, as a dialogue of argument, of research, of putting to the test, of proof) to dissociate, in our conception of the unconscious, these different elements: the primitive images, unconscious desire, and, lastly, the mode of functioning of the unconscious—the primary process.

Transpositions from one system to the other: the two hypotheses

To continue the re-examination of my 1960 text on the unconscious,[18] I will move on to chapter II, entitled: 'The Unconscious as System in Freud: The Orientations and Impasse of the Freudian Hypotheses'. The fundamental idea, in place after the first chapter, is that there are indeed two systems, two modes of functioning and two types of contents. The problem which arises in this article, just as it did for Freud in his central text of 1915, 'The Unconscious', is not only that of distinguishing the two systems (which is relatively easy and schematic) but of defining the relations between them. These are relations of conflict, relations of compromise in the symptom, but also—and this is where the problem lies—the relation of passage from one to the other.

We cannot be content with defining the preconscious system and the unconscious system as mutually exclusive, nor even with showing how the one influences the other (or rather, how the unconscious influences the preconscious, since as we have seen, the inverse is ultimately rather doubtful, and it is even this non-influence of the preconscious—even during the whole analytic process—as much on the functioning of the unconscious as on its contents, that formed the definitive basis of Freud's rock-solid belief in an unconscious thing). Beyond this problem of influence, conflict, or exclusion, we need to bear in mind the necessity of describing something else also, and of describing it in more detail: namely, the much more significant movements of passage from the preconscious to the unconscious. Here the most important is repression, for the unconscious is essentially defined as 'the repressed'—an equivalence which Freud continued to maintain throughout these papers, even if, at certain moments, the repressed no longer appeared any more than a sector of the unconscious, although the most characteristic and the most important sector.

So, on the one hand, we have the movement of repression, and on the other that of (how can one put it?) 'coming to consciousness', 'coming to knowledge', or, as we have pointed out once before, *Agnoszierung*, 'recognition', in the sense of identifying a corpse in the morgue. In my article on the unconscious I underlined the difficulty, the perplexity of Freud, in the face of two possible hypotheses: the topographical hypothesis (or that of the 'double inscription'), and the so-called 'functional' hypothesis (or rather 'economic', if you wish, but I prefer 'functional'). How are these hypotheses defined by Freud in 1915?

> Up till now, [psychoanalysis] has differed from psychology mainly by reason of its *dynamic* view of mental processes; now in addition it seems to take account of psychical *topography* as well . . . On account of this attempt, too, it has been given the name of 'depth psychology'. (Freud 1915a: 183)

This is where the definition of the two hypotheses now begins:

> If we are to take the topography of mental acts seriously [as a reality and not as a manner of speaking], we must direct our interest to a doubt which arises at this point. When a psychical act (let us confine ourselves here to one which is in the nature of an idea [*Vorstellung*])is transposed from the system *Ucs.* into the system *Cs.* (or *Pcs.*), are we to suppose that this transposition involves a fresh record—as it were, a second registration—of the

> idea in question [you see how record and registration are taken as synonyms], which may thus be situated as well in a fresh psychical locality, and alongside of which the original unconscious registration continues to exist? (Freud 1915a: 183-4)

This is the model of the topographical hypothesis, according to which each system has its own inscription (Strachey's 'registration'); it is what was already proposed in the letter of 6th December, 1896. Now here comes the other hypothesis:

> Or are we rather to believe that the transposition consists in a change in the state of the idea, a change involving the same material and occurring in the same locality? This question may appear abstruse, but it must be raised if we wish to form a more definite conception of psychical topography, of the dimension of depth in the mind. (Freud 1915a: 184)[19]

I must emphasise that this depth psychology did not come about as a manner of speaking; it is a question well and truly of knowing whether we want to formulate an idea of this 'dimension of depth'. Now, the 'functional' hypothesis is that there is only a single inscription, and that, perhaps according to the context—the kind of 'binding', the mode of 'discharge'—this representation would be part of the unconscious or the preconscious system. Once again, you can see that the so-called 'functional' hypothesis opens the door to a psychology of the field of consciousness and to an explanation by means of misrecognition, which continues to offer its services in the same way.

In my 1960 text, I gave preference to the topographical hypothesis, which seemed to me in line with the essential inspiration of the psychoanalytic experience. Here is another passage, still dealing with these two hypotheses. After an important digression, a page later, on the relations with anatomy, and having shown that the latter, even if neurological, would in no way allow us to decide between our two hypotheses, Freud reaches this point:

> In this respect, then, our work is untrammelled and may proceed according to its own requirements. It will, however, be useful to remind ourselves that as things stand our hypotheses set out to be no more than graphic illustrations. The first of the two possibilities which we considered—namely that the *Cs.* phase of an

> idea implies a fresh registration of it, which is situated in another place—is doubtless the cruder but also the more convenient. The second hypothesis—that of a merely *functional* change of state—is *a priori* more probable, but it is less plastic, less easy to manipulate. With the first, or topographical, hypothesis is bound up that of a topographical separation of the systems *Ucs.* and *Cs.* and also the possibility that an idea may exist simultaneously in two places in the mental apparatus—indeed, that if it is not inhibited by the censorship, it regularly advances from the one position to the other, possibly without losing its first location or registration. This view may seem odd, but it can be supported by observations from psychoanalytic practice. (Freud 1915a: 185)

You can see that the topographical hypothesis ends up, in a certain sense, with this *uncanny* notion that the unconscious representation can manage to put itself forth considerably *while remaining*—in spite of everything—distinct from a conscious representation. There is no question here of psychosis, but obviously it makes us think of that type of experience.

I just recalled that in chapter II of the 1960 article I showed a preference for the topographical hypothesis. Re-reading Freud's text, you can see that his oscillation between the two hypotheses (which leads him to a sort of third formulation, which is still quite close to the topographical hypothesis), and that the two types of explanation proposed for the transition from one system to the other do not refer to *the same experience*. I pointed out just now what these experiences are: on the one hand, that of a movement downward, repression; and on the other, that of a return upwards, the *Agnoszierung* of the repressed. Well, in the 1915 text, you can see that the functional hypothesis is developed around the notion of repression—which is where it seems most suitable—and it is around the notion of *Agnoszierung* that the hypothesis of the double inscription is maintained. To get straight to the essential point: it is effectively as if, when repression is in question, it is indeed a single representation which, having been conscious, becomes unconscious. However, when it is a question of bringing the repressed to consciousness again, it can never be 'disconnected' from its unconscious inscription. You can see that the double movement is absolutely not symmetrical; that there is no 'de-repression' symmetrical with the process of repression.

10 January 1978

We were examining a difficulty (perhaps the term 'impasse' used in the Laplanche and Leclaire text is too strong) raised by Freud himself: the necessity of choosing between a 'functional' and a 'topographical' point of view regarding the unconscious inscription, or, more precisely, regarding its relation to the inscription in the preconscious-conscious system. Now, my hypothesis, my current point of view, is that the choice is not quite so clear as I thought it was in 1960. Besides, if one looks more closely, Freud himself does not make a choice; he oscillates, presenting the alternatives as complementary. My own interpretation of things, though, was as follows. Freud was confronted by two types of experience when he formulated these two types of explanation. On the one hand, the experience of repression or, at least, the explanation of repression (in so far as one can speak of the 'experience' of repression, since repression is something which by definition largely escapes our direct observation) and, on the other hand, the experience of the return, the recognition, the becoming-conscious of the repressed.

The functional hypothesis and primal repression

It is in relation to the former—that is to say, repression—that what is called the functional hypothesis is put forth, and seems most appropriate. Meanwhile, it is for the latter that the hypothesis of 'double inscription'—that is to say, the topographical theory—seems to be indispensable. I was thus led to go over in succession the case of repression, on the one hand, and that of its becoming-conscious, on the other. But in order to examine the process of repression, one cannot avoid recalling and discussing the fundamental distinction Freud establishes between two very different modalities of the process: the repression which is termed 'primal' (*Urverdrängung*) and so-called 'after-pressure' (*Nachdrängen*). There is a small terminological difference here, which we might need to consider. We should translate these terms as 'primal repression' and 'retroactive pressure', something the English translate as *after-pressure*. The main thing is that in primal repression, by definition, there is not yet a distinction between the two systems, since it is this 'primal' that is supposed to *create* the distinction between the preconscious and the unconscious.

Primal repression is thus to be conceived of as a sort of initial splitting, *resulting precisely in topography*, while 'after-pressure' takes place *once this topography is constituted*. It thus seems to be a sort of logical necessity, one might say, which leads us to postulate an initial repression that creates the topographical distinction. In this sense, there is sometimes talk of the 'myth' of primal repression; one might also speak of a 'transcendental' repression. But we can see that Freud tries to rediscover, in a precise way, the trace of this 'event'. Now, this trace, by definition, manifests itself in secondary repression (*Nachdrängen*). We notice, when we analyse a secondary repression—the famous 'forgetting of names'—that there is something that resembles the pull of gravity, a kind of attraction of the idea by already-existing unconscious contents which, in short, suck it in. We could imagine a whirlpool drawing in a swimmer along with the water. Briefly, we notice that in a specific repression from everyday life, it is its unconscious connections which keep the element forgotten.

But if this hypothesis of primal repression initially seems to spring from an abstract requirement, from the necessity of a logical, or—more precisely—a transcendental foundation, what notions closer to our experience are used to describe it? Freud employs three of them: firstly, the notion of *fixation*. It is in connection with primal repression that Freud most precisely establishes the equivalence, which I mentioned just now, between inscription, repression and fixation. Primal repression is a first inscription and a first fixation, both in the sense that the subject remains stuck at a certain moment of his development, but also that a particular memory comes to be fixed in place (the way you fix in place a photograph). What is more, the drive, the force of the drive, that sort of mechanical energy, finds itself fixed to a representation, thus truly becoming 'motion' (*Regung*), and no longer merely force (*Triebkraft*). You can see how the different senses of fixation come together in our 'primal repression'.

The second notion that Freud insists upon is that primal repression, which by definition is not caused by 'attraction', since there is nothing before it which could exert an attraction from lower down, can only be maintained by what he calls a *counter-investment*.[20] In other words, this is a sort of cover, a coherent and tightly-woven weft in the higher agencies, the purpose of which is to block every possible exit, every pore through which the unconscious could seep out. Obviously, it is obsessional 'character' formations which—beyond a narrow nosological determination—best illustrate this mechanism of counter-investment.

The third concept, finally, would be that of *trauma* as a 'primary' event, contemporary with these first repressions. Here, then, are elements of description and analysis, however abstract they may be, which allow us easily to imagine this moment designated (too readily) as 'mythical': the rupture of the external barrier; the inscription, as with a branding iron, of the first signifiers; and the reconstruction of the barrier, so much more solid for having been threatened.

But in order to give life, to assign a content of experience to what remained for Freud at the limits of what can be described, it would doubtless be necessary to add to this list other aspects of theory. I myself have developed this ceaselessly: the theory of seduction and the genesis of sexuality; the theory of trauma with its 'two moments'; the appearance of the drive as an external-internal source, source-object, etc. If we relate primal repression to these first experiences of splitting, 'leaning-on' [*étayage*] or seduction, we can see that this 'myth' is not as imaginary as one might think. Certainly there is a sort of reference, as in any origin, to something like the fiction of an original separation, a primary genesis, a first split (think of the first splits in Genesis: between the waters and the sky, between the earth and the waters. . .) which would be that of the unconscious and the preconscious-conscious system.

What is important for our argument is the notion of a 'before the split'—which would not itself be purely mythical—or of a pre-splitting, or of a state without the unconscious. A state without the unconscious which we could refer to a period of earliest infancy. A state without the unconscious: does that mean a state of pure consciousness? It would be to speak, rather, of a sort of depthless presence in the world. As you know, for my part, I have the greatest reluctance to accept (something that a certain Freudianism has sometimes been led to develop) the idea that the adult world has to be extracted from a sort of monad, narcissistically closed-in upon itself. I think the state of being an object, even objectivity, is developed on the basis of modalities of presence, obviously a 'non-thetic' presence, to use the terms of the phenomenologists, but a presence in the world. Well, what is important for primal repression is that—in this state of a certain presence, a state which is preconscious-unconscious prior to there being a distinction between a preconscious and an unconscious system—there appear certain representations which are underlined, delimited, offered up, implanted—one might say—by the adult world. The first, the most important of these representations is clearly that of the breast.

Freud, in his early papers, calls these representations 'sexual-presexual', which certainly implies an initial moment at which they are still—we might say—'in limbo', prior to the distinction between heaven and hell. They are before a second moment (and it is here that the theory of trauma 'in two moments' is essential) when these representations emerge as unbearable because they have themselves become internal and autonomous sources of excitation. It is at this second moment that they are, properly speaking, repressed. You can see to what extent the theory of primal repression, and the need to distinguish two moments within this primal repression itself, lends itself to being infiltrated by what we call the first moments of the appearance of the sexual drive. There are two moments, then, in this repression dubbed primal repression: the moment that can be termed exogenous, traumatic 'in itself', but which results simply in the constitution, in a sort of still undivided world, of those fantasies without precise topographical status, and a moment when the trauma becomes self-traumatising and provokes repression. Thus, primal repression is ultimately not so mythical as some might say. If Freud neglected to study its links with other elements of the analytic discovery, then these ramifications allow us to situate a notion which in isolation might seem a little abstract.

The unconscious and the id

Just a couple of remarks concerning the consequences of this for the theory of the unconscious. The first is that the notion of primal repression, if we take it seriously, definitively disqualifies any Freudian formulations which might aim to establish between the unconscious and the preconscious, a hierarchy or a genesis, a moment of emergence. Such formulations are frequent, but always limited. In them, Freud expresses himself thus: everything that is conscious has first been unconscious; or, alternatively: the conscious emerges little by little from the unconscious. (You understand that when he speaks here of the 'conscious', Freud really has in view the preconscious-conscious system). There are formulations concerning a process of emergence which assimilates the unconscious into a pre-existing (biological?) substratum, from which the conscious gradually differentiates itself as the surface system.

Indeed, this is the danger, the richness, of the notion of id, which actually maximises the risks of just such a conception. The id, as you know, appears in Freudian thinking after 1920 and in fact, in that second topography, it appears *after* the other agencies. The second topography is first of all a modification of the metapsychological system in terms of the other agencies—that is to say, the ego, the superego, and the ego ideal. These originate much earlier in Freudian thought, well before 1920. You know how important the figure of Groddeck was in connection with the appearance of this notion and of the very term 'id'.[21] This influence of Groddeck's found something to latch on to, we might say, in Freud's thinking. This might have been a certain interpretation of the so-called 'vesicular' model, which will be put forward in *Beyond the Pleasure Principle* (1920). This is a text in which—without one ever knowing definitively what is in question, a model or the description of a certain biological reality, we are presented with a type of being which would first be pure biology, pure drive or id, and then be engulfed by a preconscious-conscious system or by an ego. Freud, to tell the truth (you can see this in the correspondence), only adopts the 'id' with a great deal of reservation, and Groddeck is aware of this, as can be seen in his correspondence with his friend, Emmy von Voigt, where his reverence for the dear professor gives way to a frankness less mitigated than in the letters to Freud:

> *The Ego and the Id* [he writes, à *propos* of Freud's book] is nice, but for me absolutely without import. It was fundamentally written to enable the use of things secretly borrowed from Stekel and myself. What is more, his id has only a limited value for neuroses. He only crosses over into the organic secretly, helped by a drive of death or destruction taken from Stekel and Spielrein. He leaves aside the constructive elements of my 'it', probably so that he will be able to bring it in fraudulently next time. There are some amusing things in it. (Groddeck 1997b: 147-8, LT's translation)

And yet, if Freud will certainly not take up the id in all its Groddeckian plenitude, he will nevertheless push further and further the absorption of his earlier unconscious into the id, an absorption which would find its last, most extreme expression in *An Outline of Psycho-Analysis* (1940):

> Id and unconscious are as intimately linked as ego and preconscious: indeed, in the former case the connection is even more

> exclusive. If we look back at the developmental history of an individual and of his psychical apparatus, we shall be able to perceive an important distinction in the id. Originally, to be sure, everything was id; the ego was developed out of the id by the continual influence of the external world [this is certainly an interpretation of the already long-established model of the vesicular system]. In the course of this slow development certain of the contents of the id were transformed into the preconscious state and so taken into the ego; others of its contents remained in the id unchanged, as its scarcely accessible nucleus. During this development, however, the young and feeble ego put back into the unconscious state some of the material it had already taken in . . . (Freud 1940: 158)

It is the same schema we find in *The Ego and the Id* (1923a): there is a part of the id which is immediately unconscious, from which all else proceeds; a primal unconscious, but also a biological unconscious. Here, we are a thousand miles from the idea of primal repression, because the latter rules out the idea of a primary biological unconscious. Thus there would be a primal unconscious which is the id, and then there would be certain contents which, from then on, would try to break through to the ego and would thus be repressed, secondarily. It is only at this point that the barrier of repression appears. Thus, there would be two parts to the id: a primal part and a secondary part, which would be the properly repressed part. The 'primal' part, in the end, comes to take the place of primal repression. In the first topography, and in the very conception of primal repression, everything we term unconscious was repressed.

We could thus, in a very schematic way, establish a choice between two conceptions, which I will define using three pairs of opposing terms: a *biologising* conception, since it invokes a biological substratum for the unconscious; an *endogenous* conception, since everything grows out of the sort of bubbling microcosm that is the id, even if secondarily, under the influence of the external world, certain contents are sent back into the id; and, lastly, a *genetic* conception, in the sense that what is produced is the effect of a differentiation.[22] Conversely, there is another conception, no longer that of the id but of a *non-biological* unconscious, since the drive emerges at odds with any pre-established biological set-up, and as a force which is not self-preservative but possibly destructive. This is a conception which is *exogenous*, for—with the notion of primal repression—one cannot pass over external influences on the biological unit represented by the infant. It is exogenous also in the sense that we understand the seduction theory. Lastly, there is a *traumatic* conception—in opposition to one of emergence—that is to say, composed of ruptures, splits and exclusions.

Obviously this opposition, as such, is not sufficient, in the sense that if one might have a certain preference for the second alternative, one certainly has to wonder why Freud nevertheless borrows the biologising language of the 'id'. To return to Groddeck, this is a language which is not authentically biologising in its own right, at least not in the sense of biological science. It is, indeed, also a universally 'psychologising' language (or, as he puts it, 'symbolic'). Groddeck connects up with a tradition which does not reduce everything to a 'biological cooking pot' out of which the 'psyche' would arise, but rather to a conception which he calls at one point *psyche-soma*, and, at another, referring to Goethe and pantheism, 'God-Nature':

> We can set up an opposition between conscious and unconscious, never between the It [*ça*] and the conscious. We can oppose the ego to the unconscious and to the drives, never to the It. For the It encompasses conscious and unconscious, ego and drives, body and soul, physiology and psychology. (Groddeck 1977b: 21, LT's translation)

'The It is resolutely *a-topic*', concludes Gantheret, who quotes and comments on this passage (in Groddeck 1977b: 21). The conceptions of Freud and Groddeck are, in fact, quite different. There is some truth in the reproach made against Freud of having stunted the id to make it fit into his topography, whilst, in Groddeck's writing (and this, inversely, is one of Freud's criticisms), it takes on a far more metaphysical, even mystical allure.

Be that as it may, the appeal to biology in Freud comes much earlier than this borrowing from Groddeck. It is a constant metaphor, so that one cannot be satisfied with an opposition between a biologising point of view and an anti-biological point of view. One could just as well say that the psychoanalytic point of view flows into a language (which is still a rather extrinsic way of speaking) which is biological or, at other times, neurological or neuro-biological. For instance, think of the 'Project for a Scientific Psychology' (Freud 1950). Or—and this is a question I cannot expand on today, but which I want to raise, in order not to remain within a pure and simple opposition, in order not to restrict ourselves to asking psychoanalysis to choose between biologism and anti-biologism—is there something deeper in this need to slip into biological conceptions? For *the unconscious, once it is constituted, is indeed an id*; it becomes a nature, a second nature which 'enacts' us—as Lacan said: which 'speaks' us . . . but is that not, already, to reduce the id-ness of the id?

There is something like a symbolic reduplication in man which makes him rediscover, or mimic, natural automatisms. Or again, and perhaps this is the same thing, there is a fertility in Freudian concepts which is an amphibology—by which we mean that they can be linked up with two different sets of concepts, two different contexts. This is an amphibology which constrains us endlessly to split up concepts and redistribute them according to two perspectives. I tried to recapture such a split two years ago, in saying that we had to apply a knife to a text like 'Instincts and their Vicissitudes' (1915b), in order to cut out the notion of the drive and the Freudian discourse on the drive, precisely in terms of these two perspectives. The same sort of knife could also be applied to a notion like the pleasure principle (and this is just one example among many) which truly takes on two significations in Freud which should be clearly distinguished from each other, but at the same time—and not without reason—we should ask ourselves why they are denominated with the same term. By this I mean, on the one hand, a pleasure principle which would be purely and simply the restitution of a certain level of non-excitation in the biological sense of the term, and on the other hand, a pleasure principle which would be a sort of unregulated circulation, at the heart of the unconscious, of sexual desire. Or again, one could use this same knife to distinguish, precisely, between the unconscious and the id.

That was my first remark concerning primal repression. My second remark concerns, precisely, the relation of primal repression to the problem with which we started, and which we should not allow to slip out of our sight—that is, the opposition of the two hypotheses: the 'functional' and the 'topographical'. The conception of primal repression *does not impose* the hypothesis of a second inscription of repressed ideas in a second place. Effectively, before the primal repression (this is not 'before' in the strictly mythical sense, yet it is nevertheless not purely chronological) we can say that there is *one single place*, and it is at a single stroke that the first ideas are repressed and that, at the same moment, an unconscious locus is created where they come to be inscribed, in particular those which will constitute something like the primordial kernel of an id.

'After-pressure'

'After-pressure' or secondary repression. What is its status *vis-à-vis* our problem: functional unconscious or topographical unconscious? After-pressure is what Freud went on to call 'repression proper' (*eigentliche Verdrängung*). Why 'after'? Because it presupposes the existence of an unconscious, and the founding moment of primal repression, which means that, clinically, it is much nearer to our experience, that of the psychoanalytic clinic, and not just to what we can reconstruct on the basis of this clinic, regarding the first moments of human life. It is the repression, let us say, of daily life, normal or neurotic. This repression is described very early on, and with a model that leaves its mark: the psychopathology of hysteria, rather than of obsessional neurosis. In the *Studies on Hysteria* (1895), you will find many examples of it: for example, the forgetting of the traumatic scene in the case of 'Katarina'. This is a very limited example but also very striking, in which it is the scene of seduction (supposedly by the uncle, but in fact by the father) which is repressed, a repressed upon which Freud effects an extraction by a sort of accelerated, extemporaneous psychoanalysis. Or again, the repression of an entire affective complex. I am thinking of the case of 'Elisabeth', where it is the whole context of the love for the brother-in-law that has to be unearthed; and in which, notably, we will find a precise illustration of the fact that this complex, 'retroactively repressed', is repressed only to the extent that it is itself attracted into the unconscious by a more fundamental love, clearly the love for the father. And then again, in Freud's self-analysis, what we could call the paradigm of repression—the symptomatic forgetting of a name: that of the Italian painter *Signorelli* (Freud 1901: chapter 1). It is certainly a question here of a discrete element, completely fragmentary, a scrap of discourse, a 'word-representation', which falls below and is cut out as if by a machine, as one could describe a geological fault occurring in a sedimentary formation.

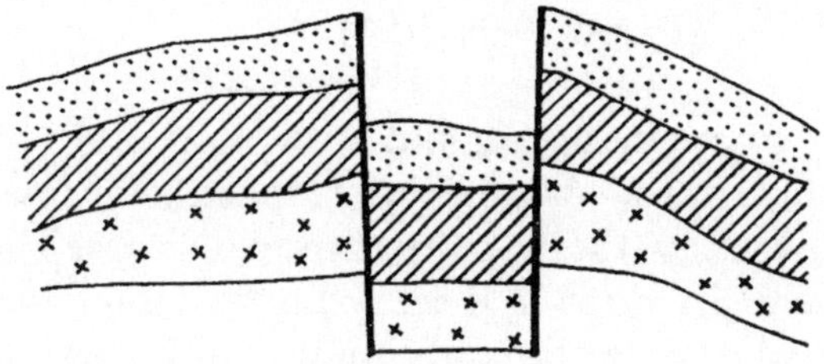

Let us see now how Freud, in 'The Unconscious' (1915a), theorises 'after-pressure':

> Let us take the case of repression proper ('after-pressure'), as it affects an idea which is preconscious or even actually conscious. Here repression can only consist in withdrawing from the idea [thus the preconscious representation] the (pre)conscious cathexis which belongs to the system Pcs. The idea then either remains uncathected, or receives cathexis from the Ucs., or retains the Ucs. cathexis which it already had. (Freud 1915a: 191)

According to our geological schema, we can easily discern the factors which repression thus brings into play. In order for there to be a localised collapse, whatever connections there were between the layers had to be broken, leading to disinvestment (Strachey's 'de-cathexis') and detachment. But there is a second reason: there was also something exercising a force of attraction, a sort of void, a subjacent cavern, corresponding to the attraction by the unconscious. Finally, the third element: there needs to be a counter-investment (Strachey's 'counter-cathexis')—that is to say, something which keeps in place that which ceaselessly seeks to rise up again.[23]

> Thus there is a withdrawal of the preconscious cathexis, retention of the unconscious cathexis, or replacement of the preconscious cathexis by an unconscious one. We notice, moreover [and this the important point in relation to our problem], that we have based these reflections (as it were without meaning to) on the assumption that the transition from the system Ucs. to the system next to it is not effected through the making of a new registration but through a change in its state, an alteration in its

> cathexis. The functional hypothesis has here easily defeated the topographical one. (Freud 1915a: 191)

I would be in complete agreement, except on one point: it is precisely not a question of the *'transition from the system* Ucs. *to the system next to it'*, but, inversely, the transition from the preconscious to the unconscious system. So much so that, in this text, there is a sort of subreption in the reasoning, for the only thing that Freud shows, and on which I lay stress, is that the functional hypothesis is eminently valuable when it is a question of describing the transition into the unconscious, but perhaps not so as regards the inverse process. In repression, therefore, it is one and the same idea upon which economic processes of disinvestment, unconscious investment and counter-investment are carried out, but the representation is the same. There is no reason to think that there are two successive representations; there is no process of *translation*, but simply a *transportation*.

16 January 1978

What interpretation can be given, ultimately, of those economic processes which Freud designates by the term 'after-pressure'? *Disinvestment*, since whatever is repressed is disinvested by the system in which it had been previously—that is, by the preconscious-conscious system. In other words, this is unconscious *investment*, since this element is snatched up by the unconscious. Lastly, there is *counter-investment*, a sort of cover which, like a tombstone, assumes its place to prevent the return of the ghost, the corpse, the repressed.

Counter-investment and 'pregnant' forms

Well, as you can see, disinvestment and counter-investment are two processes of the preconscious-conscious system. It was with these in mind particularly that I referred to—or took as a model—the picture-puzzle. A picture tells a story—of a picnic, let's say—with an element which is an integral part of this story; but if one looks at it from a certain angle, and detaches it from its context, above all with a 'disinterested', 'floating' kind of attention, one notices all of a sudden that what is in fact drawn there is Napoleon's hat—as I put it, back then. This a phenomenon that *Gestalt* psychologists have studied, in particular concerning ambiguous images, which they describe as 'pregnant' images. This is a term which easily lends itself to the interpretation of something of an economic order, since a pregnancy is a certain force exerted in relation to a certain surround, with a certain relation to 'depth', and to the 'figure'. It is a force with variations which can be registered, measured, the function of various parameters which can themselves be registered with precision. It is something which, after all, lends itself rather well to an interpretation of Freud's language of economics—at least, to a certain aspect of it. Here is what I said about it in 1960:

> The most satisfactory explanation he gives [of the independence and the cohesiveness of the two systems] is the economic hypothesis. But the only coherent interpretation we could present would have to distinguish in an absolute manner between the 'cathectic energies' involved and libidinal energy. We may for the moment give a *Gestaltist* model for this play of energies [for the investment energy in a system]. The cathectic energy of a system would be comparable to the *Prägnanz* of a 'good shape'. But it is important to note at what level the passage from one system to another operates: it cannot be the global passage of the same structure from one mode of organisation to another, similar to the oscillatory effect at work in the perception of an equivocal image. What passes from one Gestalt to another is always an isolated equivocal element, capable of being captured by the *Prägnanz* of the unconscious or (pre-)conscious *Gestalt:* repression, as Freud emphasises, 'acts . . . in a *highly individual* manner. Each single derivative of the repressed may have its own special vicissitude'. (Laplanche & Leclaire 1972: 135/p.245, below; Freud 1915c: 150).

It was at this point that I took up the model of the picture-puzzle. What I would like to say is that this model may not after all be such a bad way of providing an account, *at the very least* (although here I assume a certain distance from my earlier suggestion) of what can occur precisely at the level of the *ego*, or—if you prefer—the preconscious-conscious system. It is especially the phenomenon of counter-investment which can be described as the capacity to re-weave a coherent fabric, masking the void of what has been repressed. Here is what Freud says about this in 'The Unconscious' (1915a):

> What we require, therefore, is another process which maintains the repression in the first case (i.e. the case of after-pressure) and in the second (i.e. that of primal repression), ensures its being established as well as continued. This other process can only be found in the assumption of an *anticathexis*, by means of which the system *Pcs.* protects itself from the pressure upon it of the unconscious idea. We shall see from clinical examples how such an anticathexis, operating in the system *Pcs.*, manifests itself. (Freud 1915a: 192)

Further on we find a complementary hypothesis, which confirms the kinship, from the economic point of view, between the energies put to work in counter-investment and disinvestment, both of which belong to the preconscious system. Because if counter-investment causes coherent and well-structured reaction formations to appear in the preconscious system (I spoke a moment ago about a sort of cover, of concrete, blocking the path of the return of the repressed representation) then we need to ask about the provenance of energy deployed in this way:

> It is very possible that it is precisely the cathexis which is withdrawn from the idea [thus the energy saved through disinvestment] that is used for anticathexis. (Freud 1915a: 192)

Well, the clinical examples announced a moment ago were developed in 'The Unconscious', and taken up again in another text from the metapsychological papers, 'Repression' (1915c). These are descriptions of phobia or anxiety hysteria, of conversion hysteria and also of obsessional neurosis. I can only refer you back to these texts in all their complexity, particularly those on anxiety hysteria, which again take up, in order to theorise it, the case of little Hans (Laplanche 1980a). Let us keep things simple, in order to situate counter-investment. In animal phobia, let us recall, there is a primary repressed which is a libidinal impulse of love, an Oedipal impulse, with, obviously, representations linked to it. Moreover, when little Hans' hysteria is analysed in sufficient depth we can see that what is essential in this loving impulse is well and truly that it takes the father as its object, that it is a homosexual impulse. Let's say this is 'essential' in that the main characteristic of the symptom is its ability to condense several impulses, for which it is the substitute. To simplify we can say, with Freud, that an impulse comes to be repressed along with its representatives, and in its place—and I insist upon this—after a first moment of pure and simple anxiety (on which Freud centres his exposition, connected to his theory of anxiety, according to which it corresponds to libido freed from connected representations, a sort of libido in a pure state, and thereby destructive)—after this moment of non-symbolised anxiety correlative to a primary repression, there appears very rapidly, in its place, an anxiety-animal (for little Hans, the anxiety-horse).

Well, this anxiety-horse allows two things to happen. On the one hand, a rationalisation of the conditions for the appearance of anxiety. The anxiety which arose without cause—let us say apparently without cause—appears here in a sort of causal series which is more or less rational, with a sort of 'because . . .' It is because I see or I fear meeting this horse that I am anxious. This is clearly a 'false connection', but nevertheless allows the anxiety to be bound, to prevent it from reproducing itself in a completely anarchic way. On the other hand, it allows a structuring of space, as we don't meet the horse everywhere but only in the street, in certain parts of the city of Vienna, and not just any old parts. Thus space is oriented, polarised, structured, according to the possibilities of encountering the anxiety-animal.

As you can see, the rationalisation and especially the structuring of space call to mind very clearly the establishment of a configuration, a *Gestalt*, whose aim is to avoid any surprise. This is a figure which, moreover, will become increasingly complex as the *Gestalt* constantly threatens at certain points to crumble, to be penetrated by the original impulse and by what derives from its degradation—anxiety. In the end, it is not as solid as all that. This leads little Hans to erect more and more outer defences, in order to protect himself more and more extensively against the threat, however distant, of the appearance of the animal. Speaking in terms of counter-investment, there are two aspects to it here. In the beginning, Freud tells us, it is the symbolic substitute—that is to say, the anxiety-horse—which is counter-invested against the appearance of the original representation. As the substitute becomes excessively penetrated by the original impulse, it is the environment itself which becomes counter-invested, to prevent the very encounter with the animal. You can see that these phenomena, in so far as they are characteristics of the preconscious system (and I do mean system), or even of the ego, that these egoic mechanisms, defence mechanisms, can quite justifiably benefit from an interpretation in terms of load, of the *distribution of load*, of *pregnancy*. This does not contradict what we know about the ego, that which Freud formulates from the outset, which is increasingly confirmed in analytic experience, from the *Entwurf* (Freud 1950) via the text on narcissism (Freud 1914), right up to the last texts: the ego itself is a sort of *Gestalt*, provided with a certain level of investment. This is a level of investment which on the one hand tends to maintain itself—this is homeostasis. Yet, on the other hand, this homeostasis might be termed 'expansive', which is to say: the *Gestalt* is capable of enveloping everything which appears in its vicinity, and making it enter into its own configuration.

The problem of unconscious investment is another question, and I would say that to equate it with a *Gestalt* phenomenon seems to me far more open to question and discussion. The particulars of this question, as I explained them in 1960, could be schematised as follows. Ultimately, one speaks of the force of the unconscious, of its investment, its energy, in two ways that seem mutually opposed: on the one hand, as in this example of phobia, we see that the unconscious and unconscious representations tend incessantly to *break through*, to want to reappear, to produce in the preconscious new 'shoots', many 'offspring'. But, on the other hand, Freud tells us, it is also something which *attracts*. Every experience which somehow resonates with, becomes analogous to, makes whatever kind of connection with an earlier pattern, itself repressed—with a primal scene, for example—everything in day-to-day experience which touches (be it ever so lightly) upon a primal scene, finds itself in its turn sucked in by the whirlwind of secondary repression.

Well, this opposition between an unconscious which 'pushes' and an unconscious which 'pulls', an unconscious which in so far as it attracts, resists becoming-conscious, but which also, unceasingly, tends to provoke phenomena in the preconscious system—well, I will leave this opposition aside for the time being. Perhaps it is not as irreducible as it might appear, in spite of the 'logical' opposition which emerges here? Perhaps, above all, it is not completely foreign to the fundamental opposition between the life drive and the death drive . . . ?

Recognition of the Ucs. and the topographical hypothesis

Let me return to my argument: what is the meaning of the opposition between the topographical and functional hypotheses? I believe, with Freud, that so much is clear: in the description of repression, and equally in my model of the picture-puzzle or the equivocal image, it is surely *one and the same element* which at one moment will be illuminated by the preconscious context of the scenario, of the *Gestalt*, yet the next moment will be no longer, but will be plunged into the 'depths' of the unconscious. Repression, the process from above to below, thus does not imply a new inscription; it is the expulsion of a representation from its context and its connection to a new context.

However, the process in the opposite direction, in the direction of 'becoming- conscious', is quite different. You will notice, in 'The Unconscious' (1915a), it is at precisely this moment that the 'topographical' hypothesis, that of the double inscription, will appear so seductive:

> With the first, or topographical, hypothesis is bound up that of a topographical separation of the systems *Ucs.* and *Cs.* and also the possibility that an idea may exist simultaneously in two places in the mental apparatus—indeed, that if it is not inhibited by the censorship, it regularly advances from the one position to the other, possibly without losing its first location of registration. This view may seem odd, but it can be supported by observations from psychoanalytic practice. (Freud 1915a: 185)

Indeed, it is strange, illogical, contrary to the 'nominalist' definition of the un-conscious, that it can advance as far as consciousness without thereby abandoning its location and fundamental characteristics, and without, either, coming to coincide with the preconscious inscription to which it corresponds. Here, the topographical hypothesis breaks free definitively from the presupposition according to which the difference between the two systems would be essentially linked to a question of consciousness (in the 'conscientialist' meaning of the term). Freud leans essentially on the experience of psychoanalytic practice:

> If we communicate to a patient some idea which he has at one time repressed but which we have discovered in him, our telling him makes at first no change in his mental condition. (Freud 1915a: 185-6)

I would add: even if *he himself* discovered it (and not just if the analyst communicated it to him), if he discovered it on the basis of a certain construction (we will see in a moment how this term 'construction' comes in here), if he himself has recreated, in the conscious system, through analysis, a certain idea—well, it 'makes no difference to his mental condition':

> Above all it does not remove the repression nor undo its effects, as might perhaps be expected from the fact that the previously unconscious idea has now become conscious. On the contrary, all that we shall achieve at first will be a fresh rejection of the repressed idea. But now the patient has in actual fact the same idea in two forms in different places in his mental apparatus: first, he has the conscious memory of the auditory trace of the idea, conveyed in what we told him; and secondly, he also has - as we know for certain—the unconscious memory of his experience as it was in its earlier form. Actually there is no lifting of the repression until the conscious idea, after the resistances have been overcome, has entered into connection with the unconscious memory-trace. (Freud 1915a: 186)

Clearly Freud immediately asks the question: what is it that proves to us it is indeed *the same* idea which comes to be inscribed twice over? Is this not, perhaps, nothing but a superficial equation on our part? Nevertheless, what enables us to think, in spite of everything, these two ideas are close to each other is that they are able, *through the analytic work*, to enter into connection, to be led—as Freud puts it—to live side by side.

Working-through or ecmnesis

This unconscious representation and this conscious representation having both been acquired through analysis, the problem is then to know how they can be woven together, which is the only process by which the unconscious can be truly recovered, recognised, even integrated. In opposition to this working-through, what we have in mind (according to the beginning of this paper) is the ever-present possibility that an unconscious memory could in some way burst into consciousness, 'come into our head'—whether as an hallucination, or a dream—even though, on the contrary, it is not integrated into the preconscious system.

Well, to this question—certainly fundamental—of the possibility or impossibility of making the unconscious return, come back, through the analytic process, into the preconscious system, we will find thousands of responses, thousands of beacons, in Freud's explorations. I will point you towards only three texts: firstly, the end of 'The Unconscious' (1915a), where a kind of solution is formulated to our opposition between the topographical and the functional hypothesis, due to the distinction, which is crucial for our argument, between 'word-representation' and 'thing-representation'. Word-representation (that is, *Wortvorstellung*) and thing-representation (*Sachvorstellung*). But, even though we have got into the habit of speaking about the representation *of* a thing and the representation *of* a word, we must remember that this 'of' does not necessarily indicate the *object* of the verb—that is to say, what is represented. It is also an 'of' indicating the material, the quality, the text of the representation. The 'of', in this case, could be replaced by an adjective, and this adjectival meaning of a 'noun complement' is even more predominant when it is a question of composite nouns in German. I will use an example to explain. *Garnisonstadt*, which is correctly translated as 'garrison town' is not a town which 'belongs' to a garrison, but a town which contains a garrison[24]—a 'garrisonesque' town, so to speak. Let us remember, then, that in 'word-representation' and 'thing-representation' no doubling is necessarily implied between the word and its representation, the thing and its representation. What does Freud have to say about this nuance, which I believe to be important . . .

> The system *Ucs.* contains the thing-cathexes of the objects, the first and true object cathexes . . . (Freud 1915a: 209)

You can see that this phrase, even without my seeking it out, clearly indicates this: the investment of the 'thing-representation' is both the investment, the first and true investment of the thing *and* the object. There is at this point no distinction to be made between the thing and the representation *of the* thing. Freud's expression is: *Sachbesetzung der Objekte*, which we would have to translate, more exactly, as: 'thing-investments of objects' or even 'thing-type investment of objects':

> The system *Pcs.* comes about by this thing-presentation [or 'thing-type representation'] being hypercathected through being linked with the word-presentations corresponding to it. It is these hypercathexes [thus linked to word-representations] , we may suppose, that bring about a higher psychical organisation

> and make it possible for the primary process to be succeeded by the secondary process which is dominant in the *Pcs.* (Freud 1915a: 209)

Here we have an idea which is absolutely constant in Freud, concerning language and its function in becoming-conscious, at the level of the secondary process. If you like, thing-representation and word-representation are both representations, but word-representations—due to the very fact that they can be reproduced 'in person', that we can re-pronounce the word, and include it in our interior language—are able to reappear in consciousness, in doing so entering into connection with thing-representations: they are, one could say, able to make becoming-conscious (which is linked to the pronunciation of the word) *radiate* upon the thing-representation. (You will find these proposals, notably, in the 'Project for a Scientific Psychology' [Freud 1950], then via *The Ego and the Id* [1923a], right up to the *Outline* [1940]). It is to the extent that we can reproduce the word-representation, but cannot actively reproduce the thing-representation (although sometimes they 'return', but that is something else), that we are in a position to *weave* certain thing-representations into the context of the preconscious, to stitch them into the fabric of the preconscious.

A second beacon, much closer to treatment and its difficulties, is the 1937 article entitled 'Constructions in Analysis' (Freud 1937a). The theme of this text, as the term indicates, is the reconstruction of the unconscious through analytic work, shared by the analyst and the analysand. Its validity—which is at the same time, and indissociably, its validation—is its capacity to bring about (or not) the return of the unconscious itself. In the 1915 text this problem was already there: that when we communicate, or when the analysand discovers, through his 'work', a certain unconscious sequence, how can this sequence which he manages to formulate be connected up with what we suppose to have been repressed, and thus to form part of the unconscious?

It is in the third part of 'Constructions' that Freud studies this relation between reconstruction and memory. In the other two parts—particularly in the second—he examined above all the validity of construction: what is it that allows us to confirm our constructions? Let me recall the famous beginning of this paper. Someone makes the following objection to us: when we offer an interpretation, a construction, to a patient, it is said that we are cheating at heads or tails: 'heads I win, tails you lose'. In other words, if you confirm what I say, I have won, but if you deny it I have also won, because you can only deny it due to your resistance to the unconscious. Well, this paper goes far enough to show that this objection *falls down*, in the course of the analytic process, because an interpretation can only take on its value in the dialectic of this process. These first two chapters, which begin with the irony of 'heads I win, tails you lose', end with a fragment of comedy: a character in Nestroy (an Austrian author who has been rather neglected in our country, but who is a household name for the Viennese), a servant, has only one reply to every enigma: 'Everything will become clear in the course of events.' This comic truth also belongs to the analytic process, which constitutes an *enacted* verification or validation of the interpretations and constructions which emerge there. The third chapter, for its part, introduces a new difficulty. Even a validated reconstruction—one which has brought about a justified conviction in the patient, which is supported by all sorts of cross-checks, confirmed in experience by the illuminations and modifications of daily life that it brings—even a construction of this kind is not guaranteed to lead to recollection, and thus to the reawakening of the unconscious and the repressed:

> How this occurs in the process of the analysis—the way in which a conjecture of ours is transformed into the patient's conviction—this is hardly worth describing. All of it is familiar to every analyst from his daily experience and is intelligible without difficulty. Only one point requires investigation and explanation. The path that starts from the analyst's construction ought to end in the patient's recollection; but it does not always lead so far. Quite often we do not succeed in bringing the patient to recollect what has been repressed. Instead of that, if the analysis is carried out correctly, we produce in him an assured conviction of the truth of the construction which achieves the same therapeutic result as a recaptured memory. The problem of what the circumstances are in which this occurs and of how it is possible that what appears to be an incomplete substitute should nevertheless produce a complete result—all of this is a matter for a later enquiry. (Freud 1937a: 266)

Well, admitting that preconscious reconstruction does not necessarily manage to make the unconscious memory 'return', Freud brings in another series of facts which are ultimately far more disturbing:

> I shall conclude this brief paper with a few remarks which open up a wider perspective. I have been struck by the manner in which, in certain analyses, the communication of an obviously apt construction has evoked in the patient a surprising and at first incomprehensible phenomenon. They have had lively recollections called up in them—which they themselves have described as 'ultra-clear' . . . (Freud 1937a: 266-7)

This 'ultra-clear' (*überdeutlich*) makes us think irresistibly of what Freud, from the outset, called a 'hyperintense' idea (*überstark*) which he used to describe the *idées fixes*, even the hallucinations of hysterics:

> . . . but what they have recollected has not been the event that was the subject of the construction [it is not the *entirety* of the memory that appears] but details relating to that subject. For instance, they have recollected with abnormal sharpness the faces of the people involved in the construction or the rooms in which something of the sort might have happened, or, a step further away, the furniture in such rooms—on the subject of which the construction had naturally no possibility of any knowledge. This has occurred both in dreams immediately after the construction had been put forward and in waking states resembling phantasies. These recollections have themselves led to nothing further and it has seemed plausible to regard them as the product of a compromise. The 'upward drive' of the repressed, stirred into activity by the putting forward of the construction, has striven to carry the important memory-traces into consciousness; but a resistance has succeeded, not, it is true, in *stopping* that movement, but in *displacing* it on to adjacent objects of minor significance. (Freud 1937a: 266-7)

So there we have our phenomenon of the upward drive, the term 'displacement' which we will shortly have to emphasise. If one wished to use a more modern formulation—to which we shall also return—then memories are linked in an essentially metonymic way (that is, in a relation of contiguity) to the unconscious representation properly speaking. These are elements of proximity which appear with a disquieting intensity, quasi-hallucinatory, ecmnesic:

> These recollections might have been described as hallucinations if a belief in their actual presence had been added to their clearness. [Hallucination without belief does exist; this is what French writers call 'hallucinose'.] The importance of this analogy seemed greater when I noticed that true hallucinations occasionally occurred in the case of other patients who were certainly not psychotic. (Freud 1937a: 267)

Thus, we must insist that what becomes concrete clinically and in the treatment is this possibility of the 'unconscious' (the inverted commas emphasising here the insufficiency of the criterion 'consciousness') once certain inhibitions have been lifted, to advance right up to the preconscious-conscious system without, for all that, finding itself connected up with the latter, without being integrated. It would then appear as a truly erratic element, an ecmnesic element . . .

The third text, to which I wanted merely to allude, is contemporary with the one at which we have just looked. This is *An Outline of Psychoanalysis* (1940), where you will find once again called into question the coincidence between what is constructed and what is remembered (Freud 1940: 139). The possibility of establishing connections between the two is clearly retained, but at the same time the horizon of psychosis—that is to say of a memory reappearing in an erratic and hallucinatory fashion—albeit a limited, quasi-experimental psychosis, in the treatment—remains present.

24 January 1978

To summarise provisionally what I have tried to analyse concerning the distinction between the topographical and the functional hypotheses, you can see that they testify to an essential dissymmetry between the moment of splitting and the moment of recognition or *Agnoszierung*. (Moreover, perhaps this is a dissymmetry essential to the problem of the unconscious; perhaps we will find it in other places, in relation to other problems . . .) In the first moment, the problem is certainly that of the subtraction of a certain mnemonic or mnesic content from the illumination of consciousness, and even from the possibility of being made present. This is the moment of repression. But in the second moment, one can see that the 'becoming-conscious', as such, cannot easily take hold of what has been done and reverse it, undoing the repression. Why? Well, because the unconscious is no longer defined essentially in relation to consciousness, but rather in relation to a preconscious-conscious system (and here I must insist on the word 'system'), which has taken the place of what has become unconscious, and which constantly counter-invests it; because the reconstruction of the past is not, in itself, the rediscovery of the unconscious; because—and this is what we saw in the text on 'Constructions in Analysis' (1937a)—this work of construction can lead to some resurgences, but these are often erratic, fragmentary, allusive, metonymic, even hallucinatory. Thus arises the problem of how to 'set the seal' in the treatment on this rediscovery, between reconstruction and resurgence—the problem of a true recognition of the unconscious. Let us recall the terms successively introduced by Freud (without claiming here to reconstitute a precise historical sequence): the term 'reminiscence', in the first phase; the moment of the reawakening of affect with the memory; the term 'catharsis'; or again, the term—already present from the outset—of 'associative connection', which ought to allow the rediscovered memory to be kept on the surface, to be attached to the surface, to be taken up in the conscious system by recreating connections; then the term 'repetition'; the term 'construction', which we have briefly discussed; obviously, the *element* (in the sense of 'in one's element') of the transference; and then a term which appears later on, *Durcharbeiten*, an index of the same problem rather than its solution. What is at stake in this 'working-through'? Is it a question, once again, of establishing connecting chains, concatenations? Is it a question of a new way of symbolising? Is it a question of sublimation? As you see, we have located the principal terms of our investigation.

Chapter III of the 1960 text is, as you know, written by Leclaire. It is the analysis of his 'dream of the unicorn', and the foregrounding of representational—representatives (*Vorstellungsrepräsentanz*)—of those representations that represent the drive and upon which repression bears, since the latter is most certainly the repression of certain representations or certain complexes of representations. (We have hardly anything to add to Freud, on this point.) Ultimately it is the foregrounding of what are called the 'primary' processes, that is to say the laws of the unconscious. Leclaire's text illustrates as explicitly as possible this 'primary' mode of functioning, such as Freud defined it in a work of genius, one might say, in chapter V of 'The Unconscious' (1915a).

> The nucleus of the *Ucs.* consists of instinctual representatives [representational- representatives] which seek to discharge their cathexis; that is to say, it consists of wishful impulses . . . These instinctual impulses . . . exist side by side without being influenced by one another, and are exempt from mutual contradiction.[25] When two wishful impulses whose aims must appear to us incompatible become simultaneously active, the two impulses do not diminish each other or cancel each other out, but combine to form an intermediate aim, a compromise. (Freud 1915a: 198)

This sort of co-presence thus implies that the 'impulsional' chains, in their unconscious trajectory, are completely unaware of one another. It is only at the moment of emerging into consciousness, at the last moment, that the point of intersection of the two impulses can be discerned, that is to say, in a compromise:

> There are in this system no negation, no doubt, no degrees of certainty . . . (Freud 1915a: 198)

All this is *blindingly* clear, in its absolute, totalitarian manner (a totalitarianism which could lead one to think of the uncompromising nature of 'being' in Parmenides and the Eleatics . . .). If, in our last class, I invoked the notion of the *Gestalt* in connection with the preconscious system—well, what Freud affirms here is that at the level of the unconscious there is no *Gestalt*—or, *at the very least*, no overall *Gestalt*. There are *perhaps* partial configurations at the level of the individual impulse, drive, or complex, but not an overall configuration of complexes. Next we have a definition of the *mobility* of investments, in other words the *primary process*, which we will come back to later; this is the second major point, 'fragmentation' or 'co-presence'. Then comes the *timelessness* of unconscious processes: the processes of the unconscious system are timeless; they are not ordered in time, are not modified by the passing of time, have absolutely no relation to time. Finally, the last point: unconscious processes have no regard for reality, they are subject exclusively to the pleasure principle. This 'un-reality' allows an interesting point of linkage with the contentious issues opened up between 'unconscious' and language—namely, if more or less linguistic phenomena are present there, it is a language which is not open, in an intentional sense, onto a referent, I mean onto a view of the reality of a common world. All these characteristics of the unconscious are so unusual, so unheard-of in our experience of the psychical that Freud, in concluding, stresses his warning against the illusion of ever being able to know the unconscious directly (rather than just infer it). Unconscious processes do not reveal themselves to us; they can only be known at the moment when, the censorship having been lowered, the preconscious system finds itself led back to the modes of functioning of the unconscious. In themselves, he adds, they are thus unknowable, and even—and one can hardly conceive of going any further in this kind of 'negative theology'—'incapable of existence' (*existenzunfahïg*).

The primary process and rhetoric

I will now return to the central point: the *primary process*. Among all these characteristics of the unconscious, this is its mode of functioning. It is clearly defined in relation to the secondary process, or—and this comes to almost the same thing—as a free as opposed to a bound energy[26]:

> The cathectic intensities [in the *Ucs*.] are much more mobile. By the process of *displacement* one idea may surrender to another its whole quota of cathexis; by the process of *condensation* it may appropriate the whole cathexis of several other ideas. I have proposed to regard these two processes as distinguishing marks of the so-called *primary psychical process*. (Freud 1915a: 198)

We will have occasion to discuss the re-interpretations that have been given of these terms displacement and condensation—which thus give the closest definition of this mobility—in terms of linguistics, or, more precisely, in terms of rhetoric. Lacan, alongside Jakobson, is clearly the one who inaugurated these connections, assimilating displacement to a rhetorical device or trope known as metonymy, and condensation to metaphor. Leclaire, in the same text, takes up roughly the same equations. I myself quite often in this text—and particularly since that time, along with many others—use the terms metaphor and metonymy, but, I would like to stress, without entirely assimilating what Freud describes as displacement to metonymy, nor, for even stronger reasons, what he describes as condensation to metaphor. In a convenient manner, I use the terms metaphor and metonymy, following the rhetorical tradition of the seventeenth, eighteenth and nineteenth centuries, to designate the two types of link that can exist between two representations: a link of similarity and a link of contiguity.

In order to give some references, I will return to some authors, among others, who between them develop points of view that are somewhat contradictory. The work of Todorov which appeared recently—*Theories of the Symbol* (Todorov 1982)—is a work valuable for its clarity and for the historical perspective it offers, from classical antiquity to Freud and Jakobson. Jakobson and his *Essais de linguistique générale* (Jakobson 1963), a collection of articles which appeared between 1949 and 1956, is a fundamental, founding text of the structuralist point of view. Contemporary with Jakobson, or sometimes a little later than him, are certain texts by Lacan, of which the most pertinent for our subject would be 'The Agency of the Letter', and then the article on psychosis (Lacan 1977a, 1977b). In Rosolato's *Essais sur le symbolique* and *La relation d'inconnu* (Rosolato 1969, 1978), you will find a conception of metaphor and metonymy which, if I understand correctly, is quite directly derived from the Lacanian conception. Finally I will return to a particularly interesting work which is very dense, and runs counter to the virtual hegemony of the linguistic and structuralist orientations: I mean Lyotard's *Discours, figure* (1971), particularly in his chapter on the dream-work. Lyotard's and Todorov's are the most critical works, and those which in my view open, or re-open, certain perspectives that tended to be closed not only by purely linguistic considerations, but also by those belonging to a linguistic formalism—in other words, by what is known as the (too) famous primacy of the signifier.

A word about Todorov—you will find in his work an appendix, 'Freud's Rhetoric and Symbolics', which takes as its starting point not dream interpretation but *der Witz*, the joke. In this study, Todorov shows how Freud attempted to rediscover, in the course of everyday life, without knowledge appropriated from elsewhere, processes which spring for the most part from the procedures, the tropes, of rhetoric. So much so that one is left with the impression of a fair amount of incoherence in the Freudian classifications, and that the 'joke' doubtless needs to be rewritten, in a more convincing manner, by an analyst with a better knowledge of rhetorical descriptions. We are told, endlessly, that Freud arrived too soon, that he was not able to know Saussure, Jakobson, etc., and about what a shame that was. Well, this is not really the point, because Freud could have used a conceptual system established well before the linguistics of the twentieth century. It is not the case that Freud lacked a linguistics which was still to be discovered; he simply did not know classical rhetoric . . . Todorov gives us an idea of the way in which one could thus take up the Freudian classifications, and reduce their points of incoherence, which are very numerous: the overlapping terms, the uncertainties, the irrelevancies in analysis. He emphasises especially the ambiguity which attaches to a term such as 'displacement'. So much so, Todorov concludes (and I am pretty much in agreement with him, at least regarding the *Witz*), that Freud's original discovery lies in the invention of a method of interpretation (that is, the associative method; to be more explicit: the method of free association as the mapping of a given signifier) and not in the nomenclature of the associative pathways which he sometimes tries to establish.

The formation of the mnemic symbol

I was speaking of displacement, to which Todorov wishes to give a very restricted meaning. Well, in Freud, we have almost the chief example of this term in a passage from the 'Project for a Scientific Psychology' (Freud 1950), in a study of 'hysterical compulsion', also known as *'idée fixe'*:

> Thus, *hysterical compulsion* is (1) unintelligible, (2) incapable of being resolved by the activity of thought [obviously Freud is here designating the inefficacy of rational thought, which might aspire, in a conscious, rational way, to resolve the idea by demonstrating its absurdity] (3) incongruous in its structure . . . Now, our analyses show that a hysterical compulsion is resolved immediately it is explained (made intelligible). Thus these two characteristics are in essence one. In analysis we learn, too, the process by which the appearance of absurdity and incongruity comes about [so it is analysis which will restore this hysterical obsession to some sort of rationality. And this is stated in terms which lend themselves very directly to a sort of algorithm, so to speak]. *Before the analysis, A* is an excessively intense [*überstark*; cf. above, p.90] representation, which forces its way into consciousness too often, and each time gives rise to weeping. The subject does not know why he weeps at *A*; he regards it as absurd; he regards it as absurd, but cannot prevent it. *After the*

> *analysis*, it has been discovered that there is an idea *B*, which justifiably gives rise to weeping and which justifiably recurs frequently so long as a certain complicated psychical action has not been performed against it by the subject. (Freud 1950: 348-349)

In this 'complicated psychical work'—which will allow the effects of the unconscious representation to be eliminated—you can see that the idea of 'working-through' is already present:

> The effect of *B* is not absurd; it is intelligible to the subject and can even be combated by him. *B* stands in a particular relation to *A*. For there has been an occurrence which consisted of *B* + *A*. *A* was an incidental circumstance; *B* was appropriate for producing the lasting effect [for producing tears]. The reproduction of this event in memory has now taken a form of such a kind that it is as though *A* had stepped into *B*'s place. *A* has become a substitute, a *symbol*, for *B*. Hence the incongruity: *A* is accompanied by consequences which it does not seem worthy of, which do not fit in with it. (Freud 1950: 348-349)

Thus, between *A* and *B*, there is a bond of contiguity, a link we habitually call 'metonymic', *A* being a detail of the situation, an absolutely contingent circumstance (the colour of a garment, the number of people present, whatever . . .); *B*, the principal event which 'justified' the tears, has been eliminated, repressed, and it is onto the contingent idea, *A*, that the affect of weeping has been displaced. All this is presented to us as the formation of a *symbol*—or, as Freud calls it elsewhere, a 'mnemic symbol', 'which finds a lodgement in consciousness, like a sort of parasite' (Freud 1894: 49). You can see that *A* has completely taken the place of *B* and that *B* has disappeared, has become unconscious; that is really what has happened. Here is what Freud proposes in order to situate this hysterical symbolisation in relation to a symbolisation which—he tells us—is 'normal':

> The *formation of symbols* also takes place normally. A soldier will sacrifice himself for a many-coloured scrap of stuff on a pole, because it has become the symbol of his fatherland, and no one thinks that neurotic. (Freud 1950: 349-50)

So, it is the soldier's sacrifice for the flag which is a phenomenon that, in itself, is not pathological. We are about to see why not. This is not a value judgement about patriotism, that is not in question; Freud shows clearly how very ridiculous this flag is, in a certain sense, when he describes it quite factually as a many-coloured scrap of stuff on a pole. The sacrifice for the flag could be just as pathological as the tears of the hysteric who starts weeping each time she gets on a tram. However, that is not the case:

> . . . a hysterical symbol behaves differently. The knight who fights for his lady's glove *knows*, in the first place, that the glove owes its importance to the lady; and secondly, he is in no way prevented by his adoration of the glove from thinking of the lady and serving her in other respects. (Freud 1950: 349-50)

Here again we have a symbol: the glove. The knight will fight for the glove, he will sacrifice himself, he will accomplish all kinds of exploits for an item of clothing. Which does not mean that we are in the realm of pathology. What distinguishes this from hysteria or fetishism is that the symbol, the glove, is not a screen—neither a screen-memory nor a counter-investment. In other words, it does not stop the knight thinking of 'the lady', but rather, leads him to do so.

> The hysteric, who weeps at *A*, is quite unaware that he is doing so on account of the association *A—B*, and that *B* itself plays no part at all in his psychical [i.e. conscious] life. The symbol has in this case taken the place of the thing entirely. This assertion is correct in the strictest sense. We can convince ourselves that whenever anything is evoked, from outside or by association, which should in fact cathect *B*, *A* enters consciousness instead of it. Indeed, one can infer the nature of *B* from the provoking causes which—in a remarkable fashion—evoke *A*. (Freud 1950: 349-50)

Look at the example of courtly love, and think what would have happened to a knight who became 'hysterical'. He would no longer think of the lady at all, but he would have to keep on fighting for gloves; and each time something resonated with the unconscious memory of the lady, it would be the glove that re-emerged into consciousness:

> We can sum the matter up: *A* is compulsive, *B* is repressed (at least from consciousness) . . . [And now comes the interpretation in economic terms, which leads directly to the definition of the primary process:] The term 'excessively intense' points to *quantitative* characteristics. It is plausible to suppose that *repression* has the quantitative meaning of being denuded of *Q*, and that the sum of the two (of the compulsion and the repression) is equal to the normal. [There is a constant quantity of energy, so why not a 'quantity of tears', measurable in a 'lachrymator', investing *A* + *B*?]. If so, only the distribution has changed. Something has been added to *A* which has been subtracted from *B*. The pathological process is one of *displacement*, such as we have come to know it in dreams—a primary process therefore. (Freud 1950: 349-50)

The statement of the primary process is thus rigorously correlated with a principle of the conservation of psychical energy, exactly in accordance with the first law of thermodynamics: psychical energy cannot be created. The distribution may vary, but the sum of the energies investing *A, B, C, D,* etc., remains constant.

31 January 1978

Last time we re-read and commented on the passage in the 'Project for a Scientific Psychology' (the *Entwurf*), which compares hysterical compulsion with what could be termed normal symbolisation. Today, I will bring together the main conclusions and questions which arise from it. First of all, it is important to note that the two terms Freud uses here are, on the one hand, that of *symbol*—pathological symbol and normal symbol—and, on the other hand, that of *displacement*. Displacement is thus situated as the basis of symbolisation (or at least of a certain type of symbolisation), which authorises us to question the relation between—firstly—what concerns psychoanalysis, and—secondly—what concerns language. It was here that Lacan was the great initiator—and let us also say, the great systematiser, in a way which I certainly do not consider to be fully satisfactory—and there is no question that we must pay tribute to him for having pointed out this fruitful line of enquiry. You will see, for example, that in Freud's schema, it is a question of a connection *A* + *B* (*B* has certain points of contact with *A*), which is typically what we usually call metonymic, using rhetoric as our reference.

Displacement and the economic dimension

Our first point, then, is the relationship which needs to be established between two lines of investigation which are apparently quite different: a problem concerning psychical energy and a problem concerning psychical rhetoric. The term 'symbol' brings about the link here, but in a much broader and far more interesting sense than that of the fixed symbols (the 'symbolic') to which Freud will adhere to later on.

Our second point concerns the question of knowing *what* is displaced. Well, that which flows along the association $A \leftrightarrow B$ is not just a vague notion; it is the 'tears' which are displaced, since, normally attached to B, in the hysteric they appear in conjunction with A. Or again, in the case of so-called normal symbolisations, it is the devotion or patriotism of the soldier; in the case of the lady and her knight it is, let's say, courtly love or courtly devotion. According to the model of the 'Project' (Freud 1950) which appears to be truly founded on the clinical, what is displaced along a network of representations, that 'quantity' whose *quantum*, we can conclude, remains the same although its distribution is variable, is the quantity of an affect, apprehended, even measured, through its manifestations and its effects. You can see how plausible is the equation between the network of neurones and representations, on the one hand, and between the quantum of energy and affect, on the other. It is thus affect that is displaced, and which would therefore be (one could say, as it's a question of the symbol) the universal and unique thing symbolised or signified. One might be tempted to think that symbolisation, which is always understood as the symbolisation of a content (symbolising one representation by another), is always derived, secondary, in relation to an original task which is never understood in itself. This task consists in 'symbolising', that is, in linking, retaining—and obviously also, in mastering—the pure affect, in order to prevent it from surging forth in a non-specific, unbound form, in the form of anxiety. We can state that our hysteric's absurd weeping is the final stage, before the unveiling of a naked anxiety.

My third point is to return to the distinction between two kinds of 'displacement' which we could characterise thus: on one side, the displacement which *retains* traces of previous stages (the glove which 'keeps the memory' of the lady); and, on the other, that which *does not retain* the mark of the representation: *A* does not retain anything of *B*, at least, not consciously, and it is precisely this which designates *B* as repressed. If we no longer speak of displacement, but rather of the symbol, we would then have two symbolisations, the one symbolising another symbol. That is to say, one representation (or a complex of representations) is partially substituted for another, but retains the meaning of that other, and profits from it: the glove once more harbours the lady's perfume but, in that same way, the energy, the affect, is not transposed onto a single point in the group of representations. Instead it is divided up, spread out, and thereby bound.

The other type of symbolisation is where one representation completely substitutes another (which thus disappears). The symbolisation has caused what is symbolised to disappear, with, as a correlative (let us not say 'as an effect'; one could just as well say, 'as a cause') in the realm of affect—namely, that the latter has passed directly, leaving nothing behind, from representation *B* to representation *A*. In this case, the affect is not metabolised, is not spread across the complex of ideas; it remains non-specific or poorly specified. This is pure weeping, on the edge of anxiety, in the same way that in phobia, fear—in so far as it is poorly distributed and builds up at a single point—always tends to be transformed again, making what supports it appear—that is, anxiety.

My fourth point concerns knowing where we should situate what is described here as displacement. It could be said that at the level of a preconscious-conscious system there are displacements, but displacements regulated precisely by language. It could be said—and this is what Freud will affirm in 1915—that total, absolute displacement is characteristic of the unconscious system. However in the process which is specifically described here, it is interesting to observe that displacement should be situated not inside one of these systems—intra-preconscious or intra-unconscious—but in-between the two systems, and perhaps in order to serve as the basis for the distinction between them. It is because there is displacement—and once again, total displacement—that this element *B* falls into the unconscious; there is a forgetting of element *B*, it is not retained, it is totally disinvested. Thus, the idea of a displacement shows us the way to a model of repression, which should encourage us to complete that model.

One final remark on this passage: is this to say that in the case of symbolisations which are—what can we call them: unforgetting?

memorial?—the unconscious does not have to intervene? It would be rash of us to claim that behind the relation of the glove and the lady there were nothing more. One might clearly be tempted, very schematically, with the knowledge of later developments in analysis, to postulate behind the lady and her glove, the mother and her phallus. Or again, what is there behind the soldier and his flag? The soldier and his fatherland? The soldier and his 'motherland'? Does not every secondary symbolisation presuppose a primary symbolisation? Does not every symbolisation—even a 'rememorial' one—postulate the fundamental forgetting of a primary repression? It is in any case a legitimate question, just as it seems to me to be legitimate to attempt to reformulate a certain model of repression.

A model for repression

Returning to the article written with Leclaire, we tried at the time to formulate this model, along certain lines inspired by Lacan, as a substitution of 'signifiers', a substitution which then I dubbed 'metaphor' (a term which I will have occasion to criticise, because Lacan was not alone in designating every substitution of signifiers 'metaphor' although, from another perspective, metaphor might be considered only *one* type of substitution). Be that as it may, the model of the substitution of signifiers is not so far from what Freud describes, and the quasi-algebraic play of representations (*A* and *B*, *A* + *B*, etc.) can be linked quite naturally with certain Lacanian formulations. One of these, the formula which Lacan calls 'metaphor', as you will find in our text, is taken from Lacan's article on the psychoses:

$$\frac{S'}{S} \times \frac{S}{s} \longrightarrow S' \times \frac{I}{s}$$

(The capital letters are signifiers and the small letters are signifieds, which is in accordance with what Lacan calls the primacy of the signifier, with dignity on the side of the capital letters and inferiority, subordination, on the side of the small ones. This is a usage of capital and small letters which already implies a whole system . . .)

I will first quote the way in which, in 1960, I made use of the possible transformations of this formula:

> Let us recall here the diagram that Lacan gives of metaphor in its linguistic symbolisation:
>
> It consists in the substitution, in the relation of signifier to signified $\left(\frac{S}{s}\right)$, of a new signifier S′: used as a signifier of the original signifier S, which, by virtue of that fact, falls to the rank of signified. Thus, according to the algebraic formula:
>
> $$\frac{S'}{S} \times \frac{S}{s} \longrightarrow S' \times \frac{I}{s}$$
>
> What has happened is apparently something quite simple, a change of name: the signified s that I first named S, is now connoted by S′.
>
> But we also see, and this is what interests us, that something has fallen below, has been 'simplified out' in the algebraic sense of that term . . . [It is in fact the simplification of the product of a fraction, which consists in crossing out the terms which are the same below and above the bar.] (Laplanche & Leclaire 1972: 156/p. 262, below)

So there was a 'simplification', but what interests us—in repression—is *to know what has happened to this term 'simplified'*. That is to say, how and in what form has this term S passed to the level of the unconscious. But firstly, I think it would now be preferable to write this model the other way around. As you know, in a sum there is always a multiplicand (on which the operation is carried out) and a multiplier (which carries out the transformation). Now, that on which the transformation is carried out is the initial relationship $\frac{S}{s}$, and that which carries out the transformation is $\frac{S'}{s}$, is that which produces the effect, the transformer. It is thus more meaningful to write:

$$\frac{S}{s} \times \frac{S'}{S} \longrightarrow$$

Using this model—of something that is transformed and something that produces an effect—clearly poses many problems. Not the least of these is to know how far its legitimacy extends, and at what point one is 'going too far' with transpositions and transformations which appear mathematical. The only response to this is of an empirical kind, in terms of how fruitful such formulae can be, and how far they can help to simplify matters. Let us simply recall that the Freudian context, far from banning such efforts, rather encouraged their undertaking. Thus, the application of the formula of signifying substitution to the example of the 'hysterical tears' seems indeed to happen anyway, of its own accord. In the case of this neurotic symbolisation, we know that there is a representation at the origin of the painful affect, we have a link between *A* and *B* which means that in a certain sense term *A* can come to substitute itself for term *B*, to signify term *B*. In other words, in the complex *A* + *B*, it is the term *A* which is singled out to signify the whole of the situation *A* + *B*. In the end, the result is precisely the 'simplification' of which we were speaking. *B*, the element which is the true motive for weeping, disappears, and will be rediscovered in the unconscious. Meanwhile, it is *A* which will trigger the weeping, through a false connection whose strangeness is clearly marked, through the skewed nature of the formula $S' \times \frac{I}{s}$ (and not $\frac{S'}{s}$):

$$\frac{\text{B}}{\text{weeping}} \times \frac{\text{A}}{\text{B}} \longrightarrow \text{A} \times \frac{\text{I}}{\text{weeping}}$$

Note that *A* and *B* are in a relation of contiguity, a connection which we habitually call metonymic, and that this so-called schema of 'metaphor' is, in that sense, incorrectly designated. It would be better to designate it as a 'signifying substitution', this representing one of the most simplified modalities of symbolisation. If we now try to put into the formula one of the two examples that are given of 'normal symbolisation', we can write something like this:

$$\frac{\text{Lady}}{\text{courtly love}} \times \frac{\text{glove}}{\text{Lady}} \longrightarrow$$

Here too we are in a relation of the part to the whole, and the substitution turns on the factor of contiguity rather than that of similarity. But the essential thing is that there is no 'simplification'. The 'lady' does not pass purely and simply into the Ucs., even if she undergoes, clearly, a transfiguration. There is, in any case, *the retention of signification, which I tend to think is what defines true symbolisation*, on which I had occasion to speak three years ago, concerning rites of passage (Laplanche 1980b: second part).

A few moments previously we were wondering whether such a way of constructing things was legitimate . . . Well, here we can start to see its limitations, since we have been able to 'apply' to a case a certain rule of mathematical transformation (that of simplification), whereas in so-called normal or 'complex' symbolisation, the algebra leaves us in the lurch . . . However, on the other hand, behind the transformation of these relations, the 'calculations' symbolised here by multiplication signs—or by an arrow—there is still the value of the basic cell, for which Lacan says he is adopting what he calls the 'Saussurean algorithm', that is to say this $\frac{S}{s}$, which is supposed to be the origin of modern linguistics.[27]

The Saussurean cell

Let us remember, then, that this Saussurean 'cell' is what—for him—defined the sign. This is the unit of signifier and the signified, comprising two 'sides': the signifying side, which has to be conceived of as the phonematic side, what is purely material. This is the materiality of the 'word' in the case of language (to be precise, it is not always the 'word', because there are signifying elements which do not wholly coincide with the way words are divided). We can think of the purely material aspect of a word, which we could write and which would 'mean nothing' to us—as I wrote just now the name of that Arab logician and mathematician. On the other hand, here is the 'signified', what Saussure calls the 'mental' side (without encumbering himself with 'antipsychological' prejudices which are obligatory nowadays . . .), the mental side or simply the 'concept', or even the 'content'. This cell (so as not to repeat the inexact term 'algorithm'), this sign was written by Saussure thus:

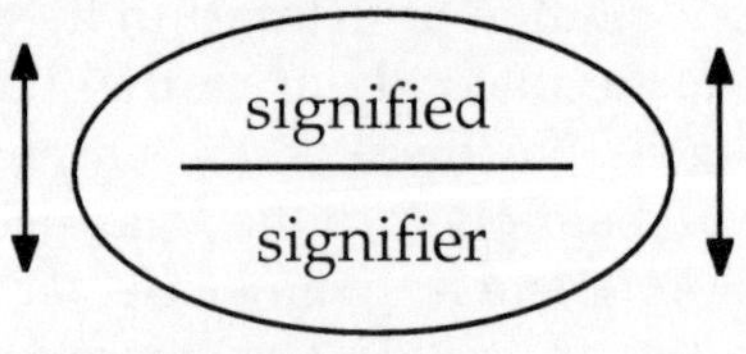

The interesting thing, the thing we need to emphasise in Saussure's work, and, we could say, in all those who have followed him on this point, including Lacan, is that the sign, at least on its 'signified' side, has nothing to do with reality. The signified does not refer to anything extra-mental. Saussure completely excludes any intentionality (and *a fortiori*, obviously, any designation) which would refer language to anything other than itself. This is very important because we are immediately shut into a formalism from which it will then be very difficult to get out.

Well, what about Lacan in relation to Saussure? As you know, Lacan, in concordance with the whole movement of that period, which already seems a little outdated, considers linguistics to be the 'pilot science' of the human sciences, but a quite specific kind of linguistics—that of *structuralism*. This is translated in the formula which we have to discuss and to analyse: 'the unconscious is structured like a language', in which each term has its weight, in particular the term 'structure'. All the terms are to be examined here: 'like', implying analogy and not identity; the article 'a' ('a language'), which authorises us to distance ourselves still further from *our* verbal language, towards a concept of language in general, of which verbal language would only be a particular case, would have to be established. How can we define 'a language' in all its generality? I will hazard a kind of formula, valid only as a discussion point, and then to be got rid of: 'A phenomenon of meaning, where something is conveyed, communicated by, or with, a material support, which is itself more or less structured.' The material support is that which, in the cell, is written 'signifier' or S. 'By' or 'with' signifies that there is certainly an 'instrumentalist' aspect of language; but the linguistic sign is never a pure means which disappears before what it communicates. A message can never be passed on without at the same time passing on the materiality of its 'support'. Obviously, we note the very approximate nature of every term in this sort of 'definition'.

But rather than getting locked straight away into the technicalities—and the obscure battles—of 'the' science of linguistics, let us take our starting point, not in 'some' language, but in this 'like-a-language' which is the *unconscious*, taking this formula 'like-a-language' as a whole, in the same way as Saussure traces a sort of outline around his linguistic sign. Starting from that, let us try to outline things, even if we have to return to language 'itself' in the end.

Are there any signifiers in the unconscious?

As for the unconscious, we will retain, at least provisionally, the distinction between a material, a materiality of the unconscious, and on the other hand, that which circulates within it. Well, first of all, on the side of the 'material' (Freud), or the 'signifier' (Saussure—Lacan), we know that the unconscious is not buzzing with words and phrases, in the sense of verbal language. We know that there, representations are representations of things, or thing-representations (*Sachvorstellungen*), often borrowed from visual sense-perception—which we call, for example, 'imagos'—but also from domains that are not necessarily visual, for instance patterns of action which could be termed perceptual-motor, and which are some of the most primitive representations: eating, incorporating, retaining, expelling, cutting up. They are at the heart of unconscious fantasies. The fact that the 'visual' appears to be predominant there (perhaps because of the dream: we have too great a tendency to infer incessantly from the dream to the unconscious) does not in the least exclude the presence of other representations, and, among them, auditory representations. This directly raises the following question: what is the status of linguistic ideas in the unconscious, of what we isolate as the 'mnemic traces' of words or phrases that have been heard? We need to be very precise here: the auditory, verbal representations are present in the unconscious only as thing-representations; they are treated there like 'things', *without respect for linguistic structure*, such as it has been described more adequately since Saussure. Here I am alluding to Martinet's description of verbal language as a 'double articulation': the first articulation is that of units broken up according to meaning, 'monemes'; and the second articulation, that of distinctive units, 'phonemes', which are not invested with meaning, at least not in their properly linguistic function (Martinet 1960).

Well, in the unconscious, the essential thing is that the elements of language found there—remnants of phrases that were pronounced, remnants of words, remnants of phonemes—feature as elements among others, taking their meaning from the particular infantile experience of the subject and not, essentially, from their insertion in a universal code and in the double structure described by Martinet. These *fragments* of language, which can be found in an unconscious complex, are without direct relation to the universal code of language; they are extracted from it, and 'cobbled together' (in Lévi-Strauss' sense of *bricolage*) into another configuration. This, by a sort of ricochet, raises a no less important question: that of the possible existence of another code, even of a structure, of the unconscious, which would be universal, trans-individual.

7 February 1978

We are continuing to put to the test, by means of a series of approximations, this formula which currently has a bearing upon the problem of the unconscious: 'The unconscious is structured like a language'. On the side of what we can, in a first approximation, call the 'signifier' in the unconscious, we have emphasised that it comprises essential differences from the signifier of a language (let's say, of a 'natural language'). It is different in so far as it appears to be out of the question to define a fixed relation with the 'signified', however one might conceive of this fixity—whether as a nominal link between a particular signifier and 'its' signified, or as a regulated correspondence within the framework of a structure (in which case this fixity would then be defined as differential in relation to other elements—as 'value'). However, the search for a code of the unconscious, for a 'fundamental language', is indeed evident in Freud's attempt to describe a symbolic system, an attempt which unfolded in the years 1900-1910, particularly under Jung's influence. This attempt, this temptation of 'the symbolic', can be discerned at the horizon of every linguistic reduction of the unconscious, to the extent that such a reduction cannot avoid what constitutes the essence of any language aiming at communication: the existence of a code. *Lacanianism does not escape this tendency*. A de-coding, in a systematic and 'wild' fashion (a rather tame wildness), is to be found in a certain posterity which recites, with open book, the monotonous anthem of the phallus and castration. In the unconscious there is no code, there is no double articulation—in the sense described by Martinet. The signifier, if we retain this word for the moment, remains stuck to the thing—even to a fragment of a thing—since it is well and truly the thing-representation, the *Sachvorstellung*, which predominates.

There is still one thing, however, which, in an unexpected reversal, reveals that we have not dealt with the relation to language by having shown that the unconscious does not have a linguistic 'structure'. This is the fact that, in so far as one can describe it, the unconscious—far from being comparable to some formless, continuous magma—appears to be composed of separate, discrete elements, of some kind of atoms. In spite of the fact that here we need to be very sceptical, because we could ask (and Freud did not fail to do so) whether this 'atomic' presentation of the unconscious is not simply the result of the methodology of our approach. Analysis is a schematisation which, by definition, gives attention to the atoms that it isolates, right down to the most elementary, the most 'indivisible'. We must, however, accept the separateness that characterises unconscious 'units' [*unités*], while holding on to the question of the origin of these units. What do they owe to perceptual 'unities', to *Gestalt* phenomena, or phenomena of form (the breast, the part-object), and what do they retain of the divisions of linguistic structure, or of 'signifying' unities?

. . . and is there any 'signified'?

Continuing our exploration, let us now turn to the side of the 'signified'. I should point out from the beginning, as an epigraph, a particularly interesting distinction—or rather, a fertile 'sliding', a drifting—which Lacan introduced into this term. Effectively, in the work of a Saussure, the signified is always the signified of a signifier, just as substantial as the latter. Yet in Lacan, sometimes, we find the following formula (testifying to a kind of liberation from a too strict and obligatory correlation): what he calls the 'signified to the subject'. Here, the signified is taken up from the expression 'I signify to you that . . .'; for instance, a magistrate who 'signifies' a judgement. To clarify things one could say that in Saussure's conception, we approach things from the perspective of concepts, and in Lacan from the perspective of judgements . . . but these are judgements equally taken to be verdicts.

We might also adopt as a framework the great opposition that has been perpetuated in a certain domain, from Saussure right up to contemporary linguistics. First of all, as it appears in Saussure, this is the opposition between language [*langue*] and speech [*parole*], language being the stock of verbal images common to a group of individuals, something at once social and structural—which is scarcely amenable to change and which is the true subject of linguistics—and speech, an individual act, which comes to inhabit this structure and make use of it. Or another distinction, which more or less overlaps the preceding one: code/message. More recently, with Chomsky, we have an opposition which also tends to align itself with the others: the opposition between 'competence'—the limitless capacity to form sentences—and, on the other hand, the 'performance' of the individual speaking subject.[28]

If you like, then, within language we can oppose the aspect of structure to that of communication—this would be another way of saying the same thing. Well, we have pointed out that the signified could take on two senses, the 'signified of the signifier' and the 'signified to the subject', in the sense in which Lacan suggests this term. The signified of the signifier would be caught up in language, a phenomenon of structure. Conversely, the signified to the subject can only be conceived of in communication, although we have to admit that there is no communication without a minimum of structure, no possibility of passing on a message without a code.

But, to return to the unconscious, it is, to say the least, problematic to bring in here the notion of 'signified', whether in the sense of a code (we have seen, in the sense of structure, that it was doubtful if we could describe a code or lexicon of the unconscious without running the risk of falling into a 'symbolic', that is to say, into a pre-established system of interpretation); or, on the other hand, in the sense of communication—that is to say, not necessarily as 'contents' with a clearly defined meaning, but in the sense of a message, albeit vague and above all enigmatic, but addressed *to the other*. In the unconscious, is there yet a signified, a message to communicate and to deliver? Well, I think we need to hold on to this, which reopens our discussion in our attempt to come up with a definition of language: the unconscious is a phenomenon of meaning, but without any communicative finality.

The unconscious communicates nothing

It might be said—perhaps metaphorically—that the unconscious speaks, but it does not aim to communicate, it does not convey any message.[29] In the dream, in the symptom, even in symptoms which are directly linguistic, such as slips of the tongue, we have to insist on the following. They are formations of the unconscious, closed in upon themselves, and not intended for communication.

Hysteria, for all that it is 'talkative', is so only as a by-product, only from the moment that it enters the analytic process; or else when the symptom is used, as Freud put it, for secondary gain, in order to be displayed. However, the symptom can exist without being shown, as a paradoxical phenomenon of *speech* that is not destined for anybody. The question is sometimes raised of knowing if a symptom can exist without being perceived by the other: 'do young girls blush in the dark'? The question, it is claimed, is insoluble, even absurd in its proposition. I am convinced that the true characteristic of the hysterical symptom, including what is called the 'conversion' symptom, is that it continues to exist even in the dark, in isolation, in the absence of all communication. Likewise, the dream is not intended to be told and, for even stronger reasons, is not the 'dream-narrative'. This latter is already association, the beginning of associations to the dream; it is the beginning of the dream's analysis.

It is analysis that transforms what is essentially closed in upon itself, in the unconscious, back into communication, and it is to the extent that it is closed in upon itself that the unconscious is repetitive. Why do I speak of transforming it 'back'—and not simply of 'transforming' it—into communication? This means that probably, at the 'beginning', in the genesis of the unconscious, there was a phenomenon of communication, which then became closed in upon itself, communication then becoming 'circulation'. The 'signified to the subject', then—to retain Lacan's fine formula, even if one does not entirely share his theory of the 'subject'. For a comprehension of what is at stake, we need to turn to the seduction theory, which is shown marvellously clearly, with a truly mythical luminosity, by a clinical example, which I have commented on more than once. This is the case of Emma, which follows the passage in the 'Project for a Scientific Psychology' (Freud 1950) on 'hysterical compulsion'.[30]

Repression and seduction

The case of Emma, let us recall, shows how 'seduction' can come into play between two scenes. In one of the scenes, the earliest of the two (Scene II, since it comes second in the analytic reconstruction) something is *signified* to the child, 'signified to the subject', but remains in her as a sequence that is absolutely not comprehended. There is certainly 'a' sexual signified in view, but what is left behind is only a thing or a sequence of things, of thing-presentations.

> Further investigation now revealed a second memory, which she denies having had in mind at the moment of Scene I [the later one]. Nor is there anything to prove this [Scene II has been repressed]. On two occasions when she was a child of eight she had gone into a small shop to buy some sweets, and the shop-keeper had grabbed at her genitals through her clothes. In spite of the first experience she had gone there a second time; after the second time she stopped away. She now reproached herself for having gone there a second time, as though she had wanted in that way to provoke the assault. In fact a state of 'oppressive bad conscience' is to be traced back to this experience. (Freud 1950: 353-4)

Everything in this description is important, in particular the fact that the child goes back. Obviously, we would say (on the basis of the knowledge Freud brought us, in the years following, concerning the existence of a precocious infantile sexuality), she goes back driven, endogenously, by her desire, so that in the end the seduction by the adult will be no more than the hysteric's allegation. Here we see a whole line of subsequent Freudian interpretation, according to which seduction is nothing but a projected reflection of a purely internal development of sexuality. However, whatever the partial truth may be regarding this reversal—in the practice of treatment as well—it does not, in my view, invalidate the prototype which represents the relation between the two scenes. She 'goes back there' not only because sexual excitement already exists for her, but in order to find the trauma again, and to try to rediscover precisely the enigmatic signified, this 'signified to the subject' which has not been delivered, in spite of an act which in itself bears signification.

As for the second scene (Scene I, the one which was first recounted by the hysteric), it comes to *interpret* and at the same time to bury, to repress, the first. It is the scene dubbed 'the scene with the shop-assistants' which for its part, in contrast to the first scene, has no manifest, surface sexual content. If you re-read this, you will see that it amounts to a complication and a concrete realisation of the *A* + *B* schema, bearing this time on *sets* of elements and not just two isolated elements, and turning on the time-lag and the 'afterwardsness'[31] between the two scenes. I have said that what is at stake is a great myth, to the extent that the play between the two scenes, the time-lag, and above all the first scene, the earliest one, were to be transposed back in time, perhaps as far as the very first days. But if we decide to push further back this 'secondary repression'—in order to make it into something closer to a certain reality we try to perceive, namely the birth of the unconscious in the first repressions—well, we will ask here, what is the signified in the unconscious? Let us say, taking as our guide this sequence of scenes, that the signified is first of all a sexual, enigmatic signified, which cannot be assimilated at first by the baby who receives it. It certainly has a relation with what is called, a little too quickly, the 'desire of the mother'. Clearly, the desire of the mother is shown in the way she takes care of the child, but it is not revealed there. It is at once conveyed and hidden, in the care, the handling, in what is given attention, in attitudes. In the most schematic terms, it is symbolised by the breast, or at least, in the unconscious. It will be taken up in the form of a certain number of representational elements (*Vorstellungsrepräsentanz*) as the breast. You can see how it is over-hasty and facile to say that the unconscious *is* the 'discourse of the other'. The child's unconscious is not directly the discourse of the other, nor even the desire of the other.

From the discourse of the mother to the unconscious of the child: a metabolism

Between signifying behaviour, laden as it is with sexuality (which one always, again, wishes to forget), between the behaviour-discourse-desire of the mother and the subject's unconscious representation, there is no continuity, nor even any pure and simple interiorisation. The child does not interiorise the desire of the mother. He neither learns the mother's fantasy nor interiorises it. Nor does the child—to refer to the learning of verbal language, concerning which one freely says that the child 'slips into it', as if from inside—slip in the same way into parental fantasy. Between these two 'phenomena of meaning' (here I use the vaguest possible term), which are, on one side, the signifying behaviour of the adult and particularly of the mother, and, on the other, the child's unconscious, which is in the process of being constituted, there is an essential moment which might be termed 'disqualification'. The unconscious is not the discourse-desire of the other, it is the result of a strange metabolism which, like any metabolism, comprises decomposition and reconstitution. It is not for nothing that we frequently speak here of 'incorporation', for incorporation resembles its metabolic model more closely that one might think. In incorporation, there is also this decomposition-reconstitution. In the beginning there is a sort of enigmatic message, a judgement or communication which is hidden behind some behaviour, a judgement which we can understand in the most Kafkaesque sense—because, concerning what is 'communicated to the subject', the subject knows neither what is expected of him nor even what the true meaning is. As in Kafka, nothing comes but the verdict. What is the verdict? We will say, to be brief, that it is pure energetics. The disqualified 'message' conveys nothing except its energy. In the same way, the first scene in Emma's case conveys nothing but the fact that it is traumatising, with no knowledge of what constitutes this traumatisation—and, moreover, that is why Emma goes back.

If we pursue this idea, we see that such a message, precisely in so far as it does not convey anything but energy or excitation, is—by its very nature—traumatising. It is in this sense that the mother—not merely due to any of her contingent characteristics but also out of necessity—is always in a sense 'bad' or 'not good enough' (to invert Winnicott's formula). Of course, it is also necessary for her to be 'good enough' to make up for this 'not good enough' which is, as it were, implicit in her very function. Thus the problem of goodness, of support, of 'holding', of attachment, is certainly not to be neglected as the background which allows this traumatisation to be not purely and simply de-structuring. However—and this is a point we insist upon, with Freud, when we speak of the disruptive character of sexuality, when we say that in the end *the truth of sexuality is the death drive*—it is the message that is necessarily traumatising, because it tends to be converted into pure energy, pure excitation. From this moment, too, you see the birth of the repetition compulsion, precisely as an attempt to produce meaning: going back to the sweet-shop to give a meaning to this message.

'Disqualification' and traumatisation are thus necessary, and for very concrete reasons: not because of some metaphysical characteristic, but as a function (as they say in other domains) of inequalities of development. What is thus designated is not, essentially, the different levels of psycho-physiological organisation and maturation in the baby and the adult. There is not only a delay (which is ordinary, for all species, and by definition, the little one is less evolved than the adult) but at the same time, in humans, there is prematurity. What counts is not immediately the developmental inequality of adult and child, but, one might say, a developmental inequality internal to the child itself, and where the child-adult disparity re-emerges.

The unconscious is certainly a 'phenomenon of meaning', and with this banal formula (after Freud) its relation to language is in question: it is born of a language (including, in language, not only the mother's articulate language, but also all her signifying and significant behaviour) and it can, perhaps, become language again. I say 'perhaps' because here we come back to the possibility of its recognition, of its *Agnoszierung*. An *Agnoszierung*, a 'becoming-message-again', is perhaps only possible in an undefined, asymptotic fashion. For the unconscious is also that which has been closed off to meaning, in order to become a means of metabolising, along only slightly differentiated paths of association, and with the aid of primitive ideas which are and remain things—thing-representations—an energy which is no more than the energetic remnant of an enigmatic signified. This is a lost signified, if you like, but 'lost' in its very nature, without any appeal to the whole 'pathos' of loss.

The Saussurean cell and structuralist hegemony

A question, then. Is it legitimate to use the formula taken partly from Saussure, S/s or signifier/signified, Sr/Sd, to understand anything at all about the unconscious? Yes, perhaps. On condition that we see what it is that it changes into, and in what way it disqualifies itself; that we use it not in the framework of a structure (because structure in the unconscious would mean the existence of a code) but as something which explodes structure—precisely the structure of coded signification which exists for adults, but not for the child—demolishing it in order to construct something else out of it.

Yet, before we make use of this formula, before we imagine how language might be de-structured in the unconscious, perhaps we should ask a preliminary question. What is it that is structured in language, and is language as structured as it is said to be? Here we should interrogate the hegemony of linguistic structuralism, which was at its height between 1950 and 1960. Structuralism in linguistics was born, as you know, with Saussure, but flourished with someone who pushed it to its limits, Roman Jakobson. Structuralism does not correspond only to the cell Sr/Sd, but to the denial (a fertile one, in a way) that between signifier and signified there is the faintest shadow of exchange, the slightest intentionality, the least agency of signification.[32]

So structuralism is not the cell Sr/Sd, but rather the ultimate attempt to reduce the phenomenon of signification which still seems to spring forth from this formula. It is precisely what is termed the reduction of signification to 'value', a term used in a completely technical sense, which is not without correspondences to Marxist theory. It is, to take up this comparison, a reduction of 'use value' to 'exchange value', in the sense that a singular, individual signification is related to nothing but the spaces between each of these cells Sr/Sd, and ultimately can only be apprehended within the framework of the structure. This means that a given signifier can only refer to a signified, can only be linked with a signified, because it is inserted in a structure where it is unable to move, because it is in opposition to other terms which fill up, so to speak, all the space.

The primacy of the notion of 'value' in linguistics returns to affirm that a direct relation between signifier and signified is just an illusion, or in any case cannot be deployed by science. The existence of a science of language begins only at the moment when the phenomenon of signifying intentionality—perhaps philosophical, perhaps vital, but which we are unable to grasp in science—can be brought back to something which can be 'dealt with', and which can be described—that is, to the gaps between each of these formulae and those surrounding it, with which it enters into opposition or composition. And starting with oppositions—in the sense in which a term like 'horse' can be opposed to all kinds of other terms in the series of mammals; or a phoneme can be substituted for other sound elements of language—with Jakobson, we soon arrive at the *binary* opposition.[33] From oppositions in a context of diversity, we move to an opposition of plus and minus, the only kind that can be entered—and this is not accidental—into a binary machine.

Well, the binarism introduced by Jakobson to describe the phonetic system, in other words, the level described by Martinet as 'secondary articulation' (the articulation of elements which have no corresponding signifieds), is then taken as far as the level of primary articulation. From a structuralist perspective, that of a reduction of signification to value—ultimately to a binary value: presence/absence—there is clearly no division of the signified upon which a division of the signifier could be modelled (according to a naïve nominalism). However, if we follow Saussure's interpretation, neither should we presuppose a prior structuration (a primacy) of the signifier. We have to imagine, from the beginning, two 'amorphous masses', that of the signifier and that of the signified, which are divided or cut out at the same time. This is the famous comparison with a sheet of paper, one side of which would represent the mass of the signifier and the other the mass of the signified. However you cut up this sheet of paper, there will be an absolute correspondence, term for term, between the discrete units thus created in the signifier and the signified. This is a seductive image, which appears to transcend the opposition between, on the one hand, a nominalism or a realism of the signified, and—on the other—an idealism, that is to say, a primacy of language in the way things are 'cut out'. Thus there would be a sort of parallelism, with no primacy awarded to either plane over the other. One and the same signifying gesture, we could say, cuts out the two planes simultaneously.

Thanks to Hjelmslev: the exposure of formalism

In fact we can see that this division or cutting-out, this interpretation, which appears unitary, can only function in so far as the two 'planes' are reduced to their mere forms. But here I am forced to appeal, in a necessarily swift allusion, to some distinctions which are particularly illuminating, introduced, on the basis of Saussure's formula, by his Danish successor, Hjelmslev. According to him, the initial two planes remain the same, except that he designates them with different terms:

signifier = plane of expression
signified = plane of content

However, each of these planes, in turn, is then be subdivided into a substance and a form, so that apparently everything is henceforth played out between four terms: the substance and form of expression (or 'of the signifier'), the substance and form of content (or 'of the signified').

14 February 1978

I find it interesting to set out Hjelmslev's distinctions in the following manner, to illustrate my argument, while still conforming to the 'cell':

substance of the expression
______________________________ (or: the signifier)
form of the expression
==============================
form of the content
______________________________ (or: the signified)
substance of the content

We notice immediately that Saussure's cell does not correspond to Hjelmslev's four terms, but only to the terms where form is involved. Only these can constitute the object of structural linguistics, which again illustrates Saussure's famous statement that language is not substance but form. Thus, only form would be susceptible to study; the only possible relation would be that of the form of a signifier (the signifier defined by the relations constituting its 'value') and the form of a signified, which Saussure called the concept, the mental image. This is to say that linguistics has no bearing upon the purely material, physical phenomena which constitute the substance of expression. Any language can be studied just as well in its written as in its oral transcription, whether the material is in sound or in writing, the systems of opposition, the 'form' of expression, remain the same. In addition, the intended aim—in other words what is currently called 'the referent'—is not taken into consideration either, to the extent that what Lacan calls 'the primacy of the signifier' is ultimately, following Saussure, a primacy of form.

So we know that language, even reduced to these two forms—that of the signifier and signified—is not, as the image proposed by Saussure would have it, a sort of recto/verso sheet of paper that is cut out in an absolutely identical way. This is almost never the case, or only in the most exceptional, most localised cases. I will take up a convenient example, of the type used by Hjelmslev, that of an animal marked by a feminine suffix: 'lioness' (Hjelmslev 1966: 136ff). The linguistic sign, as a first approximation, could be written:

/lion/ess
____
'lion' — 'female'

—which, in this particular case, is illustrated by the image of the sheet of paper, since the way the signifier and signified are cut out correspond to each other. However, on the one hand we know (according to Martinet's systematisation) that at the level of the signifier there is an extra cutting-out, a 'secondary articulation', that of the phonematic units, which are characterised precisely by their not corresponding to anything in the signified: /lie/on/ess.[34]

And on the other hand? Can we say that at least the units of the signified only come into existence if there is a cutting-out of the signifier? If there were an absolute primacy of the signifier, it would be impossible to imagine a cutting-out of the signified, of the 'concept', without this splitting having already occurred in the signifier. The signifier could certainly be 'more cut out' than the signified, but the contrary could never be true. Now let us take the example of 'female donkey', which cannot be written according to a logical, 'proportional' articulation, in the form of /donkey/ess/, but as /jenny/. The sign would be:

$$\frac{\text{/jenny/}}{\text{'female' — 'donkey'}} \quad \text{or} \quad \frac{\text{/je/nee/}}{\text{'female' — 'donkey'}}$$

From this, we see that on top of the primary articulation (which makes the units of expression correspond to the units of content), are superimposed not one (as Martinet would have it) but *two* secondary articulations, which do not correspond to each other, but which cut out, each on its own side, both the signifier *and* the signified: 'phonemes', or distinctive units of expression; 'semes' (B. Pottier) or distinctive units of content. As Hjelmslev comments:

> Our everyday languages always have this remarkable particularity, in that one single element of expression does not correspond, that is to say, has no relation with, one single element of content, and *vice versa*, but that in the majority of cases a unit composed of several elements of expression has a relation with a unit composed of several units of content. (Hjelmslev 1966: 136, LT's translation)

The only language where there would be an absolute 'signifying relevance', in which the distinctive elements of one of the two planes would correspond exactly to the distinctive elements of the other, would obviously be the famous 'well-made language', a scientific ideal which posits mathematics, ultimately, as communication without ambiguity, without any left-over or excess. However, can we still call it 'language', this formal system of transformations where the distinction between the two planes is no longer in place, where the phenomenon of 'signification' is abolished?

You see that the expression: 'structured like a language', applied to the unconscious, does not mean a great deal if one does not say *which* language is in question. Where languages are concerned, one moves from the more to the less structured, the more to the less restrictive. On both sides of 'natural' or 'everyday' languages, we have systems which are called semiotic systems, which are even less restrictive, and which modern semiology is beginning to decipher, and then also artificial languages, and finally algorithms, 'processes of calculation which link in a univocal manner a set of givens with a set of results'. It is here, and only here, that since there is an absolute necessity on the plane of transformations in the 'horizontal' or 'syntagmatic' direction, there is no longer any need to refer to a signified.

The model of the metabola and its interpretations

Let us take up this idea, using the example of the 'calculation' I proposed, to formalise, in an extension of Freud, his analysis of hysterical compulsion:

$$\frac{A}{B} \times \frac{C}{A} \longrightarrow ?$$

What would we be justified in giving as the 'result'? It is clear that it would be expressed quite differently according to the type of 'language' in which we are situated. In the 'language' of mathematics, in the 'well-made language', everything is structure but signifies nothing, so that one is within one's rights to 'simplify' the superfluous element, A, and to write:

$$\frac{A}{B} \times \frac{C}{A} = \frac{C}{B}$$

C has come, in an absolute equivalence, and without any remainder, to take A's place. In a *natural language*, what would happen? Well, this model would be that of signifying substitution—what I called metaphor in the 1960 text, and which I now prefer to designate by another term: let us say, for example, '*metabola*' (a term which is sometimes used, and which refers laterally to the idea of metabolism, which is no bad thing). For to say that it is 'metaphor' is to account for only one part of the possible substitutions, if it is true that there can exist between C and A (that is to say, between the second signifier and the first), relations of contiguity as well as relations of the order of similarity. I do not have time here to go into the distinction between metaphor and metonymy, except to mention the failure, in my view, of the attempt to reduce them to purely and simply structural phenomena. This is, of course, what Lacan tried to do, in a certain sense, but which was also attempted, with many more nuances, by Jakobson, and you will also find it in certain of Rosolato's elaborations. Metaphor and metonymy, to affirm my naïve realism, cannot be understood except in conjunction with a referent—even, in the last resort, through a relation, however distant, to some real contiguity or similarity. With this term 'real', I am postulating something which turns out to be, very probably, in the vital order. *Contiguity and similarity are divisions of life*, before they are two axes in language. This, eminently, is what, in the generation of one living being by another, makes the new living being, the living-child, at once a fragment of the maternal living being—at whatever level we are situated, even if it is at the level of the amoeba. This child is a fragment cut off from a continuity with the maternal living being and also the likeness, 'made in the image', of the maternal living being. This is what we find, in psychoanalysis, with the idea that, in the realm of desire, the child is in a certain manner a bit of the mother (which is quite *natural*!), and that it can easily be symbolised as the 'phallus of the mother'. But what we must not forget is that the child is also the somato-psychical metaphor of the mother—that is to say, given autonomy in her image.

. . . in the natural languages

Let me return to the substitution I term metabola, to make it encompass both metaphor and metonymy. We are no longer, now, in the realm of mathematical language, but in that of the natural languages, and here natural language 'splits'—as is said of an atomic reactor. It 'splits' in so far as it is, on the one hand, algorithm or structure, in which everything is relatively inter-connected. However, at the same time, it is not only that. *In so far as* it is algorithmic, we could say that—as in mathematics—if I substitute one signifier for another, then I make the first one purely and simply disappear; I effect a transfer of meaning, without any remainder. This, in a certain sense, is what is presupposed by etymological research, to the extent that etymology follows precisely these transfers of meaning, whether due to contiguity or similarity, to extension or restriction, or even to opposition, which are all modalities of substitution, in the rhetorical sense.[35] I will give two examples of this substitution which ostensibly operates without leaving any remainder.

How do we come to speak of a 'pin-head'?

$$\frac{\text{bulging upper extremity}}{\text{Sd}} \times \frac{\text{head}}{\text{bulging upper extremity}} = \frac{\text{head}}{\text{Sd}}$$

Here we have a substitution according to similarity. But there are substitutions which are of another order. For example: the French term *voler*, which came to mean *to steal*. It is thought, effectively, that /voler/ came to take on the meaning of 'to dispossess furtively of' (Old French: *rober*), because of the bird which 'steals away in flight' its prey.[36]

$$\frac{\textit{rober}}{\text{Sd}} \times \frac{\textit{voler}}{\textit{rober}} = \frac{\textit{voler}}{\text{Sd}}$$

Voler, 'to fly', is a part, a particular way, of taking something, of 'stealing' [*rober*], whence we obtain the figure of speech we call metonymy, or in a more restricted sense, synecdoche. Here, the relation between the two terms, the operator of the substitution, is a relation of the part to the whole. Here, too, the relations are 'simplified', and the old term *rober* falls away. The function of etymology is to bring to light these metabolas, these transfers, whose origin has been forgotten.

However, the process is not so simple. For one thing, there is more usually a conjunction of different kinds of relations in all the examples, the relation of contiguity or that of similarity is never entirely alone; something metaphorical always appears in metonymy, and vice versa. Thus, *voler* of course means 'to steal' [*rober*], but it means to steal with the speed, with the boldness of a falcon. As for 'forgetting', it is well known that metaphors become 'worn out', and not only metaphors but also metonymies—thus, metabolas in general. That is to say, in the end we get to something which resembles (so much that we confuse it with) mathematical simplification. These figures which entail a 'forgetting' of their history, where the meaning is only 'in the present tense', were a long time ago, in rhetoric, given the name 'catachresis':

> Catachresis consists in a sign [a 'signifier', contemporaries would say], already appropriated by a first idea, being also appropriated by a new one [thus *voler*, appropriated at the outset by the flight of the bird, will be appropriated by a new idea, that of 'to steal'; but what is important is what comes next:] which itself did not have one, or which no longer has another one of its own in the language. (Fontanier 1977: 213)

It is clearly the second of these two possibilities which is important with regard to etymology. From the moment when substitution takes effect, the previous signifier loses its usage, no longer has a place in the structure . . . *in so far as* language is structure . . . This is certainly what happens in the passage from one language to another. Where a Latin or Sanskrit etymology is given, it is clear that the term which is replaced is completely forgotten; it is no longer of any but historical interest. However, within the same language, a transfer never occurs in such a way—that is, without any remainder, and without enrichment—and it is here that we begin to move away from the mathematical algorithm. The fact that the transfer cannot take place without there being a remainder is indicated by an infinite number of things; and when we talk of a 'worn-out' metaphor, we do not take account of the extent to which metabolas are, at any given moment, ready to be reborn.

It is amusing to follow this rebirth, like a film projected backwards, at work in the joke. One of the jokes studied by Freud is the following. The first act of Emperor Napoleon III consists in seizing the property of the Crown, the property of the House of Orleans. *C'est le premier vol de l'aigle* ['It's the eagle's first flight/theft'], as the epigram puts it. Now, through this *premier vol de l'aigle*, we get precisely back on the pathway of etymology (even if the latter is 'forgotten'), since we go back in the opposite direction from *voler* = 'to steal' [*dérober*], to *voler* as applied to the falcon. But once again this shows that the transfer, most frequently, does not occur without an enrichment of meaning. Staying with our example of *vol* and *voleur*, there are unconscious correspondences which have many times been revealed in psychoanalysis, between the *vol* ['theft'] of the *voleur* and that, for example, of people *volant* ['flying'] in an aeroplane. All this seems to show that there is no such thing as total 'catachresis'—true substitution accompanied by forgetting—except when there is a change of language. That is to say, this occurs only with the passage from one structure to another, where the term replaced is no longer recognisable. The other way around, this translates as the truth that there is no such thing, within a language, as absolute synonyms.

It is due to this second aspect that language is not just an algorithm, but also creation. Lacan, and many contemporary linguists after him, speak of 'effects of meaning'. Poetry is among them, for sure, but also any elaboration, any new transfer of meaning, from slang to advertising. These are effects, displacements and enrichments which are only possible, only take effect to the extent that there is a preservation of former meaning—like a sort of aura—and are not the mathematical simplification of signifiers.[37]

. . . And in repression?

'Structured like a language'? Language, in so far as it is pure structure, appears to us ultimately, from the place of etymology, to be completely lacking in creativity. Creative language is what escapes from structure on all sides, even if it is unceasingly taken back into a code, recoded and re-codified.

So, having made all these reservations about 'linguistic structure', what is there to say now about the unconscious? What possibility is there of using a structural model for the unconscious? More precisely, I introduced the general schema of the metabola not in relation to the unconscious, but to repression. Unlike *either* algorithmic language *or* poetic, creative language, repression—on the one hand—*does not simplify*, and—on the other—*does not create meaning*. It does not simplify, but, on the contrary, it preserves. It does not create meaning because it 'preserves' what happened 'down below', just the way it is, as if embalmed. That is why I write the transformation, in this case:

$$\frac{Sr1}{Sd} \times \frac{Sr2}{Sr1} = \frac{\frac{Sr2}{Sd}}{\frac{Sr1}{Sr1}}$$

This kind of writing, belonging to a mathematical algorithm, has no meaning, but is interesting in that it shows us the strange fate of the earlier signifier which has been replaced. This signifier is preserved beneath conscious language in a most curious form, whereby, so to speak, it signifies itself. I can only attribute a quite relative value to such a schema. Just as we move away from algorithms with the unconscious, so this violence imposed on the algorithm results in no more than a suggestive value. It is a question of showing that the unconscious is the result of repression—that is, of a 'pathological' kind of substitution, a compulsive symbolisation, which neither suppresses the primary symbol nor integrates it (as the knight integrated the Lady into his devotion to the Lady's glove) but rather maintains something at a distance.

The formula above—$\frac{Sr1}{Sd} \times \frac{Sr2}{Sr1}$—can also be used in the case of Emma. $\frac{Sr1}{Sd}$ represents the first scene (or Scene II), and $\frac{Sr2}{Sr1}$ the second scene. On Freud's drawing of the network of the various associations between the two scenes, between S_2 and S_1 we find, interwoven, all kinds of links, both of contiguity and of similarity (Freud 1950: 354). The first scene in Emma's case, the scene in which the shopkeeper makes a sexual gesture that is enigmatic for the child, will continue to lead an autonomous life after the repression. Freud, on occasion, evoked the image of the nature reserve, where a piece of nature in a country is supposed to be preserved in its natural state. This autonomous life is also what my formula is intended to show, in which the repressed is of the order of $\frac{A}{A}$ or $\frac{Sr}{Sr'}$, a language which communicates nothing, which does not create any signification, which is merely a locus of circulation, that of unconscious investment.

Taking stock

In order to take stock of this year's exposition and of the unconscious, we can make a number of statements. First of all, the unconscious is not a structure. The unconscious consists of mnemic *elements*, which are repressed representations. As Freud said, they are *Vorstellungen*. On the other hand, these mnemic elements no longer refer to anything but themselves, which corresponds precisely to the Freudian term *Sachvorstellungen*, thing-representations, and not representations of things. In the end, of course, if the unconscious is not a structure but a content, a 'substance', we might say, the elements of the unconscious are nonetheless linked together in a most particular way. The term logic is only to be proposed with many precautions (it would be a logic in a 'reduced' state) and we would prefer to adopt the term Freud used—'process'.

The primary process is what we have to account for first and foremost, in any theorisation of repression and the unconscious. *Why* do these representations, from that point onwards, function according to a type of process so different from what we know elsewhere? The primary process is the reign of the pleasure principle. This is not in the sense that there is a great deal of pleasure in the unconscious, but in the sense of the Freudian pleasure principle, which is to say, the unbridled circulation of investment in the circuits of representations. It is an unregulated circulation because it is cut off from any referential aim, and from any communication. Something that might be able to give us an idea of this, more accurately than the dream, even though it is not the unconscious itself, is perhaps the screen-memory which, ultimately, is neither a screen nor significative of anything but itself (cf. Freud 1899: 301-22).

Just as the unconscious is not a structure, so there is reason to call into question the nice formula according to which 'it speaks' [*ça parle*]. One could just as well say 'it does not speak' or, at least, 'it does not speak to anyone'. The id [*le ça*] speaks of nothing but itself. It does not signify anything, in the active sense of the verb 'to signify'; it has no signifying intention, and the whole immense effort of treatment is, precisely, to get this unspeaking id to speak to someone, and to speak about something—about a forgotten past. This is also to say that the unconscious is the result of repression, and on this point we should, in my view, return completely to Freud's first intuition according to which the unconscious is not primary, but the result of repression or repressions. We have seen that these can be considered as either secondary or as originary. However, this term 'originary' should not delude us, any more than the term 'primary' in 'primary process'. The primary process is not there before the secondary process; the secondary process is not to be constructed on top of the primary process. Here I am opposed to a certain Freud, whose opinions are found in one of the texts which goes furthest in the other direction, 'Formulations on the Two Principles of Mental Functioning' (1911). Here he attempts to make the absolutely impossible deduction of the secondary from the primary process, as if the primary were the mode of functioning of an organism still unadapted, and which would have to learn, secondarily, how to live. Well—on the one hand an organism which had to learn how to live would never manage to live at all; it would already be 'dead before realising it'. (This is the truth of Darwin versus Lamarck: one does not learn to live, the organism has no time to learn how to live.) So when we try to conceive of the primary process, we should absolutely not situate it at the level of a hypothetical non-adapted mode of functioning. The primary process is only primary in a fictional sense, in the same way that primary narcissism, for its part, is only primary retroactively. The Freudian image of the 'nature reserve', which would seem to lend support to the idea that something which was there 'before', a natural state, put aside, under protection, as in the parks of the Rocky Mountains or nowadays in the nature parks of France—well, in this sense, the idyllic image is misleading. You might just as well try an image of the ghetto, or even the concentration camp, for that which brings about segregation is certainly not something which was already in existence.

There is no question, then, of situating the primary process 'before', nor of showing how a rational, secondary, well-adapted process could be established on its basis. What does need to be explained, conversely, is how it is constituted by *reduction*, on the basis of more regulated, more structured phenomena. It has to be shown that it is through the disappearance of a certain number of norms, of a certain amount of 'ballast' (a term I have sometimes used) or even of axioms (for those who feel they must refer to logic)—it is by the reduction of the rules of the game that we pass from the secondary to the primary process.

I have often used the term 'structure', or 'structuralism', and I am returning to it now to show how I conceive its truth, but above all its limitations, which have been inadequately traced, in the wave of structuralism which was unleashed twenty or thirty years ago, and whose momentum continues unabated. All human structures, fortunately, are somewhat rickety, as we saw just now in the case of language. The reduction of language to elements of binary opposition is no more than a logician's dream, as is the absolute reduction of a myth into minimal elements, 'mythemes', which only have value in so far as they can be inscribed in a kind of purely formal matrix, and which could ultimately function as elements of classification, beyond any meaning.

The text by Laplanche and Leclaire began with a critique of Politzer and of his idea that the unconscious would have neither more nor less existence than the rules immanent in a game of tennis. I opposed a 'realism of the unconscious' to this idea. But at least, let us say, in favour of Politzer—for here, in spite of everything, was something positive—this immanence of the unconscious was conceived as individual, singular. With an extreme form of structuralism, it is essentially the same 'immanentism' which emerges; the immanent element one substitutes for the singularity of the unconscious is a trans-individual immanence: language, or rather *la langue*, in the Saussurean sense.

The unconscious of a text?

Currently (in a cultural milieu tinged with 'analysis'), we hear people speaking of 'the unconscious of a text'. This is a formula at once deceptive and dangerous. The unconscious of a text—is this the trans-individual linguistic structures allowing this text to exist? Is it the 'competence' which enabled the 'performance' of this text? Or else, at the opposite extreme, is it the manifold linguistic twists allowed by this text, the multiple distortions of the code, or whatever the interpreter wishes, *ad infinitum*? In both cases, as you see, the notion of the unconscious is emptied of any reference to the individual, the author of the text. The first step towards emptying something is to despise it. To what an extent people nowadays despise any work showing an interest in the history and the unconscious of anyone producing something, at whatever level that might be! They go straight 'to the signifier', as they put it—which, once again, can have only two possible meanings.

Either one heads straight for the formal, and if so it is easy to see where this leads—to a sort of logicism, for instance, that of castration and the phallus. This is a logicism which is no less normative than any other moralism that one has condemned: that you have to 'go through castration' is no less of an imperative than the old requirement to 'adapt', for which one reproached Kris, Hartmann and Loewenstein . . . Or else, going straight to the signifier is to go into variations of subjective interpretation, and even—you can find plenty of examples of this—into the most contingent contortions, even buffooneries.

Well, in the Freudian sense of the term, there is no more an 'unconscious of the text' than there is an unconscious of the rules in a game of tennis, or an unconscious of the immanence of the laws of gravity in the fall of bodies. The unconscious is individual. To be provocative, I will say that it is *in each individual's head*. The unconscious is that part of his or her history, subtracted not only—as Politzer would have it—from the texture of conventional significations, but subtracted from any intention to communicate. I tried to capture this in my formula of a 'denominator' where there would no longer be any signified. Only the methodology invented by Freud—but not one centred on the signifier (as has been alleged)—a methodology which links indissolubly free association and the analytic situation, can allow the partial reopening—in a precarious manner, always to be questioned anew—of an unconscious always ready to close itself swiftly off again from any communication, since this closing-off is inherent in the very essence of its constitution.

II

THE PROBLEMATIC OF THE ID

21 November 1978

This year I am proposing as the subject of our reflection, for this course or these lectures, the title: The Problematic of the Id.

Each year, since this course began, I have offered a sort of methodological introduction. Without going over these introductions again today, I will just enumerate their themes. First of all, what constitutes a problematic and interpretative reflection on psychoanalysis? How can a reflection on psychoanalysis take into account—to what extent can it take into account—its own analytic method? Is it possible for an analyst to speak of analysis? A related problem, upon which I have also touched on a number of occasions, is that of the very possibility of teaching psychoanalysis at the University. And furthermore: how does an analyst-teacher choose his theme, since it is clear that the choice of a theme is never without relation to his own history—the history of the development of his thought, obviously, but also its roots, both singular and personal.

Last year I also raised the question of what could constitute research in psychoanalysis. To what extent could it be considered scientific? What 'cumulative' aspects could be required of such research? What could constitute a 'thesis', particularly in the domain of clinical psychopathology and psychoanalysis, given that the thesis has to be situated as a genre, as a kind of writing, between two other types which delimit its borders. These are, moreover, two genres which are quite esteemed: on the one hand the dissertation and, on the other, the personal testimony. I will not go through these introductions again: you will find them in the volumes of the journal of our department, Psychanalyse à l'Université, *where these lectures—along with those of other teachers at the UER—are reproduced.*

The only point over which I will linger for a few moments this year, which intersects to some degree with the questions mentioned above, is the difficulty of proposing a new theme to a new audience. A large majority of the audience which you form is new; it is renewed each year with the DEA intake. However, I do not offer a new 'introduction to psychoanalytic research' each time, but rather a theme situated in a certain thematic continuity. There is thus a difficulty, both for you and for me. For you, at least for most of you, it is a question of catching on to something already in motion, to the unfolding of a cer-

tain thought process, with certain propositions which I consider, if not fully dealt with, then at least already stated, set forth. This is obviously an invitation to you, simply in order to orientate yourselves better, to refer to the published lectures from previous years. For me, the difficulty is no less, since, without claiming to come up with something new at every moment, or even to come up with something new most of the time, I find myself caught in the double imperative not simply to re-hash, but at the same time—for those of you who are here for the first time—to contrive to lead you along lateral pathways and gangways which will allow you access to the course of my work.

Last year: the unconscious and repression

The theme I am proposing for this year, then, is 'The Problematic of the Id', and it is in direct continuity with last year's theme, 'The Reference to the Unconscious: Putting it to the Test in Practice and Theory' (and, I might add, in culture). As always, as happens every year—fortunately—this course on the unconscious is not finished. What I proposed there (if you have the curiosity to have a look at it) was to reopen the discussion of hypotheses put forward more than ten years ago—to be precise in 1966, in a paper on the unconscious.[1] These hypotheses touched, I would say, on two points: on the one hand, the realism of the unconscious: what type of reality can be attributed to what is called 'the unconscious' in psychoanalysis? And, on the other hand, the origin of the unconscious: that origin being, essentially, correlative to a term which we are going to keep constantly in view: the process which creates the unconscious, or at least separates it from the rest of the psyche—that is, repression.

Over last year's course, following on from this work of ten years ago, I offered some schemas which might be considered to have a linguistic appearance, schemas of symbolic or signifying substitution. However, obviously I talk of a 'linguistic appearance' because they are immediately beyond any narrow reference to language.

I could thus have taken my title back to the unconscious, for there were a number of things which remained unsaid, and I had spent more time on the constitution of the unconscious (to be precise, on the process of repression and on what could define this in relation to other kinds of substitution) than on its contents and its mode of functioning—more time on its 'foreign affairs' than on its 'home affairs'. And with good reason! Because, precisely, it is easier to speak of the unconscious from the outside than truly to describe it and to frame plausible formulations regarding the way it functions.

However, this year, at least in my title, I have taken up the question from another angle, and the call for this came from an argument brought by a DEA student in the annual 'dissertation' which closes the year's teaching (proof that these dissertations can be something other than copying or a purely external criticism). It consisted of a vehement but well-argued (at least in a sense) critique, bearing precisely on my own reservations, on my own critical attitude with respect to the notion of the id.[2]

The Unconscious: did it cease in 1915?

This student refers to Freud's thinking in order to make the following objection to me: you stop Freud's thinking at a given moment; you choose what is called (in our jargon) the first topography rather than the second; you stop in 1915; you neglect the later enrichments of Freud's thinking, and the notion of the id, which is an essential contribution. This criticism may not be entirely without substance. It raises lots of questions, in my opinion, apart from merely scholastic ones, a mere interrogation concerning fidelity or infidelity. How many times have we heard this argument about Freudianism, and also in spheres other than psychoanalysis, after any act of foundation, whether that of a philosophy or a religion. You often hear this: the heresies that appear are nothing but ways of choosing—in a partial, doctrinaire fashion—one particular element of the system, privileging it, allowing it to grow out of all proportion, to the detriment of a more total vision. The 'mistake' is never anything but an 'incomplete vision'. This, indeed, is the argument that Freud brandished against his adversaries, the dissidents (the Jungs, the Adlers, and even a person like Groddeck, to whom we shall have to refer to later)—that they privilege one aspect over others, and that if one would only take his doctrine as a whole . . . Well, what appears to be the originality of a disciple has a place there, but only there, within the corpus of Freudian thought.

This idea that the mistake is to make a choice within a system, looks rather different, in spite of everything, when it is no longer merely a question of a synchronic choice—that is to say, a choice within the corpus of a doctrine which is spread out, as it were, in front of us, in its entirety—but rather a historical, diachronic choice. Because, after all, to choose between the pre-1920 Freud and the post-1920—what can this mean in 1978? Well, we could put the question another way—in my view more interesting—and ask: in a thought such as Freud's, is anything ever 'new', is there an 'evolution'? Of course there's something new, if only the sudden appearance in 1923 of the term 'id'! Something new, yes, but of what order?

What is new and what returns in psychoanalysis

Does something new not always correspond to an act of refashioning? How does a thought refashion itself? This becomes a more pressing question when you happen to be a psychoanalyst, when you have knowledge of those 'events' which, beneath the appearance of something new, are returns, elements already present which repeat themselves, insist on being allowed to happen. What is it that returns when a notion such as the id is in effect advanced? What is it that returns when a notion such as narcissism, indeed of primary narcissism, or even that of the death drive, suddenly emerges, and when Freud justifies it in his own way, describing it as a discovery, while one is often able to detect—and of course it is our role to show—how this discovery has already been announced, prefigured from the very beginning.

Thus, things return. This return can take place in various ways. There can be a return from within, a pure and simple repetition. An element (I mean an element of thought, an element of theory) which has not found its place, not been retained in a solid fashion, hooked or anchored into the overall theory. Such an element re-emerges, at more or less irregular intervals, like something which has not been given satisfaction or recognition. I am thinking, for example, of something on which I have come to lay so much emphasis- that is to say, the notion of seduction—which, we might say, insists and repeats itself as something never having been given its place (in my view a privileged one) in psychoanalytic thought.

Then there are returns we could describe as different in style. In my understanding, when a thought like that of Freud transforms itself, when major balances find themselves altered, when for example his conception of the drives evolves, when his topography is modified, it is obvious that an imbalance might be created, which would then in its turn require some new creation elsewhere in that thought. To be more precise, this is something I was able to demonstrate concerning precisely that modification, around the 1920s, which from then on shifts the emphasis onto the ego and narcissism. Now, from the moment this emphasis is placed on narcissism as love of self, but also on the object-relation, on the love-relation towards objects, it became necessary to reaffirm something which appeared to have been abolished, in this kind of enthusiasm, where Eros appeared as if hitched to the chariot of the love-object; to reaffirm—in spite of everything—the unacceptable, fragmentary, fragmenting, destructive, 'irreconcilable' character of sexual desire. This was precisely the meaning of the sudden appearance of a kind of volcanic island: the death drive.

And then there are also returns, as we know, in psychoanalysis, coming from outside. A return from outside, in the doctrine, would be precisely the case of the id. The id is something borrowed. When it appears, it is brought into Freud from outside, namely by Groddeck. The id, a category of thought (if it can be called such) that Groddeck had been using for years, which he suggested to Freud from the moment he first corresponded with him, well before 1920-1923, and which was to be repeatedly rejected and then finally adopted by Freud, was borrowed, if we are to believe Groddeck, for the sole purpose of being domesticated, 'gentrified', as our contemporary jargon would say.[3]

For the time being, let us keep our feet more firmly on the ground, and return to the indispensable task of recollecting the theoretical coordinates into which the new term was to be introduced.

Thus, what is known as the first topography, let us recall, is centred upon an opposition, but one which is already ambiguous, since it can be defined in two different ways. It is sometimes an opposition of two terms, sometimes one of three, with shifting overlappings. The famous conscious/unconscious duality, as we know, is what quickly requires the introduction of a third term, the 'preconscious', but only then to settle, once again, into a binary opposition.

The first topography: the discovery of the psychical 'other thing'

Well, this first topography is put in place extremely early, from around 1895, with the *Studies on Hysteria*, or—again—the 'Project for a Scientific Psychology', and reaches its culmination in the 1915 papers, which we find collected under the title 'Metapsychology'.

To speak of a first topography, a first Freudian system, as if what was in question, entirely and essentially, were a system, is really to deprive Freud's work of its vigour. Certainly, Freud was keen to describe the functions of what he does not hesitate to call the 'apparatus of the soul' or the 'psychical apparatus', a veritable 'machine'. But what we have to keep in view, what is essential beyond the neat functioning and the endlessly refined description of mechanical parts, is the initial discovery of something within us that is radically other, which functions against our will and which determines us in a whole series of processes which had until then been considered as points of failure, as the waste-products of existence—whether the dream, the bungled action, or the symptom. The discovery of a radical other within us, not in the sense of what we have become used to writing as 'the Other' (that of 'Speech' or 'the Law') but in the sense of a neutral other, an 'other thing'. This 'other thing' (*ein Anderes*) in the realm of the psyche is the term Freud took up explicitly in the paper in which he introduced the id.

From that point on, once the existence of this radical other thing within us was admitted as irremovable, as a foundational experience—well, the difficulties really began when it became a question of defining it, 'cataloguing' it. Here we must, somewhat hastily, follow the path which Freud more than once himself retraced, as we ask ourselves: how can we possibly grasp this thing which is other than our conscious life?

A circumnavigation of the unconscious: the 'descriptive' sense . . .

Other than consciousness? This is what we call the descriptive point of view: that is to say, a definition of 'the unconscious' which would be purely descriptive, which would limit itself to noting the absence of that phenomenal element (something which is obvious to everyone, Freud says, even if we are incapable of explaining it) which is the fact of 'being conscious' (*das Bewusstsein*). To state in a banal manner that the unconscious is simply what is un-conscious, in a descriptive sense, is clearly in no way satisfactory for the requirements of the Freudian discovery. There is obviously something un-conscious or non-conscious apart from this radical 'other thing', even if only our organic life or even, in our everyday experience, the infinite number of elements we are obliged to call psychical, since at any given moment they are able to become so again. Our whole stock of memories is unconscious, in the descriptive sense of the term, without being part of the unconscious in the psychoanalytic sense.

I now arrive at the second leg of our journey. As the absence of consciousness, the descriptive criterion is completely inadequate to describe the psychoanalytic experience. We have to accept the idea that our 'other thing' is the result of a specific process very different, for example, from something simply passively slipping out of the field of current consciousness. What constitutes and enriches the 'preconscious' is the constant slippage of impressions from conscious life into memory. In order for us to be able to store away new perceptions, it is necessary, at each moment, for the memories of the previous few minutes to quit the stage, restoring to consciousness its lost virgin state (like pure wax). These memories fall into unconsciousness, but without our having to actively reject them: it is a quasi-automatic process.

. . . the dynamic sense . . .

Conversely, each unconscious element—and this is the second, dynamic point of view—is excluded, 'repressed', because it is not wanted, and for very precise, particular, individual reasons, which are precisely what psychoanalysis endeavours to bring to light. This dynamic sense of the unconscious thus implies the notion of psychical conflict. This is why, in spite of the inadequacies which may emerge, a close relationship takes root here—which will become permanent in psychoanalytic thinking—between the unconscious and the process of repression. What I don't see, what I can no longer see, is what I don't want to see—for instance, some unacceptable memory.

But things go further than this, and our route, following Freud, has to take a new turning. This is because what is excluded is not necessarily, in any direct fashion, what I do not want to see. Very often the exclusion bears on an element which has a relatively distant connection with the real object of the conflict. When I forget some name, or some face, analysis shows that it is not necessarily this name itself that I find unbearable. If it is repressed, this is only because of its connections, because of the fact that it has attracted onto it unpleasant baggage, sometimes coming from very far away and according to connections which may be entirely fortuitous. So the 'dynamic' idea, the hypothesis of an active exclusion of repressed elements, is not sufficient in itself. Thus, if some detail is excluded, but not on its own account—in a famous early example, Freud's forgetting of the name of the painter Signorelli—the repression was not motivated by the fact the Signorelli was a painter whom Freud did not like, but as a result of highly complex associations which brought together, through this name, ideas which for their part were unacceptable. The 'dynamic' hypothesis—that an element is repressed in the unconscious because of the conflict and the opposition it arouses—can only, in turn, take us further.

. . . the systematic sense . . .

With the repression of Signorelli, we are in the presence no longer of a process which excludes an element for its own sake, but of an entanglement of unconscious networks, which inevitably give rise to the idea of a true unconscious system. This is an unconscious system in which an element can find itself attracted, suddenly sucked in, as a result of extremely complex connections.

Here, then, is the third leg of our journey, that of the 'systematic' unconscious. Now, if the unconscious is conceived as a system, then along with which other systems is it articulated? You can see that now we are entering into the detail of Freudian 'machinery'. If there is an unconscious system does that mean that the conscious itself is a system? Well, Freud always maintained that the conscious as such, consciousness, could not be defined as a system, so we are not able to take the criterion of consciousness (which was the starting-point of our journey) as our support for establishing distinctions between the 'systems'. Freud never considered consciousness to be anything other than a field, an apparatus of attention, albeit a complex set-up, which allowed whatever had disappeared from its current state to return to the level of perception, via highly sophisticated connections. So that what is opposed to the unconscious, as system, is absolutely not consciousness, but rather the preconscious as a psychic locus, as a set of processes and psychical representations, quite distinct from the unconscious system in terms of its situation, of its relation to the perception-consciousness apparatus. The preconscious system is defined firstly, approximately, by its capacity to be recalled into consciousness at any given moment. It is not conscious from the descriptive point of view, but only according to its potentialities. It is capable-of-becoming-conscious (*bewusstseinsfähig*). Conversely, the unconscious is an unconscious which is not potentially capable of coming into consciousness, except through analytic processes which are highly complex, highly risky, and of which it might be asked whether they could ever be sufficient to exhaust it.

So now we have moved from the descriptive point of view to the dynamic, and from there to a point of view which we might call systematic or even topographical. There would be two psychical locations—that of what has slipped into unconsciousness from mere latency, and that of what has been excluded, repressed, and which continues to be actively kept far from consciousness.

Well, this circumnavigation of the unconscious has not yet reached its end, and it is the last leg which will bring us to the introduction of the 'id'. Our topographical distinction remains inadequate, if it is limited to affirming that there exists one system inaccessible to consciousness, and another which is excluded from it. We must get beyond these extrinsic criteria, to the essential point: the two systems are not similar in their mode of functioning. Is it because it is excluded that the unconscious functions differently? Is it because it functions differently that it is excluded?

. . . Heterogeneity

This is clearly a question which will weigh heavily on the problem of the id, because a certain notion of the id would lead us to suppose that it is excluded because, originally, it was of a different *nature*. Whatever the case may be, the next step in our gradual—and dialectical—approach to the unconscious is to show that what happens within it (in so far as one is able to describe what happens in it) does not obey the same laws of logic as those of the preconscious, but operates according to processes which we call 'primary processes'. That is to say, it has its own 'logic' in which, notably, contradiction absolutely no longer has the same function as in the secondary process, and in which the most contradictory trends can remain side by side, neither having to form a synthesis nor having to cancel out one another. Or, similarly, what is known as 'psychical energy'—which is to say, quite simply, 'affective investment', the 'affective load' of an element—can *easily* and *entirely* move to a neighbouring element. (Remember that the forgetting of a name did not occur as a result of its own affective value, but because of very distant associations, even 'forced', far-fetched ones.) These, then, are some of the classical features of the primary processes, which allow us to define the opposition between the two systems, not only in terms of the relation each of them bears to consciousness, but all in themselves, in terms of their completely different ways of functioning.

This, then, is a rough sketch of the development of the 'first topography', with its successive deepening of the notion of the unconscious, which could also be described—in a certain sense—as successive *folds* in the definition. For we must remember that the very term 'unconscious' (*Unbewusst* in German) is only an adjectival noun, a way of 'reifying' something which, at the outset, was defined by the fact of not being conscious. Yet this term 'unconscious', in spite of its notorious inadequacies, in spite of the strategic sequence of 'folds' when it comes to defining it precisely, will remain pregnant with meaning, both in Freud and after Freud. This adjectival noun, as we have seen, does not entail an essential characteristic, and we will even discover (this will be my next point) that the 'characteristic' it puts forward is not merely inadequate but—at times—inexact, even erroneous, in the sense that we shall be led to link up with the unconscious certain phenomena which are not, however, un-conscious.

Refuted in each of its successive definitions, shaken by the rough answers coming back from theory and the clinic, it persisted, and was to persist well beyond the introduction of the id (let me just remind you of the date: 1923).[4] The unconscious was to remain the authentic touchstone of psychoanalysis, maintained right up to the end, henceforth closely linked to the id—which, however, was never to dethrone it.

28th November 1978

We began, last time, to put in place our problematisation of the id, or of the id and the unconscious—in other words, of what the notion of id contributes to, or takes away from, the unconscious. This was the 'first topography', whose development I attempted to sketch, emphasising that it was never be completely dethroned in Freud's thought. If you look in one of the final systematic texts, the *Outline of Psychoanalysis,* you will find there the most complete attempt at synthesising the two points of view, without forfeiting anything of either one or the other (Freud 1940).

Motives for replacing the unconscious

So the question which emerges for us is clearly the following: does the transformation brought about by the id derive from difficulties internal to the development of Freudian thought, or is it relatively adventitious? In any event, Freud has *motives* for this replacement, this absorption of the unconscious by the id, arising from difficulties which in fact are serious, and which I will attempt quickly to set out under categories of objections (perhaps rather artificial) concerning the *limits* of the unconscious, concerning the *relation* of the unconscious to psychical *conflict*, and lastly concerning the *contents* of the unconscious. What will remain as the constant element, of course, the solid and unchanging hinge between the unconscious and the id, is neither their limits nor their relation to content, but an identical mode of functioning in both—that is to say, the primary process.

Well, firstly, *in its limits*, the unconscious system rather resembles those pictures (one thinks of Ferdinand Léger) where colours and forms do not match up, in which colours do not precisely fill out the lines marked, but rather overlap them.

Overlapping topographical borders . . .

First of all, let us recall, not everything that is unconscious is 'the unconscious'. We have emphasised this concerning the contents of what Freud, very early on, designated as the preconscious, that unconscious space which can, at any moment re-enter consciousness. However, it is a little too easy to rid ourselves of these mnemic contents, these current memories, by saying that they are not exactly repressed, subjected to a dynamic process which prevents them from resurfacing. To set up a straightforward opposition between the active forgetting of censorship and an everyday, ordinary, quasi-automatic kind of forgetting—is this not to overlook precisely the functional, defensive aspect of this everyday forgetting, which allows us to clear things away in order to be able to live? Furthermore, by the same kind of 'overlapping', it is quickly seen that in the properly, systematically, unconscious state—that state which can only return to consciousness through a struggle, through work—there exist sequences of thought which resemble (to the point of being mistaken for) our conscious thoughts. This is especially the case with certain fantasies, this term taken here in its most organised sense, namely—the day-dream. When the subject has told himself such romances as these, how can it be denied that he has entered into a privileged relation to the unconscious system, given that we see how much energy and analytic work must be put into effect to bring it back to consciousness.[5]

Next, to continue with this inventory of the non-equivalence between that-which-is-not-conscious and 'the unconscious', we must question what are called the 'mechanisms' by which we function. The eye is not conscious of its mechanism, nor—with even more good reason—of the laws of optics. One could argue that the eye *must* be unconscious of these in order to see. The Cartesians were already aware of this, but they rejected the notion of any mechanism in the body. However the question is doubly significant for psychoanalysis—namely: is that which is just about possible in the description of vision (to affirm the difference in nature between unconsciousness of our bodily physiology and the psychical unconscious) still possible when it is a question, now, of *psychical mechanisms*? The phenomenon of attention, for instance (among many others), is this not a mechanism of which, however conscious its results, we are unconscious of the process? And what can be said of the psychical apparatus itself, in its entirety? If we had to wait for Freud to gain a description of it, is this not proof that this machine, even in its most conscious parts, itself belongs to the non-conscious? We will shortly encounter this problem again in relation to the ego and its functions, which will be the turning-point for Freud in his introduction of the second topography.

Conversely, concerning the partial intersection of the systems—and this is perhaps more serious than the previous objections—we might say that everything belonging to the *Unconscious system*, precisely in so far as it obeys the laws of the primary process, is not necessarily non-conscious, withdrawn from consciousness. This is more serious because, from then onwards the very designation of the unconscious, in the adjectival sense of un-conscious, becomes not only inadequate but misleading. One thinks here of the formula which has become common currency in the description of the psychoses, according to which the unconscious of the psychotic is located on the surface. We should not claim, anachronistically, that such an objection relating to the psychoses was a determining factor for Freud in 1920. Here, perhaps, we run into major questions concerning the notion of repression; we are brought to invent and to describe other mechanisms for psychosis, and speak—for instance—of the return from the outside, of projection, even of foreclosure. The fact that in madness something of the order of drives, of the order of the 'unconscious', comes out into the open, is certainly an important objection to our simply equating drives (the id) with the repressed.

For our benefit—not for Freud's, but for the present moment—I will attempt a sort of enumeration, which is a little ahistorical, of everything that might cause the first topography to topple over into the second. Without going that far, without leaving behind the neuroses, we should clearly recall that what served Freud as a model, in the construction of his unconscious, was not the field of the neuroses in its entirety. It was essentially, in historical terms, two kinds of amnesia which allowed a particular type of disappearance to be defined, with the formation of a 'separate psychical group'. These two phenomena, narrowly linked in the emerging psychoanalytic experience, were hysterical amnesia, of the kind which the first treatments tried to overcome, and post-hypnotic amnesia, which at the time formed the object of considerable experimentation. It is this type of amnesia, cut out as if with a knife, an amnesia of plus and minus, which will inform Freud's conception of what he dubs 'infantile amnesia'. For instance, it is that which, in his view, exerts an influence on prior memories at the dissolution of the Oedipus complex and the entrance into the 'period of latency'.

Well, contrary to received opinion, Freud does not see infantile amnesia as a passive lapse of memories, or as a lack of fixation of memories in a neuro-psychical system still incomplete and weak. He considers it, indeed, as an active mechanism of repression. In a text such as 'Screen Memories' (1899), you can see how predominant is the idea that forgetting is always an active forgetting, the result of a repression. Infantile forgetting is not something automatic; what must be explained is not the memory but the act of forgetting. The model for this active, dynamic forgetting is thus hysterical or hypnotic forgetting. It is a quasi-experimental model but, despite this, should not be generalised without precaution. Very quickly, analysis was led to situate repression amongst a whole series of other defence-mechanisms, not characterised essentially by a complete escape from the field of consciousness. One may think, for instance, of what is described in obsessional neurosis. Rather than being repressed—that is to say, made completely inaccessible—the troublesome memories incompatible with the rest of the psyche are isolated, so to speak, in a corner of the psyche. Attention is diverted away from them, which Freud translates (in terms of energetics) as the withdrawal of investment-energy. In obsessional *isolation*, even if there are occasionally genuine repressions in the hysterical sense, what we observe in most cases is not the radical falling into the unconscious but a sort of disconnection of certain parts of the psyche. The work of analysis, rather than leading to a sudden lifting of repression with the re-appearance of vanished memories, is conceived as the re-establishment of the connections which have been broken. The judgement given by many analysands at the end of analysis—'what I've discovered, in fact I always knew'—well, that phrase does not substantiate a theory which would make radical repression the only mode of defence against pathogenic memories.

But we have to go further, as far as a genuine reversal. If you take a text like 'Constructions in Analysis' (1937a) you will find there, in a veiled form, the following observation from experience. It is increasingly difficult to make something radically forgotten, forgotten in the sense of repression, re-appear 'in person'. The very term 'construction' suggests that the analytic process, essentially, reconstructs the past rather than genuinely managing to make it re-appear. But there is an even more worrying aspect to this text, which I had occasion to emphasise last year. When something reappears which has been truly and radically forgotten, after extensive analytic work, this happens in a very singular way. The memory does not return 'in person', but on the fringes, in some associated memory. It returns not as the infantile scene itself but as some completely marginal, 'metonymic' detail. This detail re-appears in a way that could be termed 'ecmnesic'—in other words, without connection to the rest of the psyche—in a way that is not far from hallucination—and Freud applies this term even to neurotics. This amounts to the recognition of a radically alien quality, which from that point onwards makes the unconscious something much more heterogeneous than an 'other consciousness'. It is something which is never able to be sensibly re-inserted into the entirety of our conscious psychical life. It is . . . an id?

The unconscious is not confined to one side in the conflict . . .

A second reason for interrogating the notion of the unconscious is the consideration of its *position in psychical conflict*. In a fairly simplistic view of the 'first topography', the unconscious could have been equated with what takes the role—let's say—of the baddie in psychical conflict, of that which must be rejected because it is inassimilable, and thus on the side of repressed drives. Conversely, this would imply that, as the unconscious is identical to the repressed, one would have to seek the repressing instance in the other system, the preconscious-conscious system.[6] Well, the whole experience of analytic work, from its very beginnings, shows that this is not the case. This experience, when it exposes resistances to any coming to consciousness, shows very clearly that what represses, what defends itself, the very mode of that defence, has fallen 'into the unconscious' in the same way as that which it defends against. Analytic work often uncovers connections to what is repressed, but the history of repression itself, its very process, usually remains hidden.

This is not, we should stress, a new experience. However, in 1920 Freud gave a definitive account of it, drawing from it conclusions in respect to his 'topography'. Defence itself is unconscious, and this was one of the major reasons for shifting the accent onto the instance of the ego, which is not (like that of the preconscious-conscious) marked by a necessary relation to consciousness. The ego, in itself, is neutral regarding the distinction between the conscious and the unconscious.

The unconscious ego: un-conscious of its functions or defensive fantasies . . .

A parenthetical remark concerning this un-consciousness of the ego and its 'defence mechanisms' . . . A moment ago, I alluded to the Cartesian proposition according to which we are unaware of the mechanism by which we walk, or of optics when we see. Is this egoic un-consciousness purely and simply a non-knowledge, at the psychical level, of 'how we function'? This is indeed what a whole psychology, known as the psychology of the ego and its defence mechanisms would lead one to believe. A notion of Anglo-Saxon origin such as *insight* (which one has real difficulty in translating: 'what is seen in itself'? 'what one is able to perceive oneself'? 'becoming-conscious' . . . ? it is not quite that . . . briefly, let's for once keep an English term in our vocabulary) is sometimes understood as the subject's capacity to become aware of the way in which he functions: his defensive *habitus*, his characteristic modes of relating to what is unacceptable in himself. 'That is exactly the way you function', the analyst would have a tendency to say, and, obviously, the analysand to agree. It is relatively easy, and it allows many things to be left untouched, to simply have an *insight* into one's character, one's way of existing. You clearly see how you defend yourself each time; for instance, you isolate things, you shut them down; or again, you see that each time you project onto another what you do not wish to see in yourself. The notion of *insight*, such as I caricature it a little, is not to be entirely rejected; but it can only be considered as a stage. A 'character analysis', such as was proposed by Reich at a one point, runs the risk, like the interpretation of defences, of ending up being nothing but a denunciation, if it limits itself to highlighting a characteristic pattern of defensive behaviour, without establishing a relation to some specific contents. The notion of character takes seriously the generalisation of the obsessional, which submerges defence in a *habitus* in order to camouflage its specific, determinate aim.[7]

In any case, the notion of unconscious mechanisms or *habitus* is completely inadequate to recapture what Freud was aiming at when he spoke of the 'ego's unconscious defence'. An unconscious defence which is not, I stress, a discovery of the 1920s, for it can be seen at work from the first metapsychological developments—namely, from the 'Project for a Scientific Psychology', whose entire clinical section deals with hysterical defence, and consists in explaining how, in repression, the ego itself is led to function, contaminated by that which it would defend itself against. The ego begins to function in the mode of 'all or nothing', according to the model of total discharge, which is precisely that of unconscious fantasy or the primary process.

Here, I have just mentioned the term unconscious fantasy, which will take us on to the next stage: the discovery of *defensive fantasies*. No longer is there only the idea that the ego functions differently in pathological defence and in normal conscious functioning, but an exposure of the fact that these ego-defences, despite their appearance as abstract psychological mechanisms, are in reality under-pinned by very specific *bodily fantasies*. A mechanism like that of isolation goes back, it can be shown, to a bodily prototype which is extended in a phobia of touching. The mechanism of repression, in its very description, implies a 'bodily' work in a certain space—likewise the mechanisms of incorporation or projection. All of these 'mechanisms' are not abstract modes of functioning, in the sense I alluded to a moment ago regarding the physiological mechanism of vision. They are not only habitual, characteristic ways of functioning, but the habits are themselves based on fantasies—that is to say, on scenarios involving relations between bodies.

You can see how this progressive deepening of the notion of defence, of unconscious defence, leads us once more to a point at which the lines of defence (between the agencies involved in psychical conflict) hardly coincide with the limits of the conscious and the unconscious.

The contents of the Ucs: fantasies or drives?

Lastly, the final set of questions about the notion of the unconscious concerns the *contents* of the unconscious. Certainly, the stress laid on the model of repression (which reaches its culmination in the 1915 metapsychology) leads to the privileging of an unconscious content which is—above all—made up of representations. Here, we are taking the term 'representations' in its widest sense, including not only memories, fragments of memories, but also fantasies or even images (what we call 'imagos', of a more or less typical kind)—always on the model of one kind or another of representational contents: what Freud calls, precisely, representations of things or representation-things. In one sense, at a radical point in Freud's development, he goes as far as to exclude from the unconscious, for instance, affects; this is something apparently diametrically opposed to a conception of psychoanalysis as the bringing-to-light of hidden affects.

However, even if one accepts—and Freud will put it in question again—that the unconscious only consists of representations, one might already wonder if all these representations are the result of repression, or at least of one particular repression. Here we have the whole history of that which led Freud to discover, to attempt to bring to light, beyond the purely individual factors in each person's fantasmatic life, some more general types of structure, all of them obviously more or less linked to the Oedipus complex, and which, as you know, are given the name *primal fantasies*. Well, here again, the 'content' of the unconscious is put in question, for one must certainly wonder where these primal fantasies come from. Freud never took hold of the stick which was nevertheless held out to him by the term 'primal' [*originaire*]; in other words, he never linked the primal fantasies to what he called elsewhere *primal repression*.

Thus, rather than heading towards the idea that these primal fantasies might have something to do with primal repression, Freud set off on speculations about the history of the human species, in the direction of an unconscious which would be if not actually collective (in the Jungian sense), then at least hereditary. This was a hereditary dimension which allowed him to find in man something similar to animal instinct—that is, something which entails pre-established patterns of behaviour—that the small child has *within it* by heredity, inscribed in its biological patrimony, the pattern of love for the parent of the opposite sex and hatred towards the parent of the same sex. You can see that, via the detour of primal fantasies, we are on the way to locating, in the human being, a sort of instinctual supplement, which—however—all of psychoanalysis shows to be lacking in us, in the true sense. A contradiction? The return to the innate, to the pre-established?[8]

Let us now speak about biology in the true sense, or at least get closer to it. Well, the famous biological element that is present, as it were, on the edges of Freudian thought, cannot be easily excluded. Its point of contact is evidently the theory of drives. You are familiar with my interpretation of the history of the theory of drives—as a progressive discovery, linked to the dialectic of the thing itself—but I will not go over it again, for the time being, noting only that the moment in which it is given full scope, its ultimate adventure—in *Beyond the Pleasure Principle* (1920)—is also the point at which its formulation is linked more emphatically than ever to biology . . . or to a sort of bio-cosmology which is 'speculative', even 'mythological'. So the end-point of this bio-cosmological substratum of the theory of drives will correspond quite naturally to a transformation of topography: the affirmation that, in psychical conflict, the side against which defence operates could more adequately be described as the side of drives (the id) than the side of the unconscious.

The second topography is put in place from above

Having reminded ourselves of some of the reasons which indicate that the former definition of the unconscious needs to be revised, we have thus reached the frontier of the establishment of what is called a 'new' topography. 'New' in inverted commas, because on the one hand its roots are very old and, on the other, because it will never be able completely to dethrone the previous topography. Well, this establishment of the new topography ('id, ego and superego')—what is striking is that it is not brought about at a single moment, and especially that this does not happen from the 'bottom', but from the 'top'. It is not the id which first comes to subsume or replace the unconscious, but the notion of the ego which is introduced—or at least takes on a wholly new importance and 'character'. I can only refer you here to the article on the ego in *The Language of Psychoanalysis*, in which Pontalis and I have extensively re-traced this evolution of the notion of the ego, attempting to put to rest definitively the inaccuracies stored up by the historians of psychoanalysis, even by Freud himself as historian of his own thought.[9]

The full advent of the notion of the ego can be followed step by step, first in its progressive enrichment from 1895 to 1915, then, between 1915 and 1920, in the transformation which briskly unbalanced its problematic nature, due to the influence of three discoveries: narcissism, the importance of identifications in the constitution of the psyche, and—lastly—that of the ideal agencies. Three discoveries which, obviously, are only one.

5 December 1978

So we continue our ineluctable journey, via the construction of the second topography, towards the moment of the appearance of an id. The second topography is thus firstly constructed from the perspective of the ego, and not on the basis of a re-working of the unconscious 'foundations'. I pointed out the penultimate stage—the modifications which appeared around 1915, intimately linked with one another: narcissism, identifications, and the appearance of 'ideal' agencies. Narcissism means that the ego takes on the consistency of a love object. The identifications are another aspect of the same discovery, which could be put thus: if the ego becomes an internal object of love, then it is the precipitate, the internal residue of relations with external objects. The question raised is: does there exist an ego which is not this, which is not formed on the basis of the other. Is there any sense in speaking of an ego from the very beginning, with an origin other than that of identifications?

The third point concerns the genesis of the ideal agencies. Its principle can be summarised thus: the identifications, in the ego, do not accumulate just anyhow, one on top of the other, ending up in a sort of composite ego. Rather, they are stored up in a differentiated way, in substructures which Freud—at a certain point—designated as kinds of ministries, the 'great institutions' of the ego. Soon, this differentiation of the agencies (the ministry of moral conscience, the ministry of reality-testing, the ministry of police?) will appear, precisely, to be too 'functional'. These agencies, far from always collaborating, are most often at war with one another; there may be a raging conflict between the various identifications. The major step in this discovery was taken, obviously, in 'Mourning and Melancholia' (1917). I will not be returning to it here.[10]

Agencies: anthropomorphic, no longer functional

To conclude: before 1923, before the appearance of *The Ego and the Id*, *almost* all of the new topography was in place: the ego, the ideal agencies—and I note that these are not opposed to the unconscious any longer, since they themselves are to a large extent unconscious, although they are opposed to the repressed. How can we briefly define this new topography? Compared with the former, this one is *closer to anthropomorphism*. While for lovers of rational models it would be necessary to describe the psychical apparatus from a scientific point of view, here we describe it in magical, fantasmatic terms. We are not afraid to speak of the agencies as real people who live inside us. What was scandalous about this shift—a true scandal of analysis—accentuated further this anthropomorphism, whilst the first description of the psychical apparatus remained more abstract and more psychologising. It is also a topography which is closer to clinical experience, to the treatment of adults and above all that of children, precisely due to the fact that its structuring of the psychical apparatus allows the residues of old conflicts to show through more clearly. The conflict is now no longer between a consciousness and an unconscious, for how could there really be a conflict between a pure consciousness and a pure unconscious which would have no way of knowing each other? Thus, the conflict escapes from these difficulties bound up with a sort of psychical mechanism, and becomes a conflict between parts of the ego which each have their historical origin, their voice, their own character. Here we have, in Freud, the 'filling-out' (in a phenomenological sense) of an intuition which was present from very early on, notably in the correspondence with Fliess, in the expression 'plurality of psychical characters'.

Introducing an 'id' . . .

Well, once this topography had been established from the top down, through the higher agencies, why is there a need for an id? Why, in 1923, does this term appear? Clearly, we have to refer to what the author himself had to say about it, even if we then have to complete or explain this affirmation, which is still an affirmation directed at a given audience, at a given time:

> Now I think we shall gain a great deal by following the suggestion of a writer who, from personal motives, vainly asserts that he has nothing to do with the rigours of pure science . . . (Freud 1923a: 12)

This whole sentence is marked by a 'politics', addressed as much to the author in question as to the faithful disciples whom he wishes, in vain, to make live together:

> I am speaking of Georg Groddeck, who is never tired of insisting that what we call our ego behaves essentially passively in life, and that, as he expresses it, we are 'lived' by unknown and uncontrollable forces [let us note in passing this term 'unknown']. We have all had impressions of the same kind, even though they may not have overwhelmed us to the exclusion of all others, and we need feel no hesitation in finding a place for Groddeck's discovery in the structure of science. I propose to take it into account by calling the entity which starts out from the system *Pcpt.* and begins by being *Pcs.* 'the ego', and by following Groddeck in calling the other part of the mind, into which this entity extends and which behaves as though it were *Ucs.*, the 'id'. [And then there is a note:] Groddeck himself no doubt followed the example of Nietzsche, who habitually used a grammatical term for whatever in our nature is impersonal and, so to speak, subject to natural law. (Freud 1923a: 12)

You can see how cautiously the id is outlined, but not grasped, here, because what is in question is an 'unknown'.[11] Well, in German the id is *'Das Es'*. German has three genders: masculine, feminine and neuter, and *es* is the neuter personal pronoun, a personal which could be described as impersonal, neither the one nor the other, *ne-uter*, neither of the masculine nor of the feminine sex. The French language does not have the neuter gender. And while the psychoanalytic usage of the term ça does not cause us particular problems, let us point out all the same that there is a slight inflection: *ça* is a demonstrative pronoun, it is the contraction of *'celà'* ['this']; it is a demonstrative pronoun which, in everyday language, has become quasi-neuter. The translation is not so bad, although the translation of the *Ich* as *'le moi'* ['the ego'] in French is far more subject to reservations.

Groddeck in his own right

Which texts of Groddeck's should you look at? There are currently three texts available in translation[12]: *Le livre du ça* (Groddeck 1973a), which appeared in German in 1923; *La maladie, l'art et le symbole*

(Groddeck 1969), the most accessible and the most synthetic, a collection of the most important articles; and finally *Ça et moi* (Groddeck 1977b), primarily a collection of correspondence—mainly between Groddeck and Freud—and some documents. As for introductions to Groddeck and his thought, I refer you first of all to Lewinter's introduction to *La maladie, l'art et le symbole*. Lewinter is Groddeck's translator, and has made himself the French specialist on Groddeck. Then there is François Roustang's work *Dire Mastery* (1982) in which, among other things, the relation between Freud and Groddeck is analysed, from the very particular perspective of the mad 'relation' between master and disciple.

Well, one is fully justified in speaking of a world of Groddeck completely independent from Freud's. One of the chapters in Lewinter's text is called, not without reason, 'From Groddeck to Groddeck'. To do justice to this body of thought we must affirm that it remains, from one end to the other, faithful to its own requirements. Via a relation to Freud which is, assuredly, an important one, nevertheless it is incontestably one and the same Groddeck who encompasses Freudianism within his own parentheses.

Apart from Freud, what are Groddeck's co-ordinates? Freud compares him to Nietzsche, but Lewinter—with some justification—considers this reference to be unimportant. The fleeting allusion (in the note to *The Ego and the Id*) looks more like a touch of dishonesty. In fact, the major inheritance, traced by Lewinter, is from Spinoza, but transmitted, romanticised and rendered dialectical by way of Goethe. The terms 'God-Nature', and the expression 'die and come to be' (which is completely incompatible with the Freudian approach to death) are direct references to Goethe. Furthermore, for the historian of ideas, it would be appropriate to look more deeply at the personality and the influence of Schweninger, Goethe's master in psychosomatics, whose major work *Der Arzt* ('The Doctor') would be well worth re-examining and, first of all, translating into French.

Very briefly, today I would like to trace a certain number of dimensions in Groddeck's thought in order to try to understand what is at stake in this 'It', and to grasp exactly what Freud's (eclectic) *choice* of it might amount to. These dimensions, obviously linked to one another, are the following: monism, pantheism or 'pan-id-ism', dialectics, and finally, pan-symbolism, which is at the same time a pan-sexualism.

Groddeck's monism and Freud's anti-philosophical terrorism

What Freud highlights and immediately takes from Groddeck is his monism:

> I am afraid you are also a philosopher [Here we take into account Freud's ambivalent attitude to philosophy . . . 'Philosopher' here is taken in the pejorative sense: the 'philosopher' is the other] and of the monistic inclination which discards all the beautiful differences in nature in favour of the temptation offered by unity. Can we get rid of differences like that? (Groddeck 1977a: 38)

Groddeck replies, it has to be said, in a very convincing way:

> I do not consider myself a monist; when I am honest with myself, I notice that I take pleasure in the colourful interaction of all forces, without always realising. (Groddeck 1977a: 40)

Certainly, from the very beginning, there is an act of force, of terroristic force by Freud. It is like being transported to another world, where just by dint of calling one's adversary an 'idealist' he would disappear back underground—'philosopher!' 'monist!' 'mystic!' These objective descriptions are turned into insults, and Groddeck has some trouble in keeping his cool. His fundamental response is that one can perfectly well account for differences, whilst perceiving them as *moments* of a unity.

Monism, then, in the sense that, of course, differences are taken into account, but that ultimately they appear as superficial, resolved at another level of understanding. We will see how, in fact, most of the major sets of differences, most of the great Freudian dualities, return to a sort of unity.

Relativity of the body/soul dualism

In the highest degree, Groddeck's point of departure, and the field of the debate (or at least what seems like a debate) between Groddeck and Freud, is the duality of body and mind, or of body and soul. *Seele*, is the term Freud does not hesitate to use in order to designate the soul as a thing, something that can be described, the object of scientific proposals; as you know, we find in Freud the expression 'apparatus of the soul'.[13] The abolition of the body/soul difference is the main aim of Groddeck's attempt to find a resolution, and also of his introduction of the It (and not psychosis, as might be claimed, in a sort of retrospective illusion).

The problem of somatic afflictions and their meaning is, from start to finish, Groddeck's central interest. Groddeck, who was a doctor, aimed to treat at his clinic at Baden-Baden, in the same way and on the same level, using what might be termed a synthetic treatment, in other words, one which was both physical and psychical, for every type of disease, without distinction, all the way from neuroses and psychoses to cancer (that of Freud), or the illness that afflicted Ferenczi and which he died from, Biermer's anaemia (which is a 'somatic' illness of the first order, since it is now known that it can be cured entirely by medication).

What is important in Groddeck's thought , as Lewinter makes clear, is that, if he rejects the distinction between somatic and psychical pathology, he also rejects the notion of a 'psycho-somatic' pathology. Groddeck is absolutely not the precursor of psycho-somatics, in the sense that to speak of psycho-somatics is always to outline a third domain, as a set of conditions clearly characterised by a mixed mechanism. The contemporary tendency, as much among the Americans as in the 'French school', ends up by defining a new, discrete field, that of psychosomatics. This, by the same token, as Lewinter clearly shows, serves to maintain the opposition between psyche and soma. Now, for Groddeck, all illness is equally and simultaneously psychical and somatic, revealed in his moving proposal—repeatedly expressed—to cure Freud of his cancer by inviting him to treatment at the Baden-Baden clinic. It is not just the symptoms of an illness, but all manifestations of human life, right up to the development of an organ, which likewise takes on a psychical meaning, and subsists through this psychical meaning. This psychical sense is so omnipresent that, ultimately, the very idea of psychogenesis becomes absurd, to the extent that everything is both psycho- and somato-genetic:

> It is fashionable, nowadays, to speak of the psychogenesis of certain illnesses, and to expound upon it. The people who use this expression should, however, say once and for all what they mean by psyche. It always seems to me that they mean by it the conscious modality of man, his ideas. But what, then, do they make of the animals? Do they think, or do they not? What about bac-

> teria? Do they have a psyche, or do they not? And if they do not, where do our experts maintain that the psyche begins? . . . If they do not include in the concept of psyche unconscious life, thought and feeling, they should say so. Then we will know what we are dealing with, and we will be able to classify the whole business of psychogenesis as a thing of no importance. If, on the contrary, they include the unconscious among the forms of expression of the psyche, it is useless to speak of psychogenesis, because then all illnesses would be both psychogenetic and physiogenetic . . . For me, the question of psychogenesis does not exist . . . It is high time either to eliminate the words body and soul, or to define them anew . . . For the time being, I cannot see what psychogenesis could possibly be. (Groddeck 1969: 104-5, LT's translation)

Well, let us ponder for a moment whether the body/soul distinction, so royally abolished in the Groddeckian perspective, is as primordial in Freud as might appear. Freud, without any doubt, was convinced of this; you only have to read his correspondence to realise it. But perhaps Freud did not realise how much his own work had contributed, if not to making the whole problem of the relations between body and soul redundant, at least to overturning its terms, displacing them so that they could be dealt with otherwise than by the old solutions philosophy had fallen back on—and fallen foul of—since the time of the Cartesians.

The overturning of the body/soul problematic is missed by Groddeck

I have tried to show how the problem of body and soul came to be displaced, without of course thus being resolved, but transposed into another problem which was easier to approach, and which is grounded in the relation between sexuality and self-preservation, as two *equally* somato-psychic modes of functioning. Sexuality and self-preservation are by the same token both somatic and psychical. In this respect, Groddeck was right to want to erase any line drawn between body and soul. But, at the same time, Groddeck fails to see that the duality comes to be displaced elsewhere. The dualism—I would say, interpreting a certain Freudianism—of sexuality and self-preservation, even if this dualism is unstable, threatened by the fact that self-preservation in man (his autonomous capacity to persist in being, what one might term his instinctual potentialities) is so precarious that it is sexuality which endlessly comes to make up for its deficiencies. So, although a dualism is maintained, pansexualism is always there at the door—that is to say, the attempt and the temptation to reduce everything to a single factor in the human being, which is sexuality. From this point of view, reading Gantheret's text on 'the stakes of misunderstanding' between Groddeck and Freud is most enlightening.

Conversely, in another domain, I have tried to show that the very notion of sublimation loses its meaning (that is, a sexual contribution to non-sexual activities which can be defined as sublimation) if a non-sexual field does not maintain, at least, a minimum of consistency and appearance. Well, Groddeck does not make a frontal attack on this second polarity, that of the sexual and the non-sexual, but it is clear that it too is caught up in the whirlwind of his thought.

The absorption of sexual dualism

Another Freudian duality eliminated by Groddeck is equally important—it is, quite simply, the duality of sexuality. The only fully real being, for Groddeck, the only originary being, which is present from the beginning and towards which we aim, is a bi-sexual being. Here I can refer you to the article entitled 'The Bisexuality of the Human Being' (Groddeck 1973b). For Groddeck, bisexuality is not a metapsychological concept; at any rate, it is not only that. It is a *real* bisexuality in the beginning, which can be situated very precisely in the embryo. The embryonic state, says Groddeck, is a state which has to be called 'individual' (that is to say, in the etymological sense: 'in-divis', non-divided). The divided being is constituted through limitation and 'sexion' (which, through a double meaning of the word, is both the act of 'sectioning' and of 'sexuating', of establishing, through a violent splitting or castration, the difference between the sexes). Plato's famous androgynous being, which is referred to explicitly by Freud in *Beyond the Pleasure Principle* as the origin of the life-drives, is seen by Groddeck as something other than a myth; it is the embryonic reality at the origin of the human being. Starting from this state of pre-sexuation, undividedness and bisexuality, the fleeting moments of 'grandeur' in the life of the human being are moments of return, as bisexuality is not only behind us, but also in front of us. A number of these moments could be cited, the most striking being the *jouissance* of orgasm, of giving birth, or even of death. These moments of return to embryonic bisexuality are at the same time—to introduce another term from Groddeck's thought—moments of symbolic plenitude; they entail a fleeting coincidence of symbol and symbolised, both of these being *equally bisexual.*

Thus, at the moment of giving birth, the mother is fully bisexual with the child-phallus which fills her up. In the same way, she is as close as she will ever get to her own foetal state; a closeness which, subsequently, gives rise to resentment, for Groddeck's thought is far from a 'saintly' optimism. Hostility and hatred both have their place, especially the hostility of the mother towards the child,[14] explained in terms of the loss of fulfilment, once the delivery is over. Hatred, to be sure, finds its place both in Groddeck's thought and in his analytic practice, but it is nevertheless incontestably caught up (just as love is) in a monistic movement, so much so that another opposition—which appears in the 1920s, and on which we lay emphasis: the polarity between the life drive and the death drive—is radically relativised. Groddeck is basically uninterested in the Freudian 'death drive', to the extent that his conception of death is dialectical, while the opposition between life drive/death drive is fundamentally opposed to any dialectical interpretation. Despite all attempts to describe the Freudian polarity as a relation of two elements which interact with each other, the life and death drives clearly remain, in classical Freudianism, irreconcilable. 'Die and come to be': no-one is further from this maxim than Freud; no-one could be more vehement in denouncing it as an illusion. That which dies, in his view, never comes to be again . . .

Another opposition put in question by Groddeck is that of consciousness and the unconscious. In his work, the conscious loses all autonomy, becoming not merely subordinate but truly laughable (laughter is important in Groddeck's thought) in relation to the unconscious:

> I am of the opinion that consciousness is purely and simply a form of manifestation of the ucs.; that everything that happens in human life, everything, is ultimately created by the ucs. Consciousness is purely and simply a tool of the ucs., a servant, essentially, to roughly the same aims of communication as language or bodily attitudes, for example. Often, too, I have the impression that the ucs., through the means of consciousness, wants only to preserve the feeling of omnipotence; and that it

> plays a very amusing, and also, it is true, very cruel game with us—that is to say, with itself. (Groddeck 1977b: 45, LT's translation)

Here Groddeck, in a spirit of conciliation or politeness towards Freud, describes as the play of the 'unconscious' that which, in reality, for himself, he calls the It. That which, in *The Ego and the Id*, will return in the form of 'the ego's relations of dependence' is here a complete subordination, which removes any consistency or effectiveness from a purely illusory consciousness.

Further oppositions are encompassed by Groddeck's monism: that of the symbol and what it symbolises, since the moment of symbolic plenitude is the point at which the symbol and the symbolised are reunited. Or again, the duality of subject and object, which is so fundamental in classical Freudianism:

> The individual concept, in its effects, would thus cover all the relations of man to man, and even all the relations of man to the world as a whole. We would never have a man and a non-man, but always and only a man-god, a man-day, a man-world, we would not have a subject and an object, but a new being: a subject-object. [The following is important too:] From my point of view as a doctor, I emphasise that this formation of a new individual doctor-patient is the axis around which the treatment turns. (Groddeck 1969: 290, LT's translation)

I'm sure you can grasp the implicit consequences of such a conception, concerning the practice of the treatment and the very notion of the transference: the reconstitution of a true *in-dividuality between doctor and patient . . .*

Pan-idism

'Monism': evidently one is led to use the prefix *pan* . . . Pantheism, or 'pan-idism'? To some extent it doesn't matter. If one had to choose, I would favour 'pan-idism', even though the pantheist influence and lineage are obvious. Lewinter notes that 'It' appeared in Groddeck's work in 1909, before the reference to psychoanalysis, but at the same time as the appearance of a pantheist term, taken from Goethe: 'God-Nature'. Assuredly, one could speak of pantheism: a theory which posits an unknown entity governing the world and which perhaps, through a sort of dialectic or progression, is found in the world. However, if there is pantheism in Groddeck, or even what Freud denounces in it as mysticism, it is a mysticism which certainly has nothing to do with religiosity. As a unifying or totalising aspect of his thought, what is striking in Groddeck is perhaps laughter—and this is how he escapes from any totalistic dimension or even a narcissistic temptation to synthesise. It is a Homeric laughter, that of the It which governs everything, and which indeed laughs at all the ludicrous phenomena represented by our individual acts, our acts that are separated from one another, or - again—by symptoms, and—even more so—by so-called conscious phenomena, our reflection. Groddeck explicitly links reflection in thought to reflection in the mirror, in order to mock it. Reflection is really no more than a game played by the id with itself. We might also dub this laughter Rabelaisian: Groddeck was a man of the Renaissance, probably, and even more than a Spinozist, because Spinoza—in spite of everything—remained a Cartesian. We will be able to see this even more clearly concerning the question of symbolism.

The 'It' is certainly a more appropriate term than 'God-Nature', which calls up too many hackneyed concepts. The It is a genuinely new creation, something close to life, something that 'lives us', in an expression he repeats endlessly: we are lived by the It, particular phenomena are nothing but passivity (in the Spinozan sense) in relation to an active, universal power. Could we say that the It 'speaks' us, and could there be a plausible relation between this 'It lives us' and Lacan's 'it speaks'? Certainly, Groddeck's It 'speaks' in symbols, in symptoms, and even in language. But it speaks *only because it lives us.*

The It: the unknown

The It exceeds the individual and defies definition. Definitions of the It can only ever be negative. You can see this clearly in the article entitled, precisely, 'On the It', where Groddeck talks of the It in the way 'negative theology' talks of God, through what He is not: He has no sex, He does not exist in time, He is not . . . etc. So that it is only for the sake of convenience, provisionally, with regard for our limited intellectual capacity, that we indulge ourselves by speaking of the It as of a particular and defined person:

> The route that I have taken leads clearly to the sentence: All things are one. [Here monism is assumed, unlike in the correspondence with Freud]. Yet since this would not serve the purpose of this study, I have to assume temporarily an artificial It-individual with temporal and spatial limitations subject to life and death, a man's It. I reserve the right to remind the reader every now and then of the separation from the universe that is an artificial construction undertaken for certain purposes. On the other hand I shall make ample use of the fact that the individual is neither male nor female but both, that he is of no particular age but simultaneously one, ten, thirty years old, that everything which enters his consciousness depends on permission being given by the unconscious. Whoever doubts that my statements about sex, age and mind are true should ask the next woman he comes across whether she has ever known a man who was wholly man; or the next man whether he ever found a creature that was wholly woman. (Groddeck 1977a: 136)

12 December 1978

I am going to try to finish with Groddeck today, or at least, with this introduction, via Groddeck, of the problem of the id. Firstly I would like point out that this thought, whether pantheist or pan-idist, is driven by a sort of dialectic.

A dialectic without synthesis

Not so much in the Hegelian sense of dialectic, since there is no synthesis in Groddeck's thinking, nor anything which resembles a movement towards progress. This thought belongs more with the Oriental philosophies, and Freud's advancement of the notion of Nirvana would seem to be heading in the same direction. There is no synthesis, no progress, but rather a movement of return coming after a procession, a determination which—as must be the case—is a 'negation', where the human individual, determined (notably by his sex), 'sexioned' from the primitive unity, has to return to the whole, the latter quite clearly conceived as both foetal and maternal. Lewinter (in the preface I referred to earlier) gives a Spinozist interpretation of all this, which is very suggestive and certainly contains some truth (it is

Spinoza, but mediated by Goethe). You will notice, nevertheless, that as you progress through the text Lewinter's Spinozist interpretation is based less and less on Groddeck's writings, or on a comparison between Groddeck and Spinoza, but ends up referring solely to Spinoza.

What has Freud to do with all this? Well, obviously, Freud is a long way from Spinoza, and Freud's references to the philosopher are very rare indeed. Nonetheless, there is an clear conjunction—an elective affinity—between Freud and Groddeck. It is a conjunction which, moreover, became an object of debate in their correspondence: is it in fact a meeting of minds, a joint discovery? Or is it, as Freud would have it, a case of 'cryptomnesia', Groddeck having once had some knowledge of Freudian thought, and then having had the impression of discovering it himself? The conjunction appears in a couple of words, at two crucial points, which make of Groddeck a Freudian and an analyst, in spite of his enormous differences.

Groddeck with Freud: the prevalence of sexuality

The first point is the prevalent role of sexuality, because the whole movement of the It, its determining role and the return to totality, is obviously marked by the Freudian theory of sexuality. It is not a question of just any dialectic, or of just any return; it is a return centred on the problem of sexuality, and the symbolism of the It is itself a completely sexual symbolism. Groddeck thus accepts, and makes fully his own, all of Freud's discoveries in this register: the extension of sexuality, notably the whole 'pregenital' or non-genital dimension (a discovery that analysts never cease to call into question); also the discoveries of the Oedipus and castration complexes, although these are absorbed into a perspective at once grandiose and differently centred (the major debate in the Freud-Groddeck correspondence): the relation to the mother is conceived as primordial, while Freud, at every point, insists on the paternal function. The second, equally important point is his rallying to the Freudian discoveries concerning unconscious determinism—that is, the notion that human phenomena are to be deciphered, are symbolic of the unconscious or of the It.

This brings me to another aspect of Groddeckism, which could be termed 'pansymbolism': an universal symbolism, in which the rather extravagant influence of the great hermeneutics of history can be discerned. In particular there are two of them: the hermeneutics of the

Renaissance, and Romantic hermeneutics, while along the way all the traditions of interpretation are included, Oriental traditions to the same degree as those of the Kabbala, of Gnosticism, etc.

Symbolism: with Freud

We must not forget the role played by the term 'symbolism' in Freud's work, a role at once important and limited. This role was to assume increasing importance during precisely the period at which Groddeck made Freud's acquaintance, the years after 1910. However, it was a limited role, since, as much in what Freud terms the work of dream-formation or symptom-formation as in the psychoanalyst's opposing work, the work of interpretation, symbolism is assigned a distinct, separate place, which clearly indicates that it is not everything. Symbolism, for Freud, means the existence of symbols with a relatively fixed and universal meaning, formations to be outlined alongside the properly individual work of displacement and condensation. The 'individual work' also gives onto 'indirect representations' that are disguised or masked, but true symbolic representation is something predetermined, as if the subject selects it from a sort of symbolic stock, which is more or less inter-cultural and in any case trans-individual, and which, because of this very fact, can be deciphered in a direct fashion.

The limited character of symbolism in Freud becomes clear when we affirm a genuine opposition between interpretation through what are termed associative pathways and symbolic interpretation. It is only at those points in the treatment at which interpretation through associations falls silent, fades away, that symbolic interpretation appears. Well, Groddeck attempts to get beyond this opposition. He adopts the idea of a work of elaboration and interpretation, in the Freudian sense of the term, but at the same time he broadens considerably the place of symbolism.

Pansymbolism: beyond, or before Freud?

As proof, there is a most characteristic paper entitled 'Dream-work and the Work of the Organic Symptom' (Groddeck 1969: 135-143). Its idea is to extend to the organic symptom the processes described by Freud on the model of the dream. The organic symptom, as we have seen, cannot fail to hold meaning in Groddeck's view; nothing authorises us to treat it differently, according to another determinism than, for example, the dream. Thus, the Freudian technique of decomposition, of multiplicity, is to be extended to the organic symptom: an organic symptom, just like a psychopathological symptom, has to be taken as part of a series—one might say an infinite, or at least an indefinite, number of associative series—which give it signification and cause it to exist in the first place, and which maintain it in its consistency as symptom. The slightest symptom—an abscess, a fever, even a fracture which refuses to set properly (which is the most notable example)—has to be decomposed; that is to say, one has to follow (obviously with the help of the patient) the psychical and symbolic associations which are connected with it. This includes associations relating as much to the history of the symptom as to its actual consistency. The 'congestion' of an organ, for example, will find meaning in relation to the drives, and therefore to the desire of the subject. Interpretation here aims to model itself very precisely on Freud's decomposition of the dream process, with its displacements and its condensations. In truth these two processes, which are so important in Freud, are in the end assigned a rather limited place—if only quantitatively, for in the body of the paper the paragraph on 'organic' displacement and condensation takes up only a few lines:

> In order to keep to Freud's account of the dream-work, I will now have to speak of the use of condensation and displacement in the organic domain. Or rather, this should not be necessary, since these processes are so obvious and well-known. As an example of condensation, I would cite the abscess, which condenses in itself a long chain of organic processes. And as an example of displacement, there are those maladies characteristic of the retina which accompany renal inflammations, or the inflammations of the knee joints which accompany gonorrhoea. I will not expand further on these complex relations, but will only take the opportunity to emphasise expressly that the It, in order to transform latent organic processes into manifest symptoms and to form them through displacement, condensation or other means, very frequently, if not always, proceeds via the psyche. (Groddeck 1969: 141, LT's translation)

We should note the pluralist, polyvalent impact of this interpretation, which does not discriminate in the slightest between a displacement conceived as a change of organic location (since Groddeck does not deny that the inflammation of the knee joints which accompanies gonorrhoea is clearly due to a displacement—possibly the displacement of bacteria, or of the inflammatory process—with a pathway of migration in the organism which the doctor can trace very precisely) and, at the very same time, a displacement along the psychical pathways of associative chains—which might indicate, for example, that a gonorrhoeal infection would affect the knee in particular, because of the functional signification of that part of the body.

A methodology faithful to Freud

As for the method of interpretation, exactly as for Freud it goes back in the opposite direction along the pathways which led to the formation of the symptom. Groddeck's method, and I must emphasise this, is not purely a priori. It is not simply an interpretation of symbols according to some sort of pre-established key. It follows the associations step by step, and this comes out strongly in the most complete clinical fragments reported by Groddeck, which are those in which he speaks not of the analysis of a patient, but of his self-analysis. This is the case in the text entitled 'Psychic Conditioning and the Psychoanalytic Treatment of Organic Disorders' (Groddeck 1977a: 109-31). Here we can see how fully he uses the associative methodology—for instance, word associations—in particular around the name 'Dora'. The transference according to Freud is also taken into account so that symbolism (in the strict sense which I recalled a short while ago, symbolism in the Freudian sense) is itself decomposed. It is not tacked on as a whole, but set back in motion along lines of association.

Let us quote another passage from 'Dream-work and the Work of the Organic Symptom':

> Wounds, in the end, belong to the symbolic, and I cannot prevent myself from paying attention once more to the forces of repression, which influence the brains of psychoanalysts as much as those of neurotics or indeed my own [repression, to be exact, would be that which leads to stereotyped interpretations], for he who, instead of insisting on the castrating cut to the finger, would be bold enough to examine, for example, the whitlow psychoanalytically would discover that it is well worth while, and, on the basis of this experience, he will soon dare to take care

> of phlegmons, diseases of the joints, etc., etc., and he will discover that the symbolic of left and right, as well as that of fingers/members of the family (thumb-father), at the level of the It, contribute to the work of the symptom. (Groddeck 1969: 140, LT's translation)

This tells us, then, that Groddeck is directly opposed to a certain stereotypical way of using symbolism, to that hermeneutics current among psychoanalysts who, at the mere mention of a 'wound to the finger', react immediately with 'castration'. You can see that, where he is concerned, the work of the symbol (and we can use that expression) is much more concrete.

I wished to show how this 'symbolism' is, in more than one respect, faithful to its Freudian inspiration, to a revolution in the art of interpreting, to the point at which one cannot, in my view, speak of 'interpretation' in the same sense, before and after Freud. The idea elaborated by Ricoeur (1970), of a universal hermeneutics which simply reaches its culmination in Freud, seems to me to be quite mistaken. Thus, taking into account this revolution in the art of interpretation, which from then on becomes a step-by-step associative method, we have to say, in spite of everything, that there is a clear difference between Groddeck and Freud in terms of the therapeutic approach (even if we take no account of the extension of the method to organic symptoms).

Differences in therapeutic approach

The difference between them may appear to be paradoxical. In fact, of the two, it is Freud who never ceases to stress our limitations—the limitations of our views, the partial nature of our approaches, the need to renounce our ambitions towards universal knowledge or an exhaustive explanation of the symptom. Yet in a thinker who preaches non-totality, interpretation will nevertheless be neither direct (bearing directly on what arises in the analysis) nor limited. Not direct because, as you know, Freudian technique turned away little by little from applying itself to the point which, at the outset, demanded the attention of both the patient and the analyst. The evolution of the rule of free association meant that, ultimately, one had to refuse the shared fascination to which, in the *Studies on Hysteria*, patient and analyst evidently yield, as they combine their efforts in attacking directly the symptom to be deciphered. Soon the rule of free association no longer took the symptom as its point of departure, but took any element, possibly one suggested by the analyst. Then, still more radically, the method became a refusal of any pre-established point of departure, so as to be given over as much as possible to unconscious determinism. Freudian interpretation is indirect, then, but aims to be unfinished, non-limited. The image of a network, of a sort of indefinite mycelium of associations (Freud 1900: 525), always lurks below the surface of the unfolding treatment and of every analytic session; a network of associations can always be taken up again and completed.

I was saying, then, that there is a sort of paradox here, which we find, in an inverse form, in Groddeck, since Groddeck openly presents himself as a champion of the infinite, of the abolition of differences, of these separate domains at which the It scoffs. Groddeck rejects the idea of personal limits as a sort of transitory illusion and, for even stronger reasons, he claims the symptom itself is an illusion: it is nothing but the imperfect expression, the inadequate symbol, of something else. At the heart of this vision—which we could call infinitist, totalitarian—what is the type of interpretation proposed?

Centred on the finite symptom

Well, usually, this interpretation is centred on the symptom. Its point of departure is the symptom: it circles around it, returns to it, no doubt looking for associations, but linking them back endlessly to their point of departure. The interpretation, rather than being biographical, is symbolic, limited to the present, to present desire. If biography plays a role in it, then this is always by way of a contemporary event that is clearly outlined. Let me quote a brief clinical example. You will find plenty of others, more detailed and more interesting.

> A young girl came to see me: the right-hand corner of her mouth was irritated, a crack had formed exactly at the junction of the lips. 'It's been like that for several days,' she told me. 'When I wake up in the morning, it seems to be better, but in the course of the day it opens up again.' When I asked her if she had given someone a Judas' kiss, or if she had been a big-mouth, she replied that she hadn't. But on the other hand, a hint of a smile appeared when I asked her if she had a wicked tongue, and she told me that might well be the case. (Groddeck 1969: 103, LT's translation)

Groddeck suggests different associations for this symptom: a crack in the corner of the mouth. Several propositions that leave her indifferent: the Judas' kiss, the big-mouth . . . the patient 'takes the bait' at the idea that she has 'a wicked tongue':

> And when I point out to her that the crack is on the right-hand side, so that means she must have said something bad about someone related to her [here a pre-established symbolism intervenes, which is the ancient left/right symbolism], she recognises this: 'Yes, it was about my sister.' The following day, the wound had healed. (Groddeck 1969: 103, LT's translation)[15]

Groddeck's interpretation is diffuse and, we might say, it is an interpretation—contrary to the tenets of classical Freudianism—that is centred, limited and direct. Certainly, the opposition is not so clear-cut. Freud never denied himself the pleasure of limited and circumscribed analyses. If you take the *Psychopathology of Everyday Life*, which is often, it has to be said, a sort of fairly wild psychoanalysis, applied to everyday life; or if you take certain dream analyses in *The Interpretation of Dreams*, which are well and truly 'interpretations of the *salon*', then Freud certainly does not deny himself direct attacks on the symptom, the parapraxis or the dream. But in Groddeck we find, constantly and systematically, the transition, the almost unmediated relation he establishes between the deepest force of symbolisation—the It—and its final, concrete manifestation, the symptom in its materiality. Each particular manifestation is a mirror and a replica of the whole: not just the psychical symptom, not only the organic symptom (whether it is a symptom of so-called internal pathology or of the accidental type), but every human manifestation, and even every manifestation of the order of life, right up to a symbolic interpretation of the shape of organs, of the nose, the foot or the lungs, which would be explicitly shaped by bisexuality. Or as, another example, even a phenomenon such as the decline in visual acuity in the ageing subject, presbyopia, interpreted as the wish to see less well, and above all to keep at a distance (for, as we know, the long-sighted person continues to see at a distance, but not close up) that which is approaching—namely, death. These are some of the triumphs of 'pansymbolism'.

Lewinter, since I have referred to him, sends us back to Spinoza at this point, to what in Spinoza is defined as a 'type of knowledge'—to be precise, a knowledge of 'the third type', beyond a knowledge of the 'second type' which has a rational appearance, and which is discursive knowledge (we might say that Freud's is a knowledge of the second type). This third type of knowledge is a direct apprehension of the relation between the most defined, the most concrete, the most singular (that which Spinoza calls the finite mode) and the infinity of God. A knowledge of this third type: an intuitive science, to which Groddeck would bring his methodical concretisation.

The great hermeneutic tradition of the Renaissance: pansymbolism

We cannot fail to recognise, in this intuitive and symbolic science, a tradition which runs throughout history, which Foucault described at one of its privileged moments—the Renaissance—in the brief chapter which forms the introductory part of *The Order of Things*: 'The Prose of the World' (Foucault 1970: 17). He indicates as characteristic of this Renaissance symbolic knowledge, this great law of resemblance, certain dimensions or co-ordinates (what he calls 'similitudes'), which take the form of various sub-categories. Alongside the similitudes, there is what he calls 'the signature'. We are immediately able to find the trace of this in Groddeck, to the point where the very term 'signum'—as in signature—is emphasised by him. The signature—beyond the complex networks of similitudes between the symbolising and the symbolised—is a sort of direct mark, which short-circuits pathways that are too complicated. Another point Foucault stresses—and again we can find this in Groddeck—is that language itself, far from being the privileged medium in these systems of correspondence, or even their cause, is on the contrary their effect. Language itself is included in the system of correspondences, and is itself the effect of a sort of primary power of signification which goes beyond it:

> Language partakes in the world-wide dissemination of similitudes and signatures. It must, therefore, be studied itself as a thing of nature. Like animals, plants, or stars, its elements have their laws of affinity and convenience, their necessary analogies. (Foucault 1970: 35)

You will find more than one correspondence (certainly the right term here!) with this in Groddeck—for example, in 'The Compulsion to Use Symbols' where one of Goethe's poems, *Der Fischer* ('The

Fisherman')[16] is analysed. Groddeck, at one point, expresses himself thus:

> I have deliberately used the expression unconscious element of the poem rather than of the poet because I wanted to suggest that the work of art—like every action perhaps—has its own life, its own soul, and that, in other words, the symbol, as soon as it has emerged, throws up new symbols by means of the compulsion to associate which make up the body of the poem. The artist's conscious activity consists merely in the shaping of the form. (Groddeck 1977a: 162)

Nowadays one speaks freely of the 'unconscious of the text'. But is this not rather in the same sense as Groddeck—that is to say, in an orientation ultimately bound up with a pre-Freudian hermeneutics?

The last point, finally, of this pansymbolic view analysed by Foucault, is the famous relation between the 'microcosm' and the 'macrocosm'. Each individual formation, and notably each human individual, each human work, is ultimately a mirror of the whole world. Well, this is something else explicitly present in Groddeck—in a eulogy to Goethe, a text entitled 'Language':

> Goethe was greater as a scientist than as a poet . . . He showed science a new approach ['New'? I'm not so sure about that!], namely the approach of seeing the part in the whole, of taking the apparent whole as a symbol of the universe, of seeing the whole world symbolised in a flower, an animal, a pebble, the human eye, the sun; and to construct the world from this flower, this pebble, that is to create it anew and to investigate things not by analysing them but by placing them in the context of the whole. [You can see here how we move beyond the Freudian decomposition, belonging to the second type of knowledge, and end up with intuition.] He opened up this approach to science, which will achieve undreamt-of results in fields which have so far been untested and unknown . . . (Groddeck 1977a: 252)

and this is followed by allusions we cannot fail to recognise, both to Hindu philosophy and alchemistic philosophy.

A borrowing or a taming of the It?

Let us now pick up the thread of Freud and his adoption of the It. I reminded you of the very polemical passage in one of Groddeck's letters: 'the It is pretty . . . '. Other passages in more scientific writings, in articles, say the same thing. Groddeck never hid his judgement: the borrowing of the It from his own terminology did not do justice to the broadening he had himself wished to contribute to psychoanalytic thought. We might refer here to the text of a paper that caused a scandal at the Psychoanalytic Congress in Hamburg. There was no copy made of the text of another paper which he gave at another international Congress, such was the unanimous opposition to him! Let us quote again from the article 'Dream-work and the Work of the Organic Symptom':

> In his book *The Ego and the Id*, Freud has done me the honour of putting me forward as the inventor of the term '*Es*' (It/id), indicating that he borrowed it from me. This is true, except that the concept of the 'It' as I used it was completely unusable for him, and that he thus made of it something other than I had intended: as far as I understand, he has chosen the term to express what he understands topographically. But it has not changed anything of the essence of psychoanalysis: it has neither added nor taken away anything at all. Psychoanalysis remains what it was: the analysis of consciousness and of the repressed, that is to say, of the psyche. Now, the *Es*, whether it is a question of my It or Freud's id, which have nothing in common except the name, can be analysed as little as Ferenczi's *bios*. (Groddeck 1969: 137, LT's translation)

So again we have to call into question these accounts: Groddeck's account, when he tells us Freud understood nothing of his It, or that ultimately the two had no shared inspiration; and Freud's account, when he claims to have completely integrated Groddeck's thinking into his own discovery.

Confrontation of opinions, or problematic

I will open a parenthesis here concerning the clash and the confrontation of opinions, as they arise in my reflection, which effectively entails a comparison of diverse opinions. Is this in order to show the divisions of a fragmented psychoanalytic thought, in which the most diverse opinions coexist, where agreement on words—as we see in the case of the death drive—hides complete opposites of meaning? If that were the case, would it perhaps be enough to bring some order into these meanings? Or again, is it to lead us to make a choice, to lead us to restore a unique truth, which would be that of one of the authors being compared—that of Freud, of course, according to some sort of dogmatism? This dogmatic path is what, last year, I was reproached with not following. I was opposed in these terms: 'you talk about nothing but the unconscious, you are stuck in 1915, you don't take the id into account'. Conversely, others seem to have understood my course last year as a sort of confrontation, which would eventually result in a merely polemical, or even sceptical, conclusion. Isn't that, after all, what a person like Revel did for the philosophers, claiming to show that the history of philosophy, as it is done nowadays, ends up in scepticism?

Well, it is certainly necessary to clarify things, and I will not fail to do so. Nor will I fail to discuss, even at some length—as I have just done in the case of Groddeck—someone's thought, attempting to remain faithful to it. Sometimes choices have to be made, too. When this is necessary, I don't duck the issue, and I certainly don't always lean towards the Freudian view—far from it. I wanted to remind you, however, of this: when I bring in diverse and contrary thoughts, my goal—far from being polemical, far from wanting to set up a more or less rhetorical opposition between two opinions on a question—my aim, and I do not claim always to succeed, is essentially interpretative, or even, as I describe it, problematic. It is 'problematic' in the sense that I try to return to the exigencies (this is a term I cling to) underlying the fluctuations of a thinker and also—equally—lying behind the divergences between several schools of thought.

The exigency of Groddeck, of which I have given a broad overview, linking it also to an entire tradition which goes well beyond Goethe and even Spinoza—it is too easy to say of this Groddeckian exigency either that it was adopted by Freud, or that—on the contrary—Freud repudiated it in the cleverest manner, adopting the word so as to reject the thing itself. Let me refer you once more to Gantheret's introduction to Groddeck's last work, *Ça et moi* ['It and me'], where it is exactly this confrontation between two exigencies that is thoroughly analysed, both in terms of the irreducible opposition it conceals and, if you like, its shared foundations.

The id: four options—drive-related, genetic, impersonal, topographical

What did it mean, to introduce an id into psychoanalysis? Unless, of course, it was just another word for the unconscious. Even if, indeed, as Groddeck himself said, it sometimes is just that—another word for the unconscious? What did it mean, to introduce an id? Let us try briefly to enumerate the implications; not the meanings of the id, but what it implies as a particularity.

The introduction of an id is, first of all, a reference to the drive and, through the drive, to biology. You only have to read or skim through Groddeck's writings to realise that it is life, a vital energy, metaphysical but vital, which is at the basis of the entire theory of the It. Thus the reference is to biology, and at the same time it is a way—in relation to the very special status of biology in psychoanalytic thinking—of taking biology literally. It is to de-metaphorise it, while a whole dimension of psychoanalysis consists in using biology as something to be made metaphorical.

There is a second dimension: introducing an id is a genetic option, an option concerning the problem of origins. Here, too, there is a risk that we end up rendering univocal a problem which has always been highly complex in psychoanalysis. This is the problem of knowing if there is a first term, a last term in psychoanalysis which might be a primary term in the being—that is to say, if there is a terminus a quo, upon which one is based. We may think, for example, of the old Freudian debate between the reality of memory and the fantasmatic character of the unconscious.

Thirdly, introducing an id (I am still, for the time being, in the dimension of the particularity it conceals) is a way of emphasising the impersonal nature of that which drives us. It is thus to proceed along the path of the dethroning of the conscious autonomous subject, and to reaffirm the existence of processes which live us, the primary processes. In a curious fashion, at the very moment, in the 1920s, when a theory of the ego is affirmed in psychoanalysis which restores to prominence such notions as 'reason', if not even 'autonomy', we move as if according to a sort of balancing mechanism, in the direction of impersonality and heteronomy. The debate which finds an echo even today, as one of the current debates in psychoanalysis, even in psychopathology, is indeed that of the position of the subject, or the subject's de-centering in relation to the id and the unconscious. Obviously, I am referring you here to the entire Lacanian lineage, and to a book whose very title alone is eloquent enough: *Le sujet de la folie* (Swain 1978). Is madness a process that lives us, as the id lives us?

There is yet another demand: the id is a way of restoring order to the question of conflict at the moment when the agencies appeared, or were reaffirmed, whose elaboration in the 1920s I recalled earlier: the agencies of the ego and the ideal, superego agencies.

Well, are these four points of view, these four exigencies necessarily linked, are they of the same order, are they even compatible? I will go into them in more detail next time, starting from a reference to the drive, because it is there, in spite of everything, that the id finds its point of introduction.

The population and depopulation of topography

So I shall take the drive as my starting point, but I would like to point out here something which appears to me as a certain paradox in this new topography, a paradox or a spur to our reflection. In this second Freudian topography, the so-called 'superior' agencies (let us call them this for simplicity's sake) which had been in the previous model abstract and functional—functions of the person in the sense that one speaks of a functional psychology, or even of 'faculties': consciousness, moral conscience, whatever . . . —these 'superior' agencies have become concrete, anthropomorphic, not just furnished with memories and experiences, but populated with identifications. The superior agencies have been populated. Conversely, the unconscious, in the first topography, was 'populated'; it was anything but an unspeakable, unknown magma. What was to be found there, very precisely ('the repressed', said Freud, until the 1920s) were memories, phantasies—that is to say, always representations. Now, the introduction of the id made the unconscious more alien, closer to a vital force, more distanced from familiar objects and, at least in its extreme depths, 'more' unknown.

Could we say that the introduction of the id would end up, at least from one perspective, by depopulating the unconscious of its representations, or even by de-anthropomorphising it? (I apologise for this frightful neologism.) To deprive the unconscious of its representations, and to de-anthropomorphise it—in other words, to make it more alien, more alien to the human universe—do these go hand in hand? Or, to put the question in yet another way, do we absolutely, necessarily, have to make of the id a primal force, a force according to a vital model, in order to restore its status as impersonal, radically alien to the 'superior' system, or even to insist on the fact that it is productive, or even that it is timeless? Put another way—are there models other than the vitalist one which could account for the heterogeneity which comes to be affirmed in the second topography? Well, it is by way of the drives that I will continue next time.

9 January 1979

Assuredly, there is a certain opposition between Freud's former unconscious, teeming with representations and phantasies, and an id—in the most extreme form, Groddeck's It—which is perhaps 'depopulated' like the 'primal', lying beyond any representations that are finite, limited—or, in Groddeck's terms, sexuated, 'sexioned'. A depopulated id, rather like God. There is an echo of this—although Freud barely has time for this conception, because he considers it to be mystical—in certain Freudian formulations, in which, if not its depopulation, then at least a certain homogenisation of the id appears.

The cauldron of the id?

About the id we have very little to say, and even:

> . . . what little we know of it we have learnt from our study of the dream-work and of the construction of neurotic symptoms, and most of that is of a negative character and can be described only as a contrast to the ego. We approach the id with analogies; we call it a chaos, a cauldron full of seething excitations. We picture it as being open at its end to somatic influences, and as there taking up into itself instinctual needs which find their psychical expression in it, but we cannot say in what substratum. It is filled with energy reaching it from the instincts, but it has no organisation, produces no collective will . . . (Freud 1933: 72-3)

Clearly, a passage like this forms a contrast with the famous text 'The Unconscious' (1915a), from which we gained the impression of finding our way more easily, even if it was at the price of a certain degree of artifice. In the unconscious, said Freud, there are representations. There is even—he added—something completely opposed to the seething cauldron: there is no affect in the unconscious. At least, no affect in the proper sense of the word. There is, of course, the quantitative aspect of affect, the 'quantum'. But the term affect itself refers to a consciousness which is 'affected' and, in the unconscious, precisely, there is nothing left but the quantum, without that which is affected by it. So the very idea of affect which is qualitatively differentiated, perhaps like the idea of any quality in the unconscious, loses its sense.

Discussion of unconscious affect

I will spend a few minutes expanding on this question of affect, not in order to retrace its entire history, but to attempt to weigh up the value of the Freudian arguments. The clearest example, used by Freud, was that of the sense of guilt. He often affirms that the expression 'unconscious sense of guilt' conceals a contradiction in terms since, in the unconscious, there is nothing 'sensed', no 'affected' consciousness. One would thus have to imagine a sort of undifferentiated affect—let's say, quite simply, anxiety. The feeling of guilt would be only one of the forms of anxiety (moral anxiety, relating to other forms: social anxiety, castration anxiety, etc.) It is a form of anxiety which is specified as 'a sense of guilt' or as 'guilt' only because of a particular set of representations.

We can see very clearly what could turn an anxiety specifically into guilt: on the one hand, representations referring to sin and, on the other, those referring to punishment. This is why, when Freud claims to be expressing himself coherently, he maintains that 'in the unconscious' one could locate a *need for punishment*, but not a sense of guilt. A need for punishment is more closely linked to representations—that is, to something which can do without consciousness. In this classical view, it is precisely the fact of repression which consigns imaginary scenarios to another kind of fate—that of representing the crime and anticipating the punishment. On the other hand, this 'quantity' which circulates can be displaced and condensed *ad infinitum*, and can resurface in quite another place than that of the phantasies to which it was firstly linked.

To summarise this thesis of 1915, there was no affect in the unconscious for two reasons. The first was, in truth, rather formalist: the id, or the unconscious, by definition does not perceive. It is different and separate from the system of perception. It is on the side of what affects, and not on the side of what is affected. I say this argument is rather formal, because although he makes room for this objection to an unconscious psyche regarding affect, Freud does not maintain it where representations are concerned. As you know, Freud had more than once scoffed at the 'consciousness' objection: indeed there is perhaps a contradiction inherent in speaking of representations without a consciousness to 'represent' them, but that 'does not stop them existing'. But the same line of reasoning which he sweeps away in the name of analytic experience, concerning representations, he accommodates when it is a question of affects. One might respond to a formalist argument with a simple change of formulation (sense of guilt—need for punishment . . .) but Freud's second reason gets much closer to the heart of the matter: it concerns the very concept of repression as a defence mechanism. The *mainspring* of repression—its aim, its *principal* aim—is to separate the destiny of affect from that of representation. This mobility of affect in relation to representation is a fundamental and inaugural discovery of psychoanalysis, one which we are not going to abandon easily. From then on, if repression amounts to making affect and representation independent of each other in the unconscious, how are we to conceive of what affect becomes at that point, if not an absolutely non-specific energy, to the extent that it is no longer fixed to a particular scenario which lends it tonality. This element, repressed into the unconscious but in a form which is henceforth purely energetic, would then only re-emerge in the form of anxiety—that is to say, of the affect which itself is also the least specific.

Independent of representation, affect inclines towards anxiety

Let us turn to the clinical evidence. We encounter affects which seem to re-emerge from the unconscious as much in the treatment as in the symptom. In the treatment, from the very beginning (in the first cathartic treatments of Breuer and Freud), but also in any analytic treatment, there has always been the possibility that affective phenomena will appear independently of a precise representational context. Hatred, for example, which explodes in a crisis, with no motivation in the real, disappears as quickly as it appeared. It is devastating—more devastating, precisely, for the subject than for the person seemingly taken as the object. Or, again, an indefinite doubt, also detached from representations, with no motives, or with too many motives for the subject to be able for a moment to think that one of them is the right one. In these examples (and we could find plenty more) of affects which seem to well up from the depths of the id, one simple and banal observation cannot be avoided: such an affect, precisely in so far as it is independent of its train of representations, independent of a phantasy, is directly marked by anxiety. Indeed, we find a correlation between this despecification of affect effected by repression, and the non-specific character of affect which appears as the universal currency of affects, their lowest common denominator—that is, anxiety.

This quite particular position of anxiety is the key, without which we would not be able to take the question of unconscious affect further than merely verbal solutions. The question must, then, henceforth be formulated as follows. What are the conditions, in the id, which either cause an affect to be maintained there as an affect, so that at the moment when it re-emerges into consciousness it has its appropriate tonality; or, inversely: what are the conditions that cause the degradation of an affect into anxiety, which then re-emerges in the form of anxiety? I have already had occasion to repeat the following several times: we know how uncertain it is that an affect, once it has been degraded into anxiety, will be transformed back into a qualitatively differentiated affect. This, perhaps, is one of the major stumbling-blocks of analysis. The question is worthy of detailed examination, but only if one bears in mind the great polarity between, on the one hand, the singular affect of anxiety, and on the other hand, all the other affects.[17]

In the bag of the id: the drives

Affect, then, is the most energetic aspect of the unconscious. Perhaps what is interesting about this second theory, that of the id, is that it puts more emphasis on this energetics, under the name of the drives. What is there inside this bag, in this cauldron, in this scrip? Essentially, Freud tells us, there are the drives.

How can we situate them? It is interesting briefly to recall the schema of the psychical apparatus and, even more so, the variants on this schema. There is the schema of *The Ego and the Id*, and then that of the *New Introductory Lectures*.

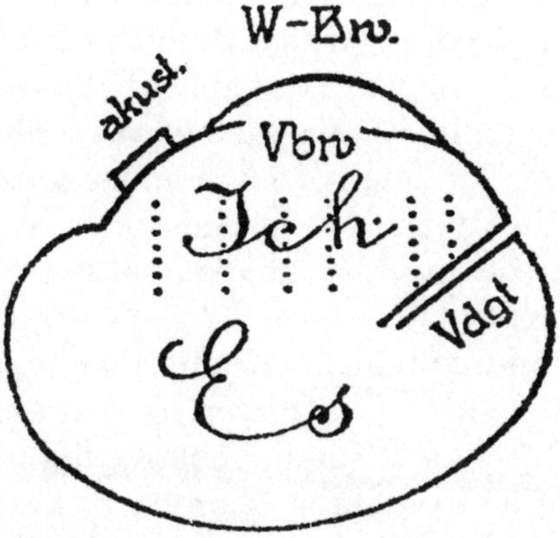

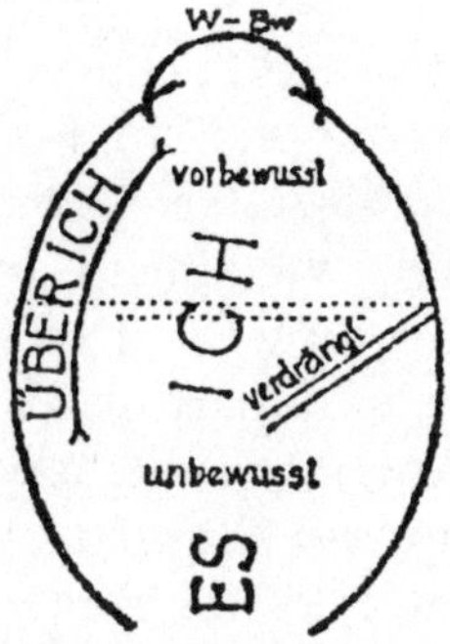

There are even three stages to the schema, if we take into account a letter from Freud to Groddeck in which something analogous had already been sketched.[18]

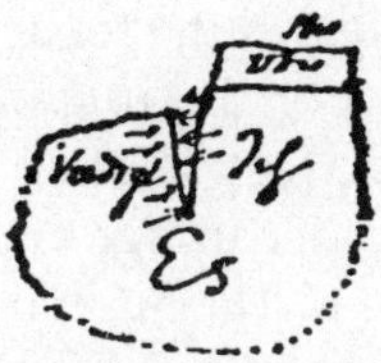

What Freud tells us in one of these texts is that the psychical apparatus is 'open at its end to somatic influences.' Now, you can immediately see that the difference (apart from the question of shape—amoeboid or ovoid—which is not really the principal problem) is that one of the schemas is open at its bottom end.

What is inside this apparatus? I would like to remind you that what typifies representations in psychoanalysis is that they are superimpositions, over-printings of completely heterogeneous domains which no reasonable person would dream of even showing on the same piece of paper. The body appears in the same schema as repression, as the ego, as the unconscious, as words, as the brain, as morality, as the id, etc. You perhaps recall the list from Borges which gives Foucault so much pleasure in the preface to *The Order of Things* (Foucault 1970: xv-xx), which places all possible animals on exactly the same plane, in a way that triggers both laughter and anxiety. Let me quote some of them: animals belonging to the emperor, embalmed animals, animals drawn with a very fine camel-hair brush, etc., etc. Well, it is precisely this way of laying down, in the same schema, things that should not be there, this anti-rational, anti-Cartesian procedure, which thumbs its nose at any distinction between the domains of being. It is precisely this laying things out on a single sheet of paper which is the method prescribed in *The Interpretation of Dreams*. A particular detail of a dream, the dream as a whole, the affect provoked by the dream, the reaction of the subject when telling the dream—all are treated on the same plane, as possible points of departure for associations.

Now, if this method achieves some convincing results, then we have to suppose that something, on the side of whatever constructed the dream, is of the same type—that is to say, fundamentally, the reality which is the basis of the work of interpretation is probably a sort of 'putting into the same bag' of completely heterogeneous things. 'Into the same bag . . . ' We encounter here the famous bag of the id again. One might well wonder—in this case—whether the psychical apparatus is not a sort of 'projection',[19] in itself perfectly anomalous; not a projection *partes extra partes*, but a projection which mixes everything up, the most heterogeneous realities, in the locus of the id. You can see that to say, for example, that the id or the unconscious is the locus of language, is to go ahead a little too fast. Certainly, language itself is found in the id, represented among other things and on the same plane as the other things. (I refer you again to *The Interpretation of Dreams*: language in the dream, linguistic representations of the dream, have no priority or superiority over the others. They are referred directly, not to the whole body of language or to linguistic structure, but to the moment on the previous day when the phrase, which returns in the dream, was pronounced). Nonetheless, perhaps this laying out is not entirely anomalous, nor doubtless as poetic, as that of Borges in *The Chinese Encyclopaedia*. I mean that this laying out, in spite of everything, has its laws. These can be designated as laws of 'derivation' (just now I was talking of 'projection') or even laws of 'representation' (*Vertretung or Repräsentanz*)—that is to say, laws of delegation.

Representation: its line is not univocal

This term 'representation' or 'delegation' is applied by Freud to the presence of the body in the id. The line along which this representation takes place is obviously the opening at the base of the second schema. Apparently, then, we are in the midst of the problem of body and soul: the apparatus—or indeed the id—would open on to impulses of somatic origin. Groddeck, the inventor of the It, refused to acknowledge this distinction between body and mind, psychic and somatic. Where Groddeck unified, we can say with certainty that Freud drew distinctions—but not, however, in the same way as Descartes. Doubtless one could find similarities with Descartes, for instance by saying that the drive, 'a concept at the frontier between the psychical and the somatic', thus the point of articulation between body and mind, might perhaps be analogous to the famous 'pineal gland'. But what we find in Freud is that there is never *only one* line of articulation. Instead, we are in the presence of a series of interlocking parts, so that the border, at the bottom end of the Freudian schema, is impossible to trace. Let us be clear on this point: as far as the drive is concerned, we have a double formulation of the relation of representation. It is stated, concurrently, that the drive is the psychical representative of forces which are in the service of the body but also, on the other hand, that the drive itself, in order to become psychical, has to find representatives in the psyche.

I believe that the best way to approach the question of the drive and of the body in the id is to set out from that which seems to be most directly linked with the functioning of any living body, of any organism. I mean the tendency to stay alive: self-preservation.

Presence of the body: where can hunger be situated?

Where, then, can self-preservation be situated in relation to the id? How does hunger (to take the main vector of self-preservation) enter into the apparatus? Hunger features rarely in Freud's writing, as is shown by the index of the *Standard Edition*. Even where you find a passage about hunger, in the vast majority of quotations you will notice that it is only present as a metaphor. It appears not directly as an urge to feed oneself in order to preserve one's being, but in the form of oral greed. With this, we are already in an entirely different register, since oral greed can and does bear on plenty of things other than food, and, even when it does aim at food, we know that it lends it plenty of other meanings. Yet hunger, in the proper, direct, non-metaphorical sense, was present from the very beginnings of Freud's work, notably in the passage of the 'Project for a Scientific Psychology' which enumerates the major needs that make the neuronal machine function. It is a truly astonishing passage since it first describes, as functioning autonomously, an apparatus with its own principle of functioning, a *non-vital* apparatus—since it is limited to evacuating the entire quantity of energy . In this fiction, it is only secondarily, as a *secondary complication*, that stimulations coming from within the organism would intervene:

> The principle of inertia is, however, broken through from the first owing to another circumstance. With an [increasing] complexity of the interior [of the organism], the nervous system receives stimuli from the somatic element itself—endogenous stimuli—which have equally to be discharged. These have their origins in the cells of the body and give rise to the major needs: hunger, respiration, sexuality. From these the organism cannot withdraw as it does from external stimuli . . . (Freud 1950: 296-7)

Physiological regulation

This list, in itself, is interesting: 'hunger, respiration, sexuality'. We shall perhaps see why respiration is included in a moment. At the end of the nineteenth century, the neurophysiology of these major needs was beginning to be well understood. The regulatory cycles of the organism were being very accurately described, as well as the systems of self-regulation in which these major needs are inscribed. Self-preservation, it was then discovered, is precisely, first of all the maintenance of a certain number of organic constants—for example, the level of oxygen or of carbon dioxide in the blood. The need (this is a system Freud describes very precisely, but without inventing anything) does nothing else but signal a disturbance of one of these constants—the fact, for instance, that the glucose level in the blood has deviated from its margin of normal variation, between 0.80 g and 1.20 g. Beyond this margin, the disturbance is signalled by a need. Or again, too high a level of carbon dioxide in the blood is signalled by another need: to activate the respiratory system.

Thus, the response to the disturbance of a constant is what Freud calls a 'specific action' which re-establishes equilibrium: the taking of nourishment or a drink, or again, the acceleration of breathing. What should be noted is that this specific action is not necessarily, or even often, an intentional behaviour, nor even one that passes via the psyche. To be sure, the satisfaction of need provokes a modification of relational life, a new orientation of the animal in its natural world. Feeding comes about through a deliberate action (we won't use the term 'consciousness' here) of the animal in seeking food. But respiration, as we know, is to a large extent regulated automatically, and it is only in moments of crisis that there is consciousness of a need for respiration. Other regulatory mechanisms, such as that of glucose levels by the pancreatic secretion of insulin, completely elude consciousness and, *a fortiori*, any deliberate action on the part of the subject. Why *three* major needs? Hunger and sexuality, fine! It is classical and literary to affirm that mankind is spurred on by these needs. But why add respiration in particular, giving it priority over so many other physiological regulatory systems? It is probably as a kind of homage to the important work of Breuer in this domain, and particularly to his discovery of the ganglion (called 'Breuer and Hering's') which is situated in the wall of the carotid, and which, like the receiver of a thermostat, constantly provides a measurement of the level of carbon dioxide in the blood, commanding, in a purely reflex action, the necessary speeding up of the respiratory rate and of the heart rate.

Let us return to the distinction we outlined just now, between automatic, reflex regulatory mechanisms—such as the one Breuer devoted himself to describing in respiration—and regulatory mechanisms that pass through the sense of need, such as hunger. This highlights that the borders between these two types of specific action are poorly defined. In the cycle of the thermostat, the moment when a psychical, or rather conscious, action must intervene is not simply the moment of imbalance (the thermostat is there to restore the balance) but the moment of pain. Mere imbalance of blood gases causes respiration to speed up. The moment when this imbalance becomes painful, there is a sensation of asphyxia; the subject rushes to the window and smashes the glass . . .

Self-preservation in psychoanalysis: the constancy and development of its status

What is the psychoanalytic status of this self-preservation which I have outlined once again? In Freud, this status certainly suffers variations. I am not saying that Freudian thought is absolutely clear: in a body of thought which evolved, and in a terminology which is not always unambiguous, we have to try to find a degree of coherence. Whether it is described as need (*Bedurfnis*) or, most often, as drive, it is always the case, if drive there is, that self-preservation is opposed (at least in terms of one of its major characteristics) to the sexual drive. This concerns the predetermined existence of an aim—a cycle of consumption, as ethologists would say—and of an object, or a type of object, which is very precise. Hunger is not addressed to just any type of object. Here we have a distinction which is still affirmed within the (too) general framework of the *Trieb*:

> The sexual drives are noticeable to us for their plasticity, their capacity for altering their aims, their replace-ability, which admits of one instinctual satisfaction being replaced by another, and their readiness for being deferred, . . . We should be glad to deny these characteristics to the self-preservative drives, and to say of them that they are inflexible, admit of no delay, are imperative in a very different sense and have a quite other relation to repression and to anxiety. (Freud 1933: 97)[20]

Thus, on the one hand, self-preservation will always be denominated *Trieb*, but with particularities which will continue to be affirmed. However, on the other hand, and this is a point which is equally important, the status of this self-preservative drive (which in the meantime has become hunger . . . respiration has faded away . . .) was to evolve in Freudian psychoanalysis. Until 1915, it was presented as taking part in conflict—that is to say, Freud attempted the impossible, to show that all psychical conflict stems from the fact that the subject *defends himself against his sexuality because it threatens the continuation of his life*. This is not unthinkable, and has been maintained by non-psychoanalysts, by theoreticians of behavioural psychology. To think that, ultimately, sexuality is suppressed via the intermediary of the threats of upbringing, parental threats and threats from the environment, is to say that if you satisfy your sexuality completely you are risking your life (obviously through the intermediary of parental threats). This has, then, a certain appearance of coherence—at any rate if one 'shifts down' a little, because it is obvious that the child does not risk his life every time he masturbates, and it is thus only through the intermediary of the threats that the risk to life looms so large.

Now, what happens? In psychoanalysis—that is to say, in the experience of psychoanalytic treatment—we see that this opposition between self-preservation and sexuality fails, because it is useless to account for the least neurotic conflict. So, can we say that after 1915 or 1920 every consideration of self-preservation disappears? I do not think it is that simple, and I have tried on numerous occasions to show that the fate of self-preservation is multiple. Firstly, it disappears from the psychoanalytic field proper. Secondly, it is made vicarious, represented (*vertretet*), if you like, in the psychoanalytic field. Thirdly, it necessarily remains present on the fringes of the psychoanalytic field. By 'the psychoanalytic field', I mean very precisely that with which analysis deals in psychoanalytic treatment.

16 January 1979

Today, I am going to finish with what we term 'self-preservation'. Last time, I mentioned its most exemplary aspect, physiological homeostasis, but obviously the domain in question is much larger. Everything connected with adaptation can, in a certain sense, be called homeostatic. The homeostasis of a human being and his environment—this is what for many psychologists, and perhaps for some psychoanalysts, the essence of the problem of adaptation entails. I would like to remind you of a work which is not yet entirely forgotten, and which only needs to be brought back into the foreground. It is the work of Hartmann, whose title alone speaks volumes: *Ego Psychology and the Problem of Adaptation* (1958). That is to say, an entire aspect of analytic theory has developed around this notion of adaptation, which obviously has little to do with Freud. Adaptivity, then, is not just maintaining one's blood glucose levels (by means of the regulatory mechanisms I was talking about last time), but it is also making progress in a career, earning a living, even choosing a partner, taking part in some politico-social activity, or driving, with due care and attention, one's *auto*mobile . . . Of course, none of these examples is purely adaptive, but it is precisely because of their adaptive aspect that they are outside the field of psychoanalysis and outside the id—if we hang on to this image of the id as a container whose contents we are trying to ascertain.

Adaptivity expelled from the field of psychoanalysis

Adaptivity (or self-preservation) disappears from the field of psychoanalysis, and is substituted by something else in the field of psychoanalysis—but necessarily remains present on the fringes of that field. Let us briefly recapitulate these main points.[21]

Disappearing from the psychoanalytic field means disappearing from two places: firstly, from Freud, and then from the reality of psychoanalysis. The disappearance from Freud was historical, in the most historical kind of history, but it is not without interest in so far as one can always wonder whether the order of Freud's discovery did not have something to do with what was discovered. Thus, in 1914 (let me remind you very briefly), with the text on narcissism, the drives of self-preservation disappear from the field of theory or psychoanalytic interest, to the advantage of what has been termed a monism of the libido, through the intermediary of a new expression—a new factor called 'ego libido'. Then, around 1920-1923, when the new locus of the drives, the id, is described, we no longer find drives of self-preservation explicitly and autonomously featured there. This is clearly history at its most superficial, as it is equally superficial to wonder, as Freud sometimes does, with a view to simply classifying things, which of the new categories of drives (life drives and death drives) would include or subsume the former self-preservative drives. The question, moreover, is so misguided when put in this way, that it can be given opposing answers—that is to say, Freud will successively rank the ego drives on the side of the death drive, and then on that of the life drives. You can see that here we are way off the mark: there is something amiss; this is not the way to put the question.

Adaptivity substituted in the psychoanalytic field

So, the second point: the drive of self-preservation is replaced within the field of psychoanalysis. The substituting organism is the ego. The ego itself is in a complex but fairly direct relation to the organism, since it is conceived of as, at once, an *apparatus of the organism* (that is, a differentiation, the part charged with the organism's relations to the external world) but also as a projection of the organism, that is as itself *a little organism*, a double. Doubling the interests of the organism, being in charge of them: that is what we mean by 'substituting'. However, the ego—and this is the fundamental discovery of the text on narcissism—from now on is animated not directly by a physiological, vital energy (as we might be led to believe by the fact that it presents itself as a sort of vital organ), but is sustained, swollen by the drives of the id. The ego can be loved (this is precisely the concept of 'ego libido'), but it can also be hated (we will have to consider this in connection with the death drive). In any case, the love of the ego is the link necessary, in man, for him to be able to struggle to keep himself alive. This is not to say that the ego is necessary for him to live psychologically, in the narrowest sense of the term. We know that an organism which has lost the love of life can keep itself alive, or can be kept alive more or less artificially. It is a question, therefore, of life in its relational aspect, and not in its most elementary aspects.

Thus it becomes possible to make a first approach towards, or a first approximation of what is called psychical 'conflict', which is not—therefore—a conflict of adaptation (although Freud thought at one point that it was, as certain psychoanalysts still do). Quite simply, it is defined thus:

The first complication is soon added to this—that, on the one hand, the ego only functions if it is invested with energy, fuelled by the drives and, on the other hand, that in the heart of the drives themselves an antagonism re-appears, essentially that between the life drives and the death drives. Also, just to make things even more complicated, one of the two categories of drives possibly has a privileged relation with the ego.

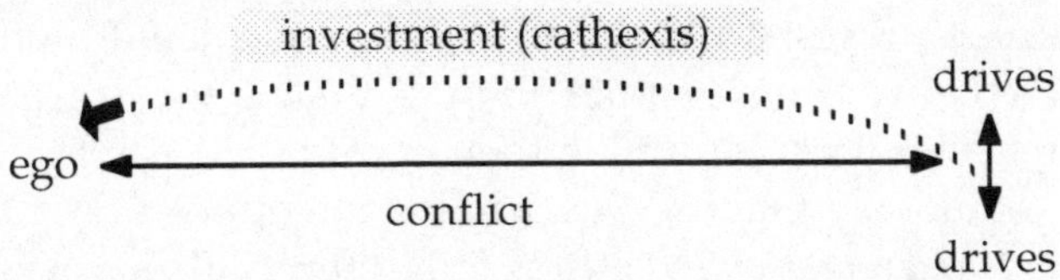

Adaptivity on the fringes of the field: three examples

Alongside these provisional schemas, it is the problem of the limits of the analytic field which preoccupies us. We could say that self-preservation is always present on the fringes, at the border, but only actually enters the field by proxy. I would like to offer quickly three examples of such situations.

First of all, the classical analytic situation, where we know that reality, adaptation, 'external' conditions are so often put forward as that which the analyst refuses (wrongly, it is said) to take into account. 'One has to live', says the patient (a schematic patient; this is a composite image, because *all* patients talk like that). 'My professional obligations mean I have to go away on such and such a day, so I won't be at such and such a session.' Often, also, to mark—as if symbolically—that it is not part of the analysis, that is it 'outside', and that nothing more can be said about it, this absence will be announced outside the session—as the patient arrives or is leaving—as if it were something which could only be part of harsh reality.

Actually the patient, the one being analysed, is both wrong and right. Certainly, he is right to say that—in a sense—there is nothing to discuss, it is not 'treatable'. The fact that you have professional obligations and are at the mercy of train timetables which don't allow you to come to a session cannot be discussed—indeed, except on the level . . . of a train timetable; or perhaps in terms of the patient's relations to his professional organisation, to its hierarchy. However, even there, if we are talking about the relation to a professional hierarchy, we run the risk of becoming caught up in love and hate—that is to say, in interpretation, and re-entering analysis. You can see that this 'one has to live', at whatever level it is presented (the level of my example is extremely simple) is not treatable, or interpretable, or potentially amenable to change, except in the modality of *'for the love of whom'* or *'for the love of what'* are you living?

Well, of course, the question that arises in the first example is that of the initial artifice or 'convention'. The analytic field is defined, in a certain way, by precise rules: nothing real is to be considered there on the level of its own reality. But it is quite obvious that, if one has laid down that nothing real should enter into it, then nothing real can come out of it. Here, I am obviously making the case for the opposition. Or again: *primum vivere deinde philosophari* ['first live, then philosophise']; from the moment you have shown the *'vivere'* the door, you now have the luxury in the analysis of *'philosophari'*, or even, which almost comes to the same thing, of 'sexualising', *sexualisari*. We have to allow this objection! We have to admit that analysis in fact reproduces a situation, *produces* a situation, which therefore leaves the problem of adaptation at the door, in the strict sense of the phrase. This is despite the fact that the development of more than one treatment is evidence of the extent to which the limits of adaptation, this *'vivere'*, can actually be modified, the extent to which these limits, which are apparently definitive, fixed in the nature of things, can appear flexible, through a simple change of perspective, even though we thought them fixed. So be it. Nonetheless, the analytic situation is sitting pretty (epistemologically!). It deliberately realises in its *setting*, in its fundamental conventions, a sort of life-size replica of what psychoanalysis, in theory, affirms regarding the life of the drives in the id—that is to say, its de-realised character.

A second example: a child is entrusted to an institution, for play therapy. There are other children in the room, a large 'team' of carers, and an assortment of apparently inoffensive toys. Quite differently from the analytic situation, on the other hand, nothing has been said to the child in the way of preliminary rules—for example, there is no rule about not doing things. At some point in the session, someone gets worried: 'Hey, where's little Peter?' He is found in a corner; he has laid bare an electric cable and he is dead. The judicial enquiry, I suppose, 'will show' that it is inexcusable carelessness to leave a psychotic child alone for a single moment. The analytic work with the team (which is traumatised) continues, nevertheless, and they begin to uncover the death-wishes that surrounded the child, death-wishes latent in the family (which obviously will be the first to take them to court), and perhaps death-wishes within the group as well. Where is the reality of the psychical conflict?

To return to my question: is it justified—or is it pure artifice—to place at the borders of our field, and not *within* our field, a direct reference to self-preservation? Naturally, the question of self-preservation will be judged by the police authorities or the judiciary, in order to come to a decision: that there must be a psychologist behind every child, at every moment. The psychoanalyst will say that the accident, real though it was, might perhaps have been avoided if the drive impulses that conditioned it had been more clearly perceived, better elucidated. In any case, you can see that the problem of the function of self-preservation in psychical conflict becomes clearer, freed of the objections relating to the artifices of the classical treatment (analysis provides itself with what it then claims to discover, and excludes on principle that which it refuses to account for).

A third example: the dream. The dream is never presented by Freud as depending on any artificial situation, notably the analytic situation. In *The Interpretation of Dreams*, reference to the analytic *setting* is virtually absent from the majority of dreams, which in any case are often Freud's own dreams, or dreams told to him in everyday life. Of course, the dream itself entails a very specific particularity, which in a sense brings it close to the analytic session—the fact, precisely, of being asleep . . .

Dreams and hunger

Well, as far as this question of self-preservation is concerned, this drive which might appear in the dream as an adaptive drive, we can take our bearings from handy references to 'hunger' which appear in the index. There are ten or so references to the problem of hunger, and more generally, to non-sexual interests in the dream, for what is generally dealt with in these passages are somatic stimuli, the diurnal causes of dreams, or even the most immediate wishes, those which can appear—on a first reading of the dream—to be obvious.

Today I am going to take up three groups of passages which are quite difficult to disentangle from their arguments, particularly in the French edition, because *The Interpretation of Dreams*, almost as much as the *Three Essays*, is a text in which editions from different dates are juxtaposed. In the French edition these additions are not distinguished, and one has to refer to the English edition to get an idea of the evolution of Freud's thought. There are two strands to the latter: on the one hand, a modification of his views on infantile sexuality (you will see with what a curious reversal) and, on the other hand, an evolution of Freud's polemical position *vis-à-vis* his entourage, his environment (a problem of 'adaptation' . . .), in relation to the objection which was endlessly levelled at him, of relating everything back to sexuality—the objection of pansexualism.

Animals and children: simply dreams about food?

Here is the first group of passages, starting with the end of chapter II on 'Dreams as Wish-Fulfilments'. It is an introductory chapter, which speaks of wish-fulfilment without, at first, defining either what type of wish is at stake, sexual or non-sexual, or whether the wish is situated at the unconscious level or not. The chapter finishes with this little sentence, which is certainly rather startling:

> I do not myself know what animals dream of. But a proverb, to which my attention was drawn by one of my students, does claim to know. 'What', asks the proverb, 'do geese dream of?' And it replies, 'Of maize'. The whole theory that dreams are wish-fulfilments is contained in these two phrases . . . It will be seen that we might have arrived at our theory of the hidden meaning of dreams most rapidly merely by following linguistic usage. It is true that common language sometimes speaks, etc. (Freud 1900: 131-2)

So we are sent back to the everyday, ordinary meaning of the word 'dream': 'I should never have imagined such a thing in my wildest dreams'. What, then, is discovered in *The Interpretation of Dreams* if all it does is prove that we dream of what we want to have? What is more, it is *hunger* that is taken as the model here, with the fowl's dream of food. The whole of the end of this third chapter reports dreams which are supposed to be transparent, the dreams of children. In particular, to return to hunger, the famous dream of Anna Freud, aged 19 months who, kept without food all day, cries out in her sleep: 'Anna Fweud, stwawbewwies, wild stwawbewwies, omblet, pudden!' Freud comments as follows on this phenomenon:

> At the time she was in the habit of using her own name to express the idea of taking possession of something. The menu included pretty well everything that must have seemed to her to make up a desirable meal. The fact that strawberries appeared in it in two varieties was a demonstration against the domestic health regulations. It was based on the circumstance, which she had no doubt observed, that her nurse had attributed her indisposition to a surfeit of strawberries. She was thus retaliating in her dream against this unwelcome verdict. (Freud 1900: 130)

The commentary continues in a rather astonishing fashion:

> Though we think highly of the happiness of childhood because it is still innocent of sexual desires, we should not forget what a fruitful source of disappointment and renunciation, and consequently what a stimulus to dreaming, may be provided by the other of the two great vital instincts [that is to say, hunger]. (Freud 1900: 130)

Are children's dreams of the 'infantile' type?

This is a passage which attracted the attention of the publishers of the *Standard Edition*, to the point that they saw in it something like the archaeological trace of a fairly old draft of *The Interpretation of Dreams*, at a time when Freud had not entirely recognised infantile sexuality, and found himself obliged to bring in 'the other of the two great vital instincts'. Here, indeed, is a note which is inserted to correct this assertion, in 1911, in order to bring the interpretation of infantile dreams more into line with what by then had been discovered in the *Three Essays on Sexuality*:

> A closer study of the mental life of children has taught us, to be sure, that sexual instinctual forces, in infantile form, play a large enough part, and one that has too long been overlooked, in the psychical activity of children. Closer study, too, has given us grounds for feeling some doubt in regard to the happiness of childhood as it has been constructed by adults in retrospect. (Freud 1900: 130 n.2)

So far, nothing very surprising, except that the dreams of childhood which had appeared to be the simplest of dreams, a kind of direct and undisguised fulfilment of alimentary need, have fallen from the primary, essential, prototypical position in which Freud (like the other 'adults') had originally placed them. In 1911, another note accentuates this about-turn:

> The fact should be mentioned that children soon begin to have more complicated and less transparent dreams, and that, on the other hand, adults in certain circumstances often have dreams of a similarly simple, infantile character. The wealth of unexpected material that may occur in the dreams of children of four or five is shown by examples in my 'Analysis of a Phobia in a Five-Year-Old Boy' . . . (Freud 1900: 131 n.1)

And then, still among the additions of 1911, here is the most complete passage, on the subject of an example which is referred to by Freud more than once: the dreams of 'the starving', of people who are subjected to serious privation of food. There are countless reports by hungry explorers of dreams of abundance, of the preparation of a banquet, etc. I will just quote one of them:

> One of us, who had a special gift for attending large luncheon parties during the night, was proud if he was able to report in the morning that he had 'got through a three-course dinner'. (Freud 1900: 131 n.1)

So, now let us highlight the real dialectical reversal that has occurred: these dreams of the starving are presented as dreams 'of the infantile type', in line with the old emphasis which considered the child's dream to be *undisguised* and of a *non-sexual* character. But the basis of this characterisation has, so to speak, crumbled away, since we have seen that the infantile, on the contrary, is also 'disguised', since little children 'soon begin to have more complicated and less transparent dreams'. Sexual = infantile = disguised (or repressed). That is exactly the equation Freud is so keen, in an analysis like that of the 'Rat Man', to reveal to his patient. You see the strange volte-face, since, starting with the animal, we have moved on to the child, considered to have completely simple dreams (dreams of self-preservation, let us say). Then we see, very precisely, the complete opposite, but we continue to maintain the idea that in the adult there might perhaps occur some of these completely simple dreams, dreams of a banquet when we are hungry . . .

Freud dreams of dumplings

Well, with the theme of the banquet when you are hungry, we reach the second passage upon which I wished to comment. It is one of Freud's dreams, the famous 'dream of dumplings', which is analysed by Freud in a complex and exciting way. This is an analysis which has been completed, notably, by Didier Anzieu (1986). Here is the beginning of it:

> Tired and hungry after a journey, I went to bed, and the major vital needs began to announce their presence in my sleep [it is truly the introduction of a so-called dream of self-preservation, a hunger dream]. I dreamt as follows: *I went into a kitchen in search of some pudding. Three women were standing in it; one of them was the hostess of the inn and was twisting something in her hand, as though she was making Knödel (dumplings) . . .* (Freud 1900: 204)

Well, let me invite you to re-read this dream, in which Freud's sexuality appears very soon in the associations and, I would say, quite candidly. Notably in the associations around names, and also in the situation of 'making dumplings', which refers directly to Freud's mother. It is one of the dreams which is analysed in some depth, an exception to Freud's habitual discretion concerning his own sexual drives:

> My dream of the three Fates was clearly a hunger dream. But it succeeded in shifting the craving for nourishment back to a

> child's longing for his mother's breast, and to make use of an innocent desire as a screen for a more serious one which could not be so openly displayed. (Freud 1900: 233)

Anzieu, in his in-depth analysis of this dream, adds, with justification, from a fairly Kleinian perspective, the idea of an elaboration of the fear of death. What is more, the theme of the three Fates, which is clearly mentioned by Freud, obviously leads to the idea of death—or in any case, to death as the loss of the mother. Be that as it may, with regard to what interests us here, you can see that things are clearer from the theoretical point of view: adult desire can appear in multiple forms, possibly even non-sexual ones, including many situations we call adaptive, or self-preservative. Adult desire can occur in many forms in both the field of sexuality and in that of adaptation, but rediscovered infantile desire leads back to the sexual source. I would even add that, in so far as it leads back to the breast, it leads us back not only to the infantile sexual source, but also, in a new twist, to the origins of infantile sexuality in its leaning-on the non-sexual—that is to say, to the birth of oral sexuality leaning-on sucking at the breast.

The duplicity or 'theoretical politics' of Freud

Well, I mentioned a third group of these passages on adaptation and on hunger. These are texts marked by the 'theoretical politics' of Freud's polemics. Their duplicity consists in, on the one hand, affirming the primacy of sexuality in the dream and, on the other, leaving a certain space for manoeuvre *vis-à-vis* the critics. One of the two principal passages is found on page 396 of the *Standard Edition*. It is a text that was written at various times, in 1909, 1911 and 1919—thus, after the original edition:

> The more one is concerned with the solution of dreams, the more one is driven to recognise that the majority of the dreams of adults deal with sexual material and give expression to erotic wishes. A judgement on this point can be formed only by those who really analyse dreams, that is to say, who make their way through the manifest content to the latent dream-thoughts . . . (Freud 1900: 396)

Here, then, is an appeal to analytic experience and no longer a reference to mere manifest content, with which Freud appeared to be satisfied when making use of the children's dreams and also the dreams of 'the starving'. The only judges are those who have experience of analysis, and not the readers armed only with their 'common sense',

> . . . this fact is not in the least surprising but is in complete harmony with the principles of my explanation of dreams. No other instinct has been subjected since childhood to so much suppression as the sexual instinct in its numerous components . . . ; from no other instinct are so many and such powerful unconscious wishes left over, ready to produce dreams in a state of sleep. [And then here is the last little sentence of this passage:] In interpreting dreams we should never forget the significance of sexual complexes, though we should also, of course, avoid the exaggeration of attributing exclusive importance to them. (Freud 1900: 396)

Such prudence, in this warning against 'exaggeration'. 'The Earth goes round', as Galileo would say, 'but we must avoid exaggeration' . . . One might conclude that Freud was risking major excommunication, that his books would be burnt, and that he himself would be delivered to the stake. Again, in 1919, you can read:

> The affirmation that *all dreams require a sexual interpretation*, against which critics rage so incessantly, occurs nowhere in my *Interpretation of Dreams*. It is not to be found in any of the numerous editions of this book and is in obvious contradiction to other views expressed in it. [But then there immediately follows this sentence:] I have already shown elsewhere that strikingly innocent dreams may embody crudely erotic wishes, and I could confirm this by many new instances. (Freud 1900: 397, my emphasis)

This was one of the first passages to show this sort of Freudian navigation, this tacking between contradictory affirmations, without taking into account the true solution brought by the analysis of the *Knödel* dream. Certainly, the most varied everyday wishes, or even the stimuli of hunger and thirst during the night, may be at the origin of a dream, but they will necessarily reawaken infantile desires, which themselves are sexual.

Rank: theoretical scapegoat

Here, then, is the second passage, in which Freud singles out a theoretical scapegoat. There is, at the end of the chapter on distortion in dreams, a note which Freud seems to value very highly, since he wrote and re-edited it in 1911, then in 1914, and then again in 1925. It is a commentary on a phrase in the text underlined by Freud and offered by him as 'the formula in which we have sought to express the nature of dreams': *'a dream is a (disguised) fulfilment of a (suppressed or repressed) wish.'* Here is the 1911 note:

> I shall anticipate questions which will be discussed later by quoting at this point Otto Rank's enlargement and modification of the above basic formula: 'On the basis and with the help of repressed, infantile sexual material, dreams regularly represent present-day, and also as a rule erotic, wishes as fulfilled, in a veiled and symbolically disguised shape'. (Freud 1900: 160)

This is the *whole* 1911 note, in which Freud cited Rank's formula as a 'development and enlargement' of his own . . . Now here is what he added in 1925, without breaking his stride:

> I have nowhere stated that I adopted Rank's formula [which was presented in the book, from 1911 to 1925, without further comment, as a complement to Freud's own thinking] as my own. The shorter version [that is to say, Freud's formula], as stated in the text above, seems to me adequate. But the mere fact of my having mentioned Rank's modification has been enough to unleash countless accusations against psychoanalysis of having asserted that 'all dreams have a sexual content'. (Freud 1900: 160)

The rest of the note is typical of that kind of defence which employs what is known as the 'kettle' argument: (1) I never said what Rank said; I quoted him, but as a 'for instance'; (2) in any case, what Rank says is perfectly defensible—above all, Rank himself has the prudence to cover himself by using the prudent formula 'regularly', which authorises us to suppose that there are exceptions (the disciple, too, knows how to protect himself against 'exaggerations'); (3) as things are in 1925, since from now on we have to deal with both sexual impulses *and* destructive impulses, the question needs to be completely re-examined, and you can see clearly that, as a consequence, I am not as sexualised as people make out.

Hunger cannot be repressed

I will conclude today with this thought: that, in spite of everything, what emerges from *The Interpretation of Dreams*—to take up this interpretative experience of the dream in the light of analytic treatment and also in the light of psychotherapy—is that Rank's formula isn't all that bad. *Adult* desire, which takes hold of the dream, is often sexual, but it may also be non-sexual. The infantile desire evoked by this adult desire is, itself, always sexual. Why? Well, because only sexuality presented the conditions for being repressed and *hunger cannot be repressed.* We do not have a single example of repressed hunger. Here, I can refer you to another text which is very interesting—to be precise, the 1915 text on 'Repression' (Freud 1915c). Straight away, as a point of principle, Freud wonders why we repress. Is it an imperative demand, as a consequence of the fact that it is painful, that an unsatisfied, tormenting hunger might be repressed because it is painful? Well, no, it is not enough that a demand of the drive (or the instinct—never mind the terminology) should be painful for it to be repressed. Other conditions are necessary, which are present only in sexuality.

23 January 1979

Have a look at Green's *Le discours vivant*—a very important and exhaustive work. Perhaps it is a little dense, but it can be approached via certain passages which directly concern us, on the subject of the id:

> The major difference between the concept of the unconscious and the concept of the id concerns the fact that at the level of the first, the drives of destruction have no place, while at the level of the second, not only do they have a determined place, but their role is held to be dominant. (Green 1973: 247, LT's translation)

Or again:

> The concept of the id, in so far as it replaces the concept of an unconscious (in the final analysis, something always organised and structured), tends precisely to recognise at the heart of this agency those blind, opaque forces, inaccessible to exploration, even more 'wild' than those which were revealed at the level of the unconscious, even more resistant to being tamed. (Green 1973: 246, LT's translation)

First of all, I will set out how far I agree and disagree with this idea that the id is in fact a deepening of the unconscious. As you see, here Green does not really invoke the idea of a biologically primal id: that is not the question.

The id and the death drive: a profound connection

Yes, the id is a deepening of the unconscious and is linked to the death drive. But in my view, the difference is that the death drive itself is not something absolutely new, an unheard-of discovery, but it is *itself* a deepening of sexuality in its most radical aspect. Assuredly, this deepening is linked to new experiences in the clinic and in Freud's reflection and that of analysts. We can cite a number of them: Green recalls the 'negative therapeutic reaction', which is the fact that certain treatments, at the same time as they appear to make progress on the level of elucidation, actually produce regressive results at the level of the very attitude of the subject towards the analysis. There is a sort of stagnation or stalling, which is in direct proportion to the degree of elucidation. This reference to the negative therapeutic reaction can be found in Freud's *Beyond the Pleasure Principle* (1920) but it is not really its central issue. Much later, in the *New Introductory Lectures* (1933), when he returns to this question of the death drive, Freud insists on the novelty—the so-called novelty—of sado-masochism, about which there is obviously a great deal to say: the problem of sado-masochism is not newly discovered in 1919-1920 . . .

Destructiveness: a discovery that goes against sexuality?

Anyway, let us take authors such as the Kleinians—whom we shall have the opportunity to speak about at greater length later on—in particular an article in the collection published under the title *Developments in Psychoanalysis* by Paula Heimann, entitled 'Notes on the Theory of the Life and Death Instincts' (Heimann 1952: 321-337). Here will find the idea that what brings the death drive centre-stage is the discovery or the experience of a destructivity in the pure state, which Heimann ultimately declares to be falsely baptised as 'sexual'. This passage is worth the effort of reading for the reversal it aims to effect. With Freud, until this point, it had been emphasised that people refused to acknowledge sexual motivations for their behaviour. Now the Kleinians claim that the reference to sexuality is itself a defence, a repression, that certain kinds of behaviour are called sexual, which allows one to refuse to see that which is not sexuality.

> It is unnecessary to give instances [the author immediately goes on to give some]. From time to time the world is shocked by reports of savagely cruel, 'bestial' murders committed by an individual or a group. Excessive cruelty is committed, either without any provocation . . . Strangely enough, such behaviour is usually regarded as perverse sexuality, [what a reversal between 1905 and the 1940s—to be able to affirm that it is a defensive banality to call these acts of violence sexual] and often such crimes are called 'sexual crimes' . . . The murdered victim of the so-called sexual crime does not die from a sexual experience, however infantile it may be, but from the infliction of maximally cruel violence. The sexual aspect of the murderer's behaviour may possibly only be introduced in order to deceive the victim and so to provide the opportunity for the aim of the urge to cruelty. Possibly the murderer starts in a state of sexual excitement, which, however, soon subsides and merely serves to open the floodgates to the violent and destructive impulses. It seems that the investigators of these crimes are aware that only the elemental power of an instinct can be their cause, but can only concede to sexuality the character of such an instinctual force. (Heimann 1952: 328-9)

Our conception: a deepening and a re-working

Here, then, is the extreme form of the thesis: that the death drive had been misunderstood, repressed, until its discovery. To situate once again my position in relation to this, let me put it this way: this deepening does not bear primarily on the unconscious, nor on the discovery of a new drive, but on the very field of sexuality and its re-working. To put things schematically, let us say that in the classical account, in that of Freud, when he writes his own history, just as much as in that of Melanie Klein, or Green, there was an unconscious whose essence was represented by sexuality. Then followed a new level of exploration or clinical and theoretical experience, which led to the discovery of the death drive, and to the advancement of an id linked to this death drive. This would be, then, a relatively linear progression, or, in any case, cumulative one. By going deeper a new field was discovered, which was added to the preceding one.

My own idea is rather different. It is a general interpretation of the discovery which, in my view, cannot be located in this way. Let us draw it, as in a cartoon or a film:

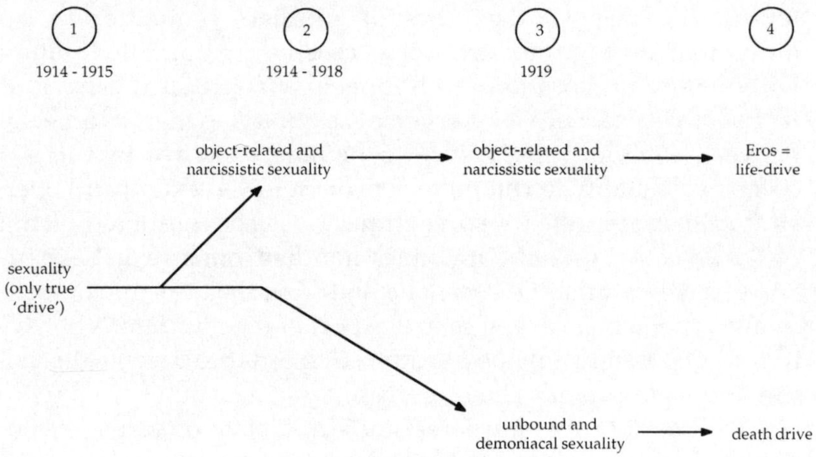

In the first phase, we certainly agree, the point of departure is the primacy of sexuality—above all, around 1915, with the texts on the unconscious and repression. Only sexuality has the right to be called a drive; the only content of the unconscious is sexuality. Then comes the second phase, which is indeed a *discovery*.

A discovery . . . but not where it was thought to be

What was discovered at that time and put forward was not the death drive but, on the contrary, sexuality invested in the object and in the ego—object-love and love of the ego. It is an absolutely new exploration: the ego as object of love, and the idea that external objects are reflections of (or in relation to) this primary investment of the ego, since we love the other according to our own image, or thanks to a potential for love which is first and foremost the potential that makes us capable of loving ourselves.

Sexuality, at this point, tended to be subsumed under this aspect of love. From this came the third phase, that of the 'turning-point', in *Beyond the Pleasure Principle* (1920). Sexuality ran the risk of being entirely monopolised; one risked seeing no more in sexuality than this bound, invested, calm and quiescent aspect. Consequently, in 1919 came the need to reaffirm something that had been lost, that is to say, non-connected sexuality, sexuality that could be described as 'unbound' in the sense of the drive—sexuality that changed its object, having only one aim, which is to move as fast as possible towards satisfaction and the complete appeasement of its desire. In other words, this is the complete realisation of desire via the shortest possible route; thus, at this moment it became necessary to reaffirm something essential in sexuality which had been lost—its demonic aspect, subjugated to the primary process and the repetition compulsion. From this point on, you can see that the content of which sexuality was comprised from the beginning was now split into two aspects, eventually to be regrouped by Freud under the terms 'life drives', or 'Eros', and 'death drives'. Eros does not represent the totality of sexuality, but those of its aspects which were attached to preserving the object, and also to preserving the ego as primary object.

Here, I am only restating things I have been saying for years, and which the diagram perhaps sums up in a slightly clearer fashion. What is the importance of all this, other than its historical aspect? That is a question you might well ask me. I hope we will have the opportunity to come back to this, but I will say right away that in my view it also has consequences with respect to our dualism of the drives—that is, the ultimate dualism between the life drives and the death drives—namely: is it a fundamental, radical dualism, or is it a dualism based on one and the same energy? You can see that it is not without economic—and practical—importance that there should be a single sexual energy which appears at the two opposite poles. It is obviously very important, in the symptom and in the treatment, that one and the same energy can be channelled, as the case may be, into activities following the direction of the life drive, or that of the death drive. This obviously suggests a possibility—for instance, in the treatment—of a transition or a return, from one to the other, but not necessarily in the right direction. Perhaps the negative therapeutic reaction is the passage of energy from the life drive to the death drive?

The death drive has to be interpreted

The id is linked, then, to the death drive. If we want to talk about the death drive and attempt to talk about it in an unambiguous way—'this is what the death drive is'—it is impossible to return to Freud without an interpretation. As for Freud himself, if we look at his words, his successive approximations, we find that he is profoundly contradictory when he wants to trace the history of his own thought, since he affirms two very different things. The first is that the death drive, in his way of thinking, is speculative in origin. This is exactly the point he makes in *Beyond the Pleasure Principle* (1920): it is a speculation, it is an exigency of the system, the consequence of a deepening of the principle of functioning of any drive. A very abstract sort of progress, apparently. But then—suddenly—we find a completely different story, for example in the *New Introductory Lectures* (1933):

> . . . we have argued in favour of a special aggressive and destructive instinct in men . . . on the basis of general considerations to which we were led by examining the phenomena of sadism and masochism. (Freud 1933: 104)

If you look closely at *Beyond the Pleasure Principle*, you will see that there is practically no place for sadism and masochism . . .

So there are some considerable contradictions! Here we find demonstrated the lack of coherence among psychoanalytic views, we witness the clash of 'opinions' in the sense discussed by Plato: one *doxa* has the same value as another, so why this one, and why not that one? This objection, which I am certainly not going to explore, could be even more clearly formulated with regard to Freud's disciples and interpreters. There, too, I think we cannot just leave it at a straightforward clash of opinions. However, I am going to mention a few of them, for how could Freud's interpreters, by which I mean the analysts who came after him, have possibly been in agreement among themselves, when the master was unable to agree with himself?

The master failed to agree with himself to such an extent that he never tried to impose his theory of the death drive at all. You might think that this is quite normal, that people don't try to impose ideas;

well, undeceive yourselves! With Freud, there is no shortage of anathemas and excommunications, nor of shibboleths, those passwords or key-words that you have to know how to utter without blinking, or else you risk being excluded from the community. For instance, you cannot call yourself a psychoanalyst if you do not admit the primacy of sexuality, if you do not accept infantile sexuality, or do not accept the transference; or, of course, if you do not accept the unconscious. Well, it is remarkable that the death drive was never made into a shibboleth. Paula Heimann, in the same article, points this out clearly:

> It is interesting to see how Freud himself hesitated to give full recognition and status, as it were, to his last discovery about the instincts, and yet how he was driven on by its impelling truth to follow his notion of an antithesis as final and cardinal as that between a primary instinct of life and a primary instinct of death. He stressed the hypothetical nature of his theory, never regarded it as a shibboleth of psycho-analysis and merely confessed to a 'cool goodwill' for it. (Heimann 1952: 321-2)

'Cool goodwill' was Freud's own term, as applied to his introduction of the death drive.

Overview of a 'divergence': from refusal . . .

Well, giving an overview would take a long time, and it is not my aim to do so. I will merely cite a few of the directions this divergence took. I am speaking of a divergence in the sense of atomic 'splitting' in a nuclear reactor (I hesitate to call these interpretations), because none of these ways of conceiving of the death drive is without its foundations in the clinic. They are not opinions based on the sheer pleasure of saying something different, but each aims at a certain segment of a reality and sticks upon it (in extreme cases, quite openly) this label 'the death drive'. Alternatively, exploring such a reality, another wonders whether Freudianism did not already have sufficient tools at its disposal to explain such-and-such a new experience.

As far as a refusal of the death drive is concerned, we can mention some of the biggest names in psychoanalysis. Jones, Freud's faithful historian, rejects the hypothesis of the death drive. His sacrilege goes even further, since he claims to show us (for all false theorisations are necessarily anchored in a subject's symptoms) that it was for entirely subjective motives, both in the general climate of thought, and Freud's own unconscious motivations, and both equally situated in this year of 1919, which led Freud to introduce the death drive. Here is a passage which is a blemish on the monument of reverence constituted by *Sigmund Freud: Life and Work*:

> If so little objective support is to be found for Freud's culminating theory of a Death Instinct, one is bound to consider the possibility of subjective contributions to its inception, doubtless in connection with the theme of death itself. (Jones 1957: 300)

After Jones, and on a completely different level, let us mention the name of Reich, who, in his dissidence from Freud, made of the death drive the fatal moment for psychoanalysis, the point at which it finally headed off into repression . I would hardly be exaggerating if I said that, for Reich, it was Freud's fascist moment. Then there is Groddeck, and here there is something of a paradox, since the patron of the notion of the It—a notion which we consider to be most definitely linked with the death drive—radically refuses this idea or, at least, the idea of the dichotomy between the life drive and the death drive. Death plays an important part in Groddeck's thought, but it is death dialectically related to life, and it is also—as you know—the illustration of Goethe's phrase 'die and become', die in order to become, and not that radical death, purely and simply annihilating, which is envisaged by Freud with the death drive.

. . . to reduction

So certain authors rejected the death drive. Those who wished to go further (rejecting a notion is not enough) attempted to reduce the facts Freud had invoked by showing that they all fitted into older frameworks of explanation. On the theoretical plane, this reduction is fairly easy, because it can be shown that Freud's so-called new formulations are re-workings of earlier formulations—the theses of *Beyond the Pleasure Principle* (1920), for instance, are re-workings of certain ideas in the 'Project for a Scientific Psychology' (Freud 1950). As for the clinical, or theoretico-clinical plane—in other words, the taking into account of the repetition compulsion, of sado-masochism, or of the negative therapeutic reaction—well, we might say that in this reduction to an earlier theoretical framework (which avoids the necessity to introduce new concepts) Freud himself had shown the way. Before *Beyond the Pleasure Principle*, we could take a paper such as 'Instincts and their Vicissitudes' (1915b), where it is demonstrated that so-called aggressivity is, perhaps, in reality, the 'aggressive' character of all drives, a way of hypostatising this active and aggressive aspect. But above all the meaning of *Beyond the Pleasure Principle*—the whole of its first chapter—consists in trying to explain the phenomenon of repetition, using nothing but earlier 'tools'. Is it not possible, after all, thanks to the earlier conceptual apparatus, to bring back into line the facts which apparently contradict the pleasure principle? But then there is also something very odd: even after the introduction of the death drive, in a text such as *The Ego and the Id* (1923a), Freud declares that it was introduced for speculative reasons, and that if one look for traces of it in reality and in the clinic, then one will never find it—at least, not in its pure state. It is, he tells us, 'silent', whereas 'the clamour of life proceeds for the most part from Eros' (Freud 1923a: 46).

There are two examples of this 'reduction', in which Freud himself thus showed the way. In France: Nacht. In America: Fenichel. Nacht, with his first text *Le masochisme* (1971a), and then a later text which took up the same ideas: 'Manifestations cliniques de l'aggressivité' (in Nacht 1966). Let me quote a few passages:

> The results of observation demonstrate sufficiently well, as much in man as in the animals (Cannon, Massermann and others) that the aptitude for aggressive reaction of all living creatures is a result of the constant tendency to eliminate that which, through its state of excitation, and thus of tension, would disturb the equilibrium/repose of the organism. (Nacht 1966: 50, LT's translation)

Thus, aggressivity is a necessary form of activity, it is the active aspect of the activity undertaken by an organism to restore its equilibrium. He goes on:

> The fundamental biological principle which tends toward the suppression of any tension felt by the organism as displeasure or suffering is manifest not only by reactions of defence against the source of this displeasure, but also by reactions suitable for eliminating the excitation responsible for the tension, which from then on leads to pleasure . . . Thus, to avoid dissatisfaction, as

> much as to obtain the satisfaction of needs—*briefly, in order to live*—aggressivity comes into play. It is present in diverse forms in most of the actions of existence . . . It is in displeasure, in dissatisfaction or suffering, that aggressivity seems to find its source. Well, displeasure, dissatisfaction, in a word, the partial frustration of instinctual needs, constantly mark the development of the human being in civilised societies . . . This report will thus be centred on the notion of *aggressivity*, the *result of frustration*. (Nacht 1966: 50-1, LT's translation)

In principle, this reasoning is very simple, but it has some fundamental consequences: firstly, that aggressivity is present in every drive. This was the typically Freudian thesis before 1919. Secondly, that this aggressivity is laid bare—one might say—in the state of frustration at the moment when it no longer seems to act simply for itself, having forgotten its aims, but in order purely and simply to destroy the obstacle. This is the moment at which—if you like—it becomes hatred. It is a very astute theory, not at all simplistic, and in particular it incorporates what Freud—and other authors after him—attempted to bring to light: a sort of passive, latent masochism, a masochism which seems to expand of its own accord. It is a masochism which Nacht at times calls 'organic', but which he tries to show, nonetheless, is always secondary.

The drive to die

Just now I cited Fenichel. We could cite the whole of Anglo-Saxon, and particularly American, psychoanalysis, at least up to a certain date. In these authors, in Fenichel, the situation is fundamentally the same. In any case, let us say that there is a refusal of Freud's essential thesis affirming that the death drive is, initially, directed not outwards (as aggressivity) but towards the subject; that it is absolutely not a drive to cause death, but a *drive to die*, or to *cause oneself to die*. Having rejected that idea, one might well admit external aggressivity, at the level of clinical practice, as an independent given which becomes more and more important, taking up a more and more prominent position in the treatment. This occurred to such an extent that analysis in those countries, during the period from 1930 to 1940, became the analysis of aggressivity, but without anyone feeling the need to formulate hypotheses concerning the ultimate question of the 'metaphysics' of this aggressivity.

As you know, the American authors, and the Anglo-Saxons in general, have little but disdain for problems of 'theory', even of metapsychology. Aggressivity may be the prerogative of all drives, but it doesn't really matter whether it is created by frustrations or simply 'revealed' by them. It is a scholastic debate, because frustrations are there from the beginning. The apparent acceptance of this discovery—or this apparent discovery—of aggressivity in Freudianism, leads to an widespread deflation of the analysis of sexuality. In a sense, this could be considered a powerful return of Adlerism, a return to what Freud had himself rejected at the time when he was criticising the idea of a drive of aggression: that is to say, the notion that the essence of psychical conflict is quite simply a conflict concerning the struggle for existence.

Modalities of 'rallying'

To return to the history of the movement, one might say that in relation to the death drive there was at first a tendency, among the old guard, or at least a part of the analytic old guard, towards a rejection of the very idea. There was, and still is, an attitude which watered down the death drive (the analysis of 'aggressivity'). Nowadays, and perhaps above all in France, there is a sort of fashionable acceptance or re-affirmation of the death drive. I will mention three modalities of this re-affirmation because, even if one claims to give the death drive its place, things are not so coherent, the various aspects are not so easy to synthesise.

Nirvana and Epicureanism

The first modality emphasises the aspect of the reduction of tensions, which can be summed up in the single word 'Nirvana', a term taken directly from Hindu philosophy. Effectively, a certain aspect of Freud's thinking owes a great deal to Hinduism: the idea that existing, desiring, is ultimately the worst of all evils. To exist in a state of desire is the very worst of all, and one must reach the state of non-desiring being, through the best possible means, through the strictest discipline. We are speaking of Hinduism, but we could equally well think of Epicureanism which, in its true sense, aims at nothing but the death of desire. This aspect, which is sometimes called the death drive, has its models in clinical experience (more evidently than the tendency to resolve conflicts, or to reduce the excitation inherent in pleasure) in those cases where the avoidance of conflict predominates, the seeking out of situations where excitation cannot even reach you.

A few examples: the *obsessive*, about whom it is said, not without reason, that he installs death in his life, he 'plays dead', that he creates for himself a sort of shell precisely so that these excitations cannot reach him directly, but only in a filtered form, completely reconstituted. Excitations are taken up into a system that aims to deaden them ('to deaden' is to put a sort of cushion in their way, so as ultimately to reach a state close to death). There is also *moral masochism*—taken in the sense of the state of stagnation discussed by Nacht—which is not the race towards pain of perverse masochism, but a masochism which, on the contrary, seeks out situations of passivity.

Along these lines of interpretation, I will quote Lagache, who in his papers on masochism tends to reduce it not to the seeking of pain as in erogenous masochism—a Dionysian, frenzied search for pain, itself so closely related to the drive—but rather to something it would be quite wrong to call by the same name, the search for pure and simple passivity. Lagache shows that this dimension of passivity is a fundamental dimension of life. From birth, but above all afterwards, activity can be divided into two opposing psychological tendencies, which Lagache calls the tendency to reduce tensions and the tendency to realise possibilities. In this general psychological opposition, we see (in passing) that sexuality has rather disappeared from the horizon.

Let us note, however, that the idea of the reduction of tensions is perhaps on its own inadequate to account for what Lagache is aiming at with his idea of a fundamental passivity. The reduction of tensions is inscribed in a vital rhythm: possibilities are realised, which themselves create new tensions which have to be reduced. Then, again, there is a new possibility which is accepted, and so it goes on . . . But, on the contrary, 'the avoidance of tensions' short-circuits this vital circuit. It is a way (to take up an expression of Freud's) of running towards death by the shortest route, without accepting the alternations of tension and relaxation, of pleasure and unpleasure, which constitute the core of the opposition described by Lagache.

To remain within this first perspective, which is to place the death drive on the side of Nirvana—in other words, of a short-circuit of psychical conflict—it is interesting to cite another text by an author I mentioned just now: Nacht. In a passage from *Guerir avec Freud*, all of a sudden he displays doubts about his own theory. I have always developed arguments—he says (to paraphrase him)—to show why the death drive did not seem to me to be necessary to account for what happens in clinical practice. However, there are some cases which can be quite unsettling in this regard. If there is something that resembles the death drive, here are two cases which perhaps might justify the hypothesis: they are two cases of suicide which appear to be profoundly related to the drive, inscribed in a destiny (Nacht 1971b: 39-40). This way of speaking about the death drive, of allowing oneself to be unsettled by clinical evidence which cannot be reduced to theory, is very much the way Freud introduced the repetition compulsion or the 'fate' neurosis. All these facts could be reduced and explained, but in spite of everything something is left out, an impression, a final irreducible element, which provokes us into looking for another explanation.

Be that as it may, this 'Nirvana-like' or Epicurean interpretation of the death drive could in a certain sense fit in with one of the aspects of the Freudian death drive. But in other respects, it must be admitted that it corresponds very little to the violent, brutal, frenetic appearance taken on in Freud by the kind of fury of destruction and pain he attributes to the death drive. In other words, Nirvana (even the Nirvana of the suicide) and destructiveness make an uneasy couple. How can we conceive of a desire for inner peace—even if it is the peace of the cemetery—when it is directed outwards, is transformed into a violent desire to destroy, to cause suffering, to break and crush?

Confronted with these apparently simple aspects of 'death in life' in the obsessional, or in the moral masochism of the eternally dominated, the eternal dogsbody, one is right to wonder whether analysis does not express a slight repugnance. That is to say, having spent years working methodically on symptoms, on cases, to show that they are not what they think they are (that is the very essence of analysis: to show that the immediate impression is deceptive), all of a sudden an analyst yields, for a moment, to an immediate impression. Here, it is the immediate impression of stagnant water, of dreamless sleep, of a suicide driven by no phantasy other than that of peace, the silence of the depths. This sudden acceptance of abandoning oneself to the illusion of the impression, this sort of temptation of repose and—it must be said—the momentary abandonment of the analytic tool, can be found, as much as in Nacht, in a well-known article by Winnicott: 'Fear of Breakdown' (1989). I would link this article to Nacht's because of the sudden incursion of a temptation, that of the immediately obvious. However, if the feeling of obviousness is not to be dismissed, it is to be taken as a *feel-*

ing, as an index of our resonance with something; but it would not be a sign of the simplicity of the phenomenon. The whole of psychoanalysis—like any science—is constructed in opposition to the obvious.

Another modality, the second,[22] of accounting for the death drive, can be found in Kleinianism, and in the next lecture we will refer to one of Melanie Klein's later articles, 'On the Theory of Anxiety and Guilt' (Klein et al. 1952 [1948]).

30 January 1979

With Melanie Klein

Melanie Klein. I suppose everyone is familiar with the essentials of her thinking, which at first sight seems fairly simple, because it relies on the interplay of a small number of concepts. If you are not careful, all her writings have the air of saying the same thing, the theoretical texts and also the interpretations. On this question of interpretation we can turn to Dayan's article, entitled 'Madame K. interpréta' (1977), where this technique of interpreting is clearly demonstrated. Concerning the principal concepts, we just have to look at Klein's writings and *Developments in Psychoanalysis* (Klein et al. 1952). These are texts which, if they are approached in a closer and more 'historical' fashion, may well add nuances to our initial impression of uniformity.

I will take anxiety as my point of departure. It is a central concept in Melanie Klein's work and essential for our study of the id, because perhaps the only way to speak of the id is to envisage the way that it affects us, that it affects the ego. Perhaps, after all, the bag of the id—the famous bag drawn in several of Freud's diagrams—is just the bag of the ego? The way in which the inside of this bag is affected by the id is precisely through anxiety.

What is interesting about Klein's 1948 article entitled 'On the Theory of Anxiety and Guilt' (Klein 1952a) is that we find in it something which goes beyond the schematic opposition between paranoid anxiety and depressive anxiety. Furthermore, we find in it a reflection which takes us further in the attempt to grasp the foundations of the Freudian death drive.[23] Ultimately, these are views centred on a truthful enough apprehension of the choices that have to be made, in Freudianism, concerning anxiety.

I do not intend to go into detail about what I said on the subject myself a few years ago, starting from the basis of the theory that Melanie Klein herself took up, known as Freud's 'first' theory, a theory of anxiety as transformed libido, as a last form or avatar of libido. I will only return very briefly to the possible interpretation of Freud's thought and of, roughly, his crucial development (I say 'roughly' because I completely agree with Melanie Klein's demonstration that this development is not quite as fundamental as some would say). It is a development which, nevertheless, pivots around the 1926 text *Inhibitions, Symptoms and Anxiety*, with its innovation of an anxiety termed 'anxiety-signal', triggered by the ego. In this idea of an anxiety-signal, there is something artificial *vis-à-vis* the very notion of affect. The fact that signals are used—let us say 'by the ego', if we wish to keep to this way of describing things—to signpost anxiety, is particularly obvious in phobia. Maybe even castration is merely one of these signals destined to signpost anxiety? (Although here I am just putting out a feeler!) However, the ego triggers anxiety as a signal at its convenience . . . I would say that, when this theory appears, one wonders whether Freud had encountered anxiety in the clinic. If we leave out this theory of the anxiety-signal—which we might describe as rather unfortunate—then what we have in 1926 are more like clarifications (which we can perform with Freud, and continue beyond him) than a real transformation.

Clarification of the question of anxiety

Let us quickly list these clarifications—first of all, concerning the 'location' of anxiety, and the so-called 'id anxiety' which was supposed to be opposed to 'ego anxiety'. My way of formulating this clarification is as follows: all anxiety belongs to both the id *and* the ego; it originates in the id, but the ego is where it is produced. A second clarification concerns the relation between repression and anxiety. As you know, the 'first' theory claimed, in a fairly dogmatic manner, that anxiety was the result of repression. From this arises the apparent contradiction: is it anxiety that provokes repression, or repression that provokes anxiety? Essentially, the choice was made in 1926, that it is indeed anxiety which is the motive of repression, and not the other way round. But obviously there are nuances. First of all, we have to wonder what happens with primary repression; is the situation the same? However, it is clear, in spite of everything, that repression can break down the affects bound up with the events on which it has a bearing, turning them into anxiety. Lastly, the final clarification concerns the very idea of a 'transformation' of libido into anxiety. To describe anxiety as transformed libido is a formulation somewhat lacking in rigour. The libido is a theoretical and energetic concept—as such, it cannot be perceived directly. Anxiety, by contrast, is an *affect*, and it can perfectly easily be the way, or one of the ways, that the libido affects me—in other words, affects the ego.

Well, what Melanie Klein emphasises in the first part of her article is precisely that this fundamental theory, linking anxiety to the libidinal attack, was perpetuated by Freud beyond the avatars of the signal, particularly in the *New Introductory Lectures*, a text written by Freud after 1926:

> In the *New Introductory Lectures*, referring to the theory that anxiety arises from a transformation of unsatisfied libido, Freud said that it has 'found some support in certain almost universal phobias of small children . . . Children's phobias and the anxious expectation in anxiety-neurosis serve as two examples of one way in which neurotic anxiety comes about; *i.e.* through direct transformation of libido'. (Klein 1952a[1948]: 272)

In spite of the so-called second theory, Freud's thought continued to gravitate around the libidinal, energetic origins of anxiety:

> Two conclusions, to which I shall return later on, can be drawn from these and similar passages: (a) in young children, it is unsatisfied libidinal excitation which turns into anxiety; (b) the earliest *content* of anxiety is the infant's feeling of danger lest his need should not be satisfied because the mother is 'absent'. (Klein 1952a[1948]: 272)

What interests Melanie Klein above all else is infantile anxiety, the infantile origins of anxiety. This is not merely because she is a child analyst, but because she is seeking, like any analyst, what is most primary in the situation experienced by the adult.

The 'primacy' of infantile sadism

In my reading of this article, I will move straight on to paragraph III, where she immediately (for it is a very rapid text) introduces her great clinical discovery: the precocity of sadism and masochism. I will remind you of one famous and key sentence, which begins an article that is inaugural for Melanie Klein: 'A Contribution to the Psychogenesis of Manic-Depressive States', first published in 1935:

> My earlier writings contain the account of a phase of sadism at its height, through which children pass during the first year of life. (Klein 1975[1935]: 262)

If you wanted to draw a sort of graph of the force of the drive, the curve of sadistic aggressivity would therefore find its highest point in the very first months. It is the first to appear, whereas love grows more slowly, in a more uneven fashion:

> In the very first months of the baby's existence it has sadistic impulses directed, not only against its mother's breast, but also against the inside of her body; scooping it out, devouring the contents, destroying it by every means which sadism can suggest. (Klein 1975[1935]: 262)

The primacy of sexuality, Freud's heroic discovery, is replaced by Melanie Klein with a 'different' discovery, which might appear no less scandalous, even in the analytic milieu: the primacy of destructiveness. Klein reminds us that Freud certainly introduces the death drive, and that he situates it as a danger to the individual:

> The dangerous death instincts are dealt with in the individual in various ways: in part they are rendered harmless by being fused with erotic components, in part they are diverted towards the external world in the form of aggression, while to a large extent they undoubtedly continue their internal work unhindered. (Freud 1923a: 54)

But, Klein continues, he does not draw the inevitable conclusion concerning anxiety:

> Following this line of thought I have put forward the hypothesis that anxiety is aroused by the danger which threatens the organism from the death instinct; and I suggested that this is the primary cause of anxiety. Freud's description of the struggle between the life and death instincts . . . would point to the conclusion that anxiety has its origin in the fear of death. (Klein 1952a[1948]: 275)

Attack by the death drive equals attack by libido

Well, here I myself have to intervene in the debate with these two great—but absent—thinkers, and I ask you to follow me in this proposition starting from the pivotal situation represented by anxiety (pivotal both for Freud and for Melanie Klein). The proposition is that the threat in question, the internal attack which takes the ego as its object (what Freud terms the internal attack on the ego by the libido) is *exactly the same* as the threat of the death drive and its internal attack on the ego, according to Melanie Klein. This leads us to conclude that the death drive takes, in effect, the central role in the id which was formerly taken by the libido for Freud. In my view, both of them are aiming at the same phenomenon.

Let me quote a term of Melanie Klein's, which is not in the text we are discussing here, but which is no less characteristic and is a fundamental concept: the notion of 'hatred of the id'. Particularly in the text quoted above, 'Psychogenesis of Manic-Depressive states', it is shown that the ego hates the id, an id which pays it back with its unceasing attacks. The id is regularly placed on the side of bad objects, amongst the persecutors. When the object is split into good and bad, it is the id which absorbs the bad part, and any excitation in the subject, of whatever nature—including erotic excitation, in the true sense of the term—any excitation, internal or external, increases the violence of the id's attack. Any excitation in the child, Melanie Klein observes, augments its paranoid anxiety, adding its extra charge to the energy of the persecuting id. You have to recognise, then—as I do—that Melanie Klein's death drive represents nothing other than the most destructive aspect of the libido, that which is most irreducible to the ego and most demonic!

To return to the article in *Developments* (Klein 1952a)—on the basis of this substitution, within the question of anxiety, of Freudian libido by the Freudian-Kleinian death drive—a double series of problems arises, for us as much as for Melanie Klein. On the one hand, the question of the 'idea of death' (as well as the death drive) in the unconscious; and, on the other hand, an even more difficult problem: that of the priority (or otherwise) of the self-destructive moment in the death drive.

The question: the 'idea' of death

An idea of death in the unconscious? Melanie Klein seems to oppose Freud quite radically here, by accepting what Freud had always denied. Freud's position, firstly, is recalled in these terms:

> In *Inhibitions, Symptoms and Anxiety*, Freud discussed his reasons for not regarding the fear of death (or the fear for life) [you will see how important this distinction is] as a primary anxiety. He based this view on his observation that 'the unconscious seems to contain nothing that could give any content to our concept of the annihilation of life' (SE XX, p.129). He also pointed out that nothing resembling death can ever have been experienced, except possibly fainting, and concluded that 'the fear of death should be regarded as analogous to the fear of castration.' I do not share this view . . . (Klein 1952a[1948]: 275-6)

Within this position and this Freudian argument, it is possible, if you like, to consider two aspects. The first (which comes second in Klein's argument) is that, in the unconscious, there is nothing but representations, representatives of representations which are necessarily residues of locatable experiences. On this basis, what experience could remain in the unconscious as a trace of—and to become the representative of—the idea of death—'except, perhaps, fainting', says Freud? But fainting does not itself subsist as such, as a trace. The memory of a fainting-fit attaches itself to some detail of the moment of loss of consciousness: a detail, an object, a particular circumstance in the surroundings. All these are perfectly positive traces, which can perhaps refer to an experience but which, in themselves, are not ideas of death. Have there been others? The idea of a mute person, as in the 'Theme of the Three Caskets' (Freud 1913b); the image of the mother, in the very same text, who in one of her aspects represents death; or again, more socialised images of death, even including the mundane skeleton?

Well, all these images, when they are located in the unconscious, can feature there only in an absolutely positive fashion. This is the second part, the most important aspect of the Freudian argument: that in the unconscious there is no negation, there are only positive representations; the idea of 'no life', the annihilation of life, cannot be represented. Let us recall the famous philosophical critique of the idea of nothingness, as it was renewed by Freud's contemporary, Bergson: I cannot think of nothingness, I can only ever think of some *other thing*. The thought of nothingness is always the thought of some positive other thing, while the idea of an absolute negation cannot be represented. Well, this critique of the idea of nothingness, undertaken classically by Bergson and by plenty of others before him, at the level of a conscious thought, is even more pertinent when we try to find a model which might apply in the unconscious. In fact the 'no', the *not to* live, is for Freud by definition of the order of language—that is, a secondary system. The 'symbol of negation' is something which appears at the moment when repression is lifted, while the very idea of a negation is incompatible with the logic (if we can still speak of logic), and with the circulation of representations in the unconscious. In the unconscious there would be nothing other than representations—side by side, on the same plane—none of which would exclude its neighbour.

Anxiety (of) death, idea of death: Klein's ambiguities

So, in spite of this argument of Freud's—an argument concerning both fact (such as, what would be the experience of death reproduced in the unconscious?) and principle (such as, the unconscious does not have the means to think negation) how does Melanie Klein find the resources to 'not share this view'? Let us firstly note that in this passage she plays on the two English terms, 'fear' and 'anxiety'. *Fear* has a theme; it is the fear of something. But the fact that she plays on these two terms does not make things easier, in so far as the idea of a fear of something is precisely what is so difficult to assign to the unconscious. The unconscious functions in such a way that affect and representation, fear and the thing one is afraid of, are led to work separately, to be displaced in relation to each other, so that the link between fear and the thing feared is dissolved. Here, I will quote some of the formulas from this passage by Klein, formulations which are ambiguous, juxtaposing correct intuition with conclusions whose thematisation is more or less erroneous:

(I) 'Anxiety is aroused by the danger which threatens the organism from the death instinct' (Klein 1952a[1948]: 275).

There is very little to say about a formulation like this. Except simply to comment that 'the organism' is both the living creature in the ordinary sense of the term, and also the organism representing the organism—that is to say, the ego. It is both the physical organism and the psychical organism. Anxiety arises from a danger. Anxiety is the subjective translation of a danger, and the formula 'due to the death drive' is sufficiently cautious to keep at a distance, for the time being, the hypothesis according to which it would be appropriate, as such, to posit an *idea* of death in the unconscious.

The second formulation is as follows:

(II) 'Anxiety has its origin in the fear of death' (Klein 1952a[1948]: 275).

This formula brings into play two terms which I mentioned just now: fear and anxiety. Fear is that which is more thematised, which 'intentionally' aims at something. But the formula, if we think about it, clearly turns out to be to Melanie Klein's disadvantage, since what is more thematised—we might say 'more secondary', the fear-of-something—is posited as being at the origin of what, elsewhere, Melanie Klein, following Freud, designates as the most primary—that is, anxiety. Far from anxiety being at the origin of fear, according to this formula it is rather a fear—one with 'a precise object one is afraid of'—which is at the origin of the most primary—that is, anxiety. Moreover, we will find the opposite of this formula appearing shortly.

(III) 'I would also think that if we assume the existence of a death instinct, we must also assume that in the deepest layers of the mind there is a response to this instinct in the form of fear of the annihilation of life. Thus in my view the danger arising from the inner working of the death instinct is the first cause of anxiety' (Klein 1952a[1948]: 276).

Here is a formulation which at last reverses the rather disconcerting hypothesis put forward in (II), that anxiety has the fear of death as its origin. Here things are put completely back on their feet. What is primary is the internal work of the death drive; it is this work which is the primary cause of anxiety or which 'converts into anxiety' according to the more debatable formulation belonging to the 'first' Freud. There is nothing to argue with here. What is presented as secondary is a fear, a *response* to that drive in the form of the fear of annihilation of life.

Fear, then, is a response and not, as she had told us just before, that which was primary in relation to anxiety! But whose response? (Here,

I have to add to Melanie Klein's text). It is a response from the one who is 'worked on', who is attacked—that is to say, the ego. Certainly, Melanie Klein situates us 'at the most profound levels of the psyche', but we have got into the habit, with Freud, of considering that the ego, too, exists down in the depths. So what exactly is this response to the work, to the attack by the death drive? It is not a fear of death, but a 'fear of the annihilation of life'. Beware! In German (cf. *Inhibitions, Symptoms and Anxiety*) you will find *Lebensgefahr*, which is transposed into French as *'danger de mort'* ('danger of death'). This *danger de mort*, which features as a warning on electrical transformers, is 'danger of life' in German, 'threat to your life'. Let us say that the danger of death is what is objective, and that fear for one's life is what is subjective; or, if you like, as Melanie Klein puts it, a fear of annihilation, not just a fear for one's life but, in a much more precise fashion, a fear of the annihilation of life. People will object that these are just quarrels about words! But what has to be conceived, beyond words, is the *affect in the ego*, its *response* (I want to hang on to this term) on contact with a drive which fragments it, overwhelms it, annihilates it. Once again, the idea of a no, of a 'not to live' or 'no longer to live', can only be situated at the most secondary levels, where the symbol of negation appears.

Anxiety is the anxiety of annihilation. In annihilation, there is nothing, but *the fear of annihilation does not necessarily presuppose the idea of nothing*. Anxiety is the anxiety of annihilation as experience. There is no need to go looking for the very particular experience of fainting, as Freud would have us believe; it is a continual experience, constantly renewed, the threat to the ego of being annihilated, fragmented by the attack of the drive. The annihilation of life is not present in the unconscious as an idea, any more than the idea of death; nor is it a thematic object of fear. However, this does not prevent primary anxiety from being linked with the death drive, from being radical and from being itself an experience of annihilation.

Melanie Klein is hardly a dialectician. It is not a question of putting her in contradiction with herself, from one passage to the next, just as it is not a question for me of putting different authors into some sort of enclosure to watch them mercilessly slog it out. The problem does not lie there! It lies, for us, in showing the only possible sense of this affirmation of the priority of the anxiety of death—namely, that this anxiety is not anxiety-about-death, but something like death-anxiety, annihilation-anxiety. As you can see, this question, ultimately, of whether the idea of death is present or not in the unconscious, is not as obscure as one might think, and the opposition between those who allegedly affirm or deny it is not a radical one.

Melanie Klein and the 'auto'-moment: projection or deflection?

Now we confront a more complex problem, the second problem I mentioned a little earlier: does Melanie Klein, or does she not, agree with the fundamental Freudian idea that the death drive is the drive of *my* death? That is to say, does she agree with the priority of what I call the auto-moment, the *Selbst* moment (whether auto-eroticism or auto-destruction, it doesn't matter). To what extent is the death drive a SELBST *vernichtungstrieb* ('*self*-destructive drive')? First of all, since it is Melanie Klein of whom we are speaking, let us clear up one misunderstanding. If you look at a few essential passages of Melanie Klein or, in a more synthetic approach, to the entry 'Good object—bad object' in *The Language of Psychoanalysis*,[24] you will soon become convinced that the 'bad' in Melanie Klein does not originate in the external world (for example in a mother who is objectively aggressive, even though obviously this may be the case), but instead aggressivity is always primarily and essentially that of the child. The bad object, for Melanie Klein, is *what I attack* and onto which I project my own aggressivity. Having cleared up this potential misunderstanding, the problem is then to know if it is *my own aggressivity* or *my own auto-aggressivity* that comes to be externalised. Let us use two convenient terms—'projection' and 'deflection'. Projection corresponds to the most common schema in Klein: the breast hates me and is, by projection, in a mirror-image, bad, because I hate it and I attack it. This is hetero-aggression, which is thus projected:

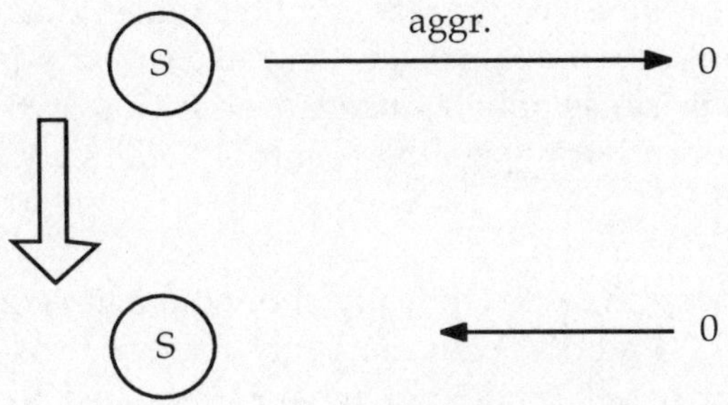

With deflection (a term Klein uses in a commentary on Freud), the process is very different and can be schematised not by a 'mirror-image', but by a sort of rotation through 180°:

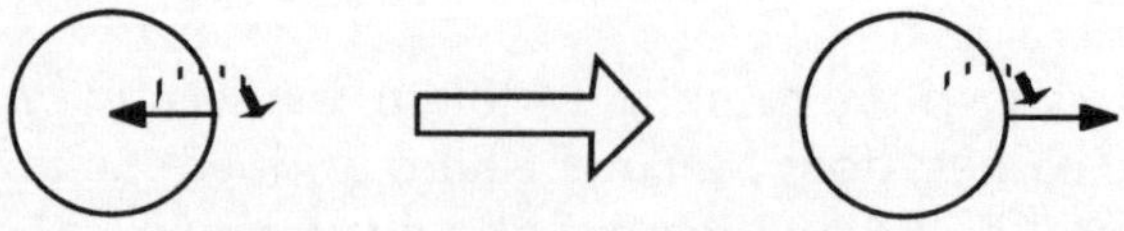

in order not to hate myself — I hate the breast

This process does not exclude the possibility of a subsequent projection (in other words, the properly Kleinian moment). But it is appropriate to distinguish clearly between the two movements: deflection (in order not to hate myself and destroy myself, I hate and destroy the breast); followed by projection (I hate the breast, the breast hates me, the breast is bad).

Melanie Klein, in this 1948 article, thus claims to adhere totally to the Freudian theory of the death drive, as a drive that is originally self-destructive. She provides two theoretico-clinical examples, and today we will focus on the first of these. It comes from a book which is already rather old, *The Psychoanalysis of Children* (Klein 1932). It is the ultimately rather banal observation of a child who claims, in his psychotherapy, to have at his command fierce wild animals which he can use at will against his enemies. These are, obviously, substitutes for his own aggressivity or sadism. Well, here is the conclusion Klein draws, in a couple of lines, after describing, with similar haste, this horde of aggressors kept on a leash:

> He sometimes became very frightened that the wild animals he had tamed would turn against him and exterminate him. This fear expressed his sense of being threatened by his own destructiveness (as well as by internal persecutors) (Klein 1952a[1948]: 276-7)

Does this observation, as such, really show the primacy of an auto-destructive moment, Freud's *Selbst* moment? This should be discussed at two levels. First of all, could not what is reported to us here be described from another, much simpler perspective, which was Freud's for a long time: the turning of aggression into auto-aggression, rather than a proof of the original auto-destructiveness of the subject.

Nothing proves that this turning of the wild animals against the child was a return to a stage at which the wild animals would have attacked the child from the inside.

However, above all (and this is our second level), the problem becomes more complex with the personification (the representation) of the drive in the form of internal persecutors. Now, what Freud was aiming at in his most theoretical texts on the topic of the death drive, was a drive as if in its raw state, a drive with no fixed representation of either aim of object—a sort of blind, auto-destructive force. Indeed, that is why one has been able to say that a principle is in question there, a quite particular mode of functioning of psychical energy, rather than a true drive, with a specific aim and objects.

Well, what is described here by Melanie Klein is not that. They are persecutory objects, internal persecutors, whose image is manifestly borrowed from the external world. It is a death drive whose representatives, whose 'representational representatives' in the Freudian sense of the term, are secondary in their specific features. They are wolves, leopards or elephants, all of them objects the child once saw in his picture book.

What can we conclude from this clinical illustration, other than that Melanie Klein was able to do perfectly well without the primary deflection assumed by Freud, and for the very good reason that, for her, everything comes from the to-and-fro between introjection and projection, and that in the end it matters little where it all 'started'. That is true not only for her, but for any analyst at the moment of interpretation: one can only interpret in terms of fantasies—that is, of representations—and, by definition, representations are borrowed from the external world . . .

7 February 1979

Today I shall try to conclude this question of anxiety in Klein, while keeping to the step-by-step rhythm of our own project. Concerning the death drive, I had raised two questions that were suggested by Klein's article: that of the *idea of death*, and the second—which will occupy us now—that of knowing how Melanie Klein goes about it, how she can take seriously the idea of a priority, in the death drive, of a moment that I term the 'auto-moment', a moment when the drive takes the individual itself as its object and, in the case of the death drive, as its object of destruction.

The internal devourer

The second example offered by Melanie Klein is what she calls, with Freud, one of the primal situations of anxiety: 'the fear of being devoured by the totem animal' (the father), a fear she rediscovers in numerous analyses. What is the route taken by Klein? She has no difficulty in showing that this fear is 'displaced'; its archaic aspect has a bearing on the mother, or even on a part of the mother.

> In this way, first the mother's breast (and the mother) becomes in the infant's mind a devouring object. (Klein 1952[1948]a: 277)

Examples are easy to find—such as 'the boy who said his mother's breast had bitten him', or 'the girl who thought her mother's shoe would eat her up', etc. (Klein 1952a[1948]: 277 n.2). What is more, the devouring breast is itself internal, a destroyer from within, and does not threaten just from the outside:

> The threat to the self from the death instinct working within is bound up with the dangers apprehended from the internalised devouring mother and father and amounts to fear of death. (Klein 1952a[1948]: 277)

With these internal dangers, this internalised and devouring father, mother, or breast, we are certainly dealing with the 'auto-moment': I attack myself from within, or rather, my bad internal objects attack me (that is, attack my ego; we are used to this equivalence). But the question of knowing which comes first, projection or interiorisation, is not completely futile in this discussion of the auto-moment. In a certain sense, Melanie Klein absorbs herself in the pursuit of this question and precisely, in this passage, concludes that the self-destructive moment is not primal:

> The fear of being devoured by the father derives from the projection of the infant's impulses to devour his objects. (Klein 1952a[1948]: 277)

From time to time Melanie Klein has been, to an extent, accused of idealism. It is said that she wished to extract every object-relation from what was first contained inside; the world of the child would then be a completely projected world. This objection was formulated some time ago, in a article that has remained famous, by Pasche and Renard (1956). Idealism? It is not quite that. It seems, rather, to be a question (at least in passages like the last one) of a primal hetero-aggression in Melanie Klein, an aggression which only shows itself and takes on specific features by finding objects in the external world, by 'pro-jecting' itself.

In any case, in a passage like the last one, what is described as an internal attack, as auto-aggression, is always a secondary moment, a turning against the self, the introjection or internalisation of the bad breast against which, *in a primal moment*, the child's aggression has already borne. Whereas in Freud, in his description of the movement of the drive (I am not necessarily preferring one argument over the other), there is instead a sort of mythical primal moment, which we could call reflexive, or more precisely (since 'reflexive' implies a re-flection) a 'middle' moment in the grammatical sense of the term: 'I eat myself', 'I attack myself'. This is without there being *presented* any representations *either* of that which attacks, *or* of the ego, the 'myself' who is attacked. It is a moment one can describe as 'mythical', and it is certainly very difficult to conceive or to represent. In fact, as soon as 'I eat myself' or 'I attack myself' take on a specific form in fantasy, it implies that one has already gone looking in the external world for the fantasy or the image of the thing that attacks (the breast, the penis . . .) and also of that which is attacked—the ego—for the ego, too, is constituted by a movement of introjection. This time, it is the introjection of a 'good' object, a 'good' mother, a 'good' breast, to speak Klein's language. That is, as we shall see, a breast which is already 'whole' in some sense, even though it is classically a 'part' object. Thus, every time one wants to speak of this auto-fantasy, one is indeed forced to imagine it as finding its representational contents in the external world, and thus to conceive of it—in a sense—as reflexive or reflected in relation to a primary relation to the external world.

Thus in these two examples from Melanie Klein, there is a play of introjection and projection, but without any real trace of the process of 'deflection'. However, this is not the last word on the subject. Melanie Klein will return to this search for the primal, for the originary. It is a quest, a characteristically psychoanalytic exigency. In anxiety, what are the primal anxieties, what is the initial anxiety on the basis of which all other anxieties are modelled? Like Freud, like Rank, Klein is led to posit, as a paradigm, a model that is primal, enigmatic and hypothetical, a paradigm extrapolated 'beyond the limits of a first draft', the model of birth.

The schema of an original deflection?

Melanie Klein explicitly draws the schema of a deflection of the death drive onto the external world, at the moment of birth, with all the inevitable contradictions which arise when one talks about 'birth fantasies':

> We may assume that the struggle between life and death instincts already operates during birth and accentuates the persecutory anxiety aroused by this painful experience. It would seem that this experience has the effect of making the external world , including the first external object, the mother's breast, appear hostile. (Klein 1952a[1948]: 278)

This is a painful experience, which is immediately translated into persecution, with the result that it makes the first external object appear to be persecutory:

> To this contributes the fact that the ego turns its destructive impulses against this primary object. The young infant feels that frustration by the breast, which in fact implies danger to life, is the retaliation for his destructive impulses towards it and that the frustrating breast is persecuting him. [And here is where the notion of deflection appears:] In addition he projects his destructive impulses on to the breast, that is to say, deflects the death instinct outwards; and, in these ways the attacked breast becomes the external representative of the death instinct. (Klein 1952a[1948]: 278)

There is an extrapolation 'beyond the limits of a first draft' every time one tries to speak from a psychoanalytic point of view about birth, or indeed about the prenatal state. The 'implausibility' (I am *not* making this an objection here) which arises when one speaks of the very moment of birth in a strictly historical sense, of the objective loss of that protective milieu constituted by the mother's belly—well, the implausibility concerns including there objects like the breast and, still more so, including the ego, as Melanie Klein wishes to do. This is so even if we admit that in speaking of birth we also have in view the moments 'immediately after' it, the primal moments of reunion, and of the loss of the mother, such as suckling.

The implausible Klein, and Klein the 'observer'

The implausibility of this first perception of the breast as being purely persecutory, entirely bad . . . It is interesting to compare, in the same collection, Melanie Klein the theoretician (whom I have just quoted) and Melanie Klein the observer, who expresses herself in an article entitled: 'On Observing the Behaviour of Young Infants':

> The new-born infant suffers from persecutory anxiety aroused by the process of birth and by the loss of the intra-uterine situation [here we find the same model: all the unpleasure of loss is immediately transformed into persecution]. A prolonged or difficult delivery is bound to intensify this anxiety . . . These feelings are in some degree relieved by the various measures taken to give him warmth, support, and comfort, particularly by the gratification he feels in receiving food and in sucking the breast. These experiences, culminating in the first experience of sucking, initiate, as we may assume, the relation to the 'good' mother. It appears that these gratifications in some way also go towards making up for the loss of the intra-uterine state. From the first feeding experience onwards, losing and regaining the loved object (the good breast) become an essential part of infantile emotional life. (Klein 1952b[1952]: 238)

What is the reason for this divergence between the theoretical position and that of observation? We have to be clear about this: there is a contradiction in Melanie Klein which we find over and over again, between the baby or the child observed directly, and the baby described in the analyses. The former is calm, often smiling, and sometimes—but only temporarily—in a rage. This is the child, after all, that we know. The other child seems to be constantly prey to the most violent internal struggle. This real discrepancy makes Melanie Klein's descriptions sometimes appear to be the creation of a separate world, completely at odds with what we perceive of the child—or anyway, taken to the *n*th degree.

This is the difference between the objective infant and the infant interpreted retrospectively, in the retrospectivity of analysis, even if this retrospectivity comes only a few seconds later. What is given by the Kleinian interpretation is a sort of theoretical model which telescopes into one moment, into a single mythical moment, what is actually constituted over a number of moments, in the constitution and the internalisation of fantasmatic images. This contradiction appears to be most flagrant with respect to birth, where we are offered two versions from very different perspectives. According to one of these, at birth the breast is essentially the object of the projection of the death drive. Conversely, in the other version, the infant finds in the breast the compensation for this irruption of the death drive from within. I would say that, as for Freud, the moment of birth at which we are not ourselves, any more than we will be at our death,[25] becomes the retroactive model for traumatisation, which is always a traumatisation *from within*. Here, then, is the model: no more object for the drive, because the maternal womb has been lost; an internal attack, since the drive, no longer having an object, comes to be stuck inside destructively; and thirdly, it needs an object on which to project this attack. It is on the basis of this model—which does not contradict what is observed, but is at a certain distance from it—and this model alone, that Melanie Klein is able to subscribe to the Freudian idea whereby the death drive would firstly relate to *my* death, before being deflected to the outside. This is how the passage quoted in the article on anxiety concludes:

> The 'bad' breast is also introjected [after there has been a projection onto the breast], and this intensifies, as we may assume, the internal danger- situation , i.e., the fear of the activity of the death instinct within. (Klein 1952a[1948]: 279)

It is a question of intensifying and not of creating. The X of the bad breast comes to reinforce the internal action which already existed:

> For by the internalisation of the 'bad' breast, the portion of the death instinct which had been deflected outwards, with all its associated dangers is turned inwards again and the ego attaches its fear of its own destructive impulses to the internal bad object. (Klein 1952a[1948]: 279)

A mythical genesis

This time the schema is typically Freudian, the one we find in *Beyond the Pleasure Principle* (1920) or in *The Ego and the Id* (1923a). These are three moments which are, by the way, purely theoretical, and only the third of which begins, as it were, to speak to us. A first moment of the drive's stagnation, without representation, a 'silent' moment, as Freud puts it in *The Ego and the Id*: the death drive is silent in its origin. A second moment of deflection and of the projection of the death drive onto the breast, which then becomes, in Melanie Klein's expression, its 'first external representative'. This is the first moment in which the death drive finds a representative, in other words—a fantasy: it is the moment of external aggressivity. Then finally the third moment, the introjection of the bad breast: this is the internal attack.

So, this moment of the drive (I am deliberately calling it simply *the* drive without, at this stage, distinguishing between the death drive and the sexual drive), a moment without representation, this first, silent moment—is it anything other than a retroactive myth, in the same category as all other suppositions about birth? Or, if the term myth is unacceptable (it has become a little hackneyed in psychoanalysis), is it at least a sort of analogue, a physiological model, reinterpreted retroactively, of what is to take place on the psychical level? But concerning the second moment, in turn—the moment of originary destructiveness turned to the outside, or what Melanie Klein calls the 'sadism at its zenith' of the first few days and months—we have seen that, in a sense, one can wonder if it is consistent with what is observed. Does she not confuse the active character of any relation to the world on the part of an organism with true sadism, which is sexual?

If you can follow how I set out and criticise this sequence, then the *only assignable moment, the moment of emergence, would be that of the constitution of the attacking-internal-object*. This internal persecutor is what I have sometimes called the source-object, which is at once stimulating and persecutory. It is the 'bad' object, or even the seductive object, recalling everything that can be drawn from our theory of seduction as the implantation, internally, of an image which becomes a source of energy which it is impossible to escape—the drive itself. This 'bad' object (bad for the ego) arises and becomes internalised through splitting, the splitting into good/bad perhaps being nothing other than the opposition between the object as exciting and the object as pacifying. Each time the pacifying and satisfying object goes away—whether in the abstract model of birth or, later on, in a more concrete fashion, in the first relations with the mother or the carer—it is, as a consequence, the exciting object which is internalised. As you know, in my view this 'bad' exciting breast is a sexual breast, and the death drive it stimulates by its attack—which is nothing but *its* attack—can be termed the *sexual death drive* as opposed to a *sexual life drive*.

Kleinian oppositions: a kind of Meccano?

Let us return to Melanie Klein, to try to situate the opposition between the life drives and the death drives in her thought. Well, there is no lack of dualisms and dichotomies in Kleinianism. One has the impression of being confronted with a sort of building game in which, with the help of a very small number of matching pieces, screws and bolts, with the help of a very small number of binary oppositions, the whole world can be reconstructed. Let us recall the principle of 'matching pairs': firstly, the opposition introjection/projection, and the preliminary question it raises: does this opposition presuppose that there is already an ego? What does it mean to introject if there is not yet an 'intro'—that is to say, the establishment, physically, of an initial border between an inside and an outside? Concerning this 'pair', I can only mention a more fundamental objection, and one which was raised by Lacan: is it really a question of such a symmetrical opposition as the terms would have us believe? Might there not be some processes which are of a heterogeneous nature or order?

The second pair is that of 'good' and 'bad' (always put in inverted commas by Klein, to show that they are qualities attributed subjectively by the infant to his objects; it is not the objective goodness or badness of the breast or of the mother which are at stake, it is what the child makes of them, through his attack or his love). 'Good' and 'bad', which I tend to interpret, as you have seen, as the opposition of the pacifying and the exciting. Then there is the further opposition: part/whole, which I will come back to in a moment. Finally, there is the opposition of the two great phases or positions: paranoid or paranoid-schizoid, and depressive or manic-depressive. These pairs interconnect, there is interplay between them, in the sense of the Homeric combats which Melanie Klein describes within the psyche. Within these interconnections, where can we situate the drives of life and of death?

Without doubt, we could find that they have affinities with the core of each of these pairs of opposites. One might maintain, for example, that the life drive would be more on the side of introjection; on the side of the 'good'; on the side of the whole, as opposed to the part. Then, in relation to the 'positions', the death drive is most dominant in what Melanie Klein describes as the paranoid phase, the life drive beginning to overcome it in the depressive phase.

Paranoid position and depressive position . . .

Perhaps, in order better to locate the meaning of the life drive and the death drive, the most concrete, most developed opposition is in fact that of the paranoid and the depressive positions, which could act as our guide. There is, on this subject, in the article on anxiety which I am considering, a sort of revision of the Kleinian theses, or at least the final stage of a revision. Melanie Klein never ceased to add still further nuances to the opposition of the two types of position, to the point where she saw them not as two succeeding phases cut off from one another, but as the same relation with a different emphasis.

Let us first of all recall the schematic contrasts between the two phases, so that we can then show how they are in fact complementary. Their opposition can first of all be situated in time: the very earliest (three or four) months correspond to the predominance of sadism in the paranoid phase, while, in the depressive position, sadism is moderated by love, which tends to repair the object. In the paranoid phase, the major mechanism is splitting (whence the denomination 'paranoid-schizoid', a term to signify 'the phase of splitting and persecution'), the splitting of the object leading to a sort of Manichean struggle between entirely 'good' objects and those which are entirely 'bad'. Conversely, the depressive phase is described as a stage of synthesis, in which the object is *both* 'good' and 'bad', both hated and loved, the most difficult thing to achieve and to bear being to hate that which one loves at the same time. The opposition between part object and whole object is also divided into two phases. In the paranoid phase the only objects in play are parts of the body—breast, penis, milk, excrement. On the contrary, in the depressive phase, it is the whole object, the whole body of the mother, which is at stake. Lastly, as far as the type of fear is concerned, we can say that at the paranoid stage it is a fear of destruction, of annihilation, in all sorts of modalities: burning, chopping up, drowning, etc. In the depressive stage it is the fear of a loss which is one's own fault—that is, guilt at having to lose the object because of one's attacks on it. As to 'the reason why' there is fear, Klein defines as follows. There is fear for the ego at the paranoid level, and an increasing fear for the object as one moves into the depressive position.

. . . their dialectical complementarity

Now, this 1948 text, devoted to *anxiety in general* and not specifically to depressive or paranoid anxieties, definitively relativises this opposition. The temporal sequence is put in question: depressive anxiety, says Melanie Klein, can appear very early, even from the so-called paranoid stage, and conversely, paranoid anxieties, anxieties of destruction, form an integral part of depressive anxiety. So what happens to the opposition part/whole? When it is described, as just now, as being the opposition of a part of the body to the whole body, this has clear connotations of constructivist geneticism. The whole person of the mother, according to a certain Kleinianism, is constructed, synthesised, out of bits of the mother. Instead, it should be observed that the part is always cut out from the background of the whole and that, in the perceptual and emotional world of the child, the two take shape progressively and correlatively in relation to each other, rather than the whole being put together by assembling the parts. Melanie Klein does not, subsequently, go so far as to reject this sort of geneticism, which would construct the whole out of the sum of the parts, but in this article she takes an essential step: the opposition part/whole is no longer vital for the distinction between paranoid and depressive anxieties. There can be an anxiety caused by loss, a depressive anxiety, in relation to 'part' objects (the breast) in so far as that which is threatened is a breast which, very early on, can be both loved and hated, a breast which I would term an 'object', a unitary object. Here is a passage which clearly situates this revision of Kleinian thought, and which in my view is important. It makes Kleinian thought more supple and—above all—dialecticises the couple 'part'/'whole':

> In such states of integration [which can thus exist very early on], a measure of synthesis between love and hatred in relation to part- objects comes about, which, according to my present view gives rise to depressive anxiety, guilt and the desire to make reparation to the injured loved object—first of all to the good breast. That is to say that I now link the onset of depressive anx-

> iety with the relation to part-objects. This modification is the result of further work on the earliest stages of the ego and of a fuller recognition of the gradual nature of the infant's emotional development. There is no change in my view that the basis of depressive anxiety [it is this which is important] is the synthesis between destructive impulses and feelings of love towards one object [thus, an object which can be synthetically aimed at by love and by destruction]. (Klein 1952a[1948]: 283)

The opposition part/whole is dialecticised, that is to say, it is no longer conceived mechanically as a relation of part to whole. A breast can be, in this sense, a 'whole' object, 'one' object, and one can feel guilt about attacking it while one loves it. Conversely, let us say, a person can be a part-object—that is, a completely 'bad' persecutor, separated by splitting from any 'good' aspects. To the extent that this geneticist hypothesis has arisen, in which the part /whole difference takes on a different meaning, it is the very distinction between the two forms of anxiety, paranoid and depressive, which tends to become blurred. It is founded, says Melanie Klein in this text, on a border concept. It remains very useful for untangling emotional situations in analysis, but it is no longer anything more than the differentiation of a type of anxiety that is perhaps singular. I will remind you here of a passage which in my view is essential. It is already very old, as it is in the article on manic-depressive states, which was interesting for showing clearly the link between the depressive and the persecutory, and in doing away with any mechanistic opposition between the two.

> The absence of the mother [schematically, we should be in the 'depressive' position] arouses in the child anxiety lest it should be handed over to bad objects, external and internalised, either because of her *death* or because of her return in the guise of a *'bad'* mother. (Klein 1975[1935]: 266)

At the very heart of depressive anxiety—and perhaps its ultimate explanation—is this persecutory aspect which means that when a mother goes away, when the object disappears, by virtue of that very fact, the object is split and its bad aspect (as Freud had said very precisely regarding depression) 'falls onto the ego'. Well, what Melanie Klein in a sense rediscovers here, in the wake of Freud's intuition in 'Mourning and Melancholia' (1917a), is—briefly—that the anxiety of loss is in no way independent of depressive anxiety. All anxiety of loss is at the same time, indissolubly, an anxiety due to the return of the 'bad'.

I had said that the old quarrel between 'anxiety of the ego' and 'anxiety of the id' in Freud could be understood in this way. All anxiety is *for* the ego, and all anxiety comes *from* the id, comes from the attack of the id. Well, in the same way, in a very similar formulation, I would say that in Melanie Klein all anxiety has a paranoid aspect if one considers the attacker, or the bad object; and all anxiety has a depressive aspect, if one considers that which is threatened with annihilation and loss—namely: the object which is both loved and hated, and the ego, itself an object, identified as it is with this synthetic synthesised object, the so-called whole object. All anxiety is both paranoid and depressive, but obviously the accent can be either on the attacking pole or on the pole of what is attacked.

Sexual life drives and sexual death drives

'Sexual life drives', then, and 'sexual death drives'. Melanie Klein, as you know, refers very seldom to the economic system of the drives—I mean, the way in which drives function. She is little concerned with knowing whether they function differently, or in an equivalent fashion (although with different aims). There is, however, a distinction in the economic regime of the drives, in their way of working, and it is only on this basis that one can conceive of how the same libido could be at work in the two types of drive. It is only on this basis that one can follow the hypothesis, which you will find everywhere in *The Ego and the Id*, according to which the death drive has no energy of its own, but that the two types of drive are fed by one and the same libido.

Sexual life drives: we know how these should be described. They are drives relating to an object, tending to maintain and unify the object. 'The object', clearly including the ego, is the first major object of this drive of life, which then becomes what—in Freudian language—is known as narcissistic libido. But how can we define the sexual death drive? If the so-called paranoid aspects are what characterise it best, we can see that it is marked by a form of splitting, leading to the reduction of the object to a single, one-sided, fragmentary aspect. The object is split, and one of its aspects is detached—the exciting aspect, and therefore even a dangerous, possibly a destructive aspect.

How, in relation to a 'whole object drive' which would be the life drive, can we define a death drive? Can we speak of the 'drive of representation'? The mother who goes away, the mother of the life drive, and the 'bad', the exciting mother who returns when the pacifying mother goes away—are they made of the same fabric? The one is an object in the synthetic and probably also narcissistic sense of the term; the other is a source of excitation. Can we formulate, regarding the death drive, something like the 'drive of the signifier'? From this perspective the whole of Lacanianism—with the emphasis on the signifying, split, 'unary', unilateral aspects of the object, in so far as it is taken from then on as signifier and not as synthesised object—this accent which Lacanianism puts on the signifier is perhaps nothing more than a new accentuation of the death drive in relation to the life drive, which, for Lacan, is relegated to the side of narcissism and the imaginary. Be that as it may, in relation to the synthetic, regulatory aspects of Eros or the life drive, it is certainly the sexual death drive which gives us the closest image of what we call the primary process in the id—that is to say, compulsive and indefinite displacement along chains of association between 'objects' reduced to their signifying aspects, aiming towards discharge by the shortest possible route, with no regard for the survival of the object.

The drive of the (whole) object and the indexical drive

At this stage in our reflections, what has emerged is thus the opposition between the 'drive of the ("whole") object' and the 'drive of representation' or of 'the signifier' or better, perhaps, the 'indexical drive'.

I have had to rush rather, not simply in order to finish, but to finish for this year. Next year, we will be taking up the question of the id again and, I imagine, I shall be presenting something around the notion of what the psychoanalytic method teaches us about its object. What we can construct, imagine, concerning the way the id functions, on the basis of the analytic method, a method which—I think—is nowadays at risk of falling into disuse. What I mean is that the proper way to approach the unconscious, as codified by Freud in *The Interpretation of Dreams* onwards, is tending to be replaced by something that preceded it, alas, for thousands of years—that is, a pure and simple hermeneutics. What does the analytic method teach us, when it is taken seriously, about the object it helps us to discover?

THE UNCONSCIOUS: A PSYCHOANALYTIC STUDY[1]

Jean Laplanche and Serge Leclaire

I. *Three Approaches Toward a Realism of the Unconscious*

(A) Meaning and Letter. An Examination of Politzer's Critique

That we accord the *Critique of the Foundations of Psychology* a privileged place here at the beginning of our study should be taken as a tribute to an author—or at least to the original phase of his thought—whose influence on the development of psychoanalysis in France has not been sufficiently appreciated.[2] His work has served as a veritable 'introduction to psychoanalysis' for an entire generation, and even now its shock value is far from diminished. For who will deny the liberating effect of the cry: 'down with metapsychology!' at a time when Freud's metapsychological concepts continue to exist primarily for the secondary gain they provide as a means of defence against thinking.

It would be difficult to find a clearer introduction to the problem of the unconscious than a discussion of this text. Is the unconscious a meaning or a letter? Politzer answers this question in exemplary fashion with a radicalism of meaning that pretends to take over the whole of Freud's discovery while simultaneously eliminating the unconscious. His attempt immediately takes us beyond the old objections raised by a psychology of consciousness, such as the ones Freud refutes in the first section of 'The Unconscious'.

If we take up the terms of Politzer's critique, we find the metapsychological hypothesis of the unconscious attacked on two levels: for its *abstraction* and its *realism*.

Abstraction is the first of these approaches. It would seem that Freud was inconsistent with the consequences of his own discovery; this situation would appear to be most evident in the way his thinking progresses in *The Interpretation of Dreams*. For while the essence of the Freudian discovery consisted in replacing impersonal mechanisms with a way of explaining dreams as acts of a particular subject in a 'first-person' drama, Freud, in all his metapsychological essays, and in particular in the last chapter of *The Interpretation of Dreams* ('The Psychology of the Dream-Processes') falls back to the level of abstract psychological entities whose interplay would occur mechanically and no longer at the level of subjectivity. What then comes to the fore are impersonal factors, agencies, psychical forces whose machinery attempts in vain to reconstitute the phenomenon in its concreteness. According to this analysis, Freud was not true to his fundamental aim: what is expressed in the manifest content as the act of an *I* should not be reduced at the latent level to an interaction of psychical things. The latent content, the dream-wish must not leave the domain of subjectivity, the domain that defines psychology.

We will try to say later how we might consider Freud's machinery, when we come to the metapsychological developments of 1915. We pause here only over the expression 'first person' in order to indicate the deviation or at least the restriction it imposes on Freud's discovery: is there no other alternative than between a mechanism—a process operating at the level of a thing—and the first person? Is it not precisely Freud's discovery, under the name of 'dream-thoughts,' that an utterance may take place 'in person'—without, however, being in the first person, but in the alienated form of the second or third person? If the subject of the utterance is at first only a grammatical one, it is none the less a subject: when 'it talks' [*ça parle*] in the unconscious, we do indeed find the dramatic unity so dear to Politzer, but this drama does not necessarily take place 'in the first person'. We may even wonder whether the defining characteristic of unconscious structures is not that they include voices other than that of the 'first person'.

Realism is the second principal approach. Let us follow here Politzer's demonstration in the case of the dream.

A dream analysis gives the impression that we move from a manifest content to a latent one. Now, 'to speak more precisely, a dream has only one content' (Politzer 1968: 184), the latent one, just as we can say that there is only one narrative, the manifest one: the text of the dream only expresses in an unconventional language meanings [*intentions significatives*] which have not found an adequate sign. Dream interpretation is, of course, a translation, but the mistake of Freudian realism consists in assuming the actual independent existence of this translation, at the moment when the dream is elaborated, in the form of unconscious thoughts. Under the pretext that the 'significant intentions' of the dream can be expressed in the language of waking life, it is assumed that they are already embodied, at the time of the dream, in a text distinct from the manifest content.

Politzer opposes this realism of signification with a theory of the immanence of meaning which, if it does not borrow its elements from phenomenological doctrine, could certainly be justified in terms of it. Politzer uses various comparisons to make us see the connection between the manifest and the latent: the dramatic relationship that links a play to its theme, without our having to assume that this theme is already written-in somewhere (Politzer 1968: 73), the immanent relation through which the rules of tennis are present in a match in implicit fashion (Politzer 1968: 190), the linguistic relation . . . but here let Politzer speak for himself:

> In the dream of Irma's injection, 'Irma has a sore throat' means 'I wish there were an error of diagnosis'. Now first of all, there can only be 'explanation' at the level of meaning, since we are faced with the explication of a text, or rather, with the analysis of a dramatic scene. Thus the wish for an error in diagnosis explains the sore throat just as the Latin term 'pater' *explains* the French word 'père', or rather, as jealousy explains Othello's action (Politzer 1968: 176).

This double 'or rather' by which Politzer quickly abandons the 'linguistic' relation for a relationship of another order, more specifically the expression of an emotion in a gesture, is significant: for how could Politzer be at ease in his linguistic example, in a relation which is not the immanence of a hypothetical intention to a sign, but the substitution of one sign for another?

But let us close for a moment the door that opens on to the linguistic dimension of the substitution of signifiers, in order to indicate the perspective in which Politzer intended to 'found' psychology.

What Freud reified in the term 'unconscious' is, in this view, only a particular instance of the general category of signification or of the 'first person drama', a category destined to replace that of causality in psychology. For Politzer, this category is a scientific category in the full sense of the term, since it is the result of an objective elaboration: the subject is in no way privileged in relation to this knowledge. Of course, the subject may himself be the one who interprets his own actions, but for this act of learning his subjective situation is, in fact, unfavourable:

> Indeed, it does not seem to us legitimate to expect of the subject anything other than the actual accomplishment of the action: the meaning of the act may be known to him, but dreams and the

> facts of mental pathology show sufficiently that he may also not know it. (Politzer 1968: 211)

And 'precisely because it does not consider that the ignorance of the subject as to his own being is a particularly remarkable thing,' concrete psychology 'has no need for the notion of an unconscious' (Politzer 1968: 214).

'The facts of the unconscious are no longer given directly but constructed, like those of the other sciences' (Politzer 1968: 215).

We should not conceal from ourselves the aspect of these texts that finds an echo not only in Freudian experience and teaching, but in a certain philosophical tradition as well: the blindness which by virtue of his very position affects the subject in regard to the meaning of his actions, the radical opacity of the *cogito*—this Malebranchian thesis finds its correlate in Freud's theory.

And as to the other facet of Politzer's position, the notion that the unconscious is only the construction of the other as knowing subject, we may juxtapose this with Freud's article on 'Constructions in Analysis (1937), where the importance of this 'intellectualist' mode of approach is demonstrated.

And yet, however satisfying and stimulating a perspective which sweeps out the old metapsychological arsenal may be; however close, too, it may seem to a modern thesis which would emphasise the similarities between the field of analysis and that of linguistics or cryptography—how can we fail to see the reduction, indeed the flattening that Politzer imposes on the dimension of subjectivity as discovered by Freud. In other words, the mere opposition of the manifest narrative or gesture and the drama or meaning immanent to them, and which analysis has only to reconstruct—all this seems to us incapable of accounting for the data of psychoanalysis. This can be demonstrated both at the level of manifest behaviour or of the manifest text and at the level of latent meaning.

At the level of the manifest text: our experience goes against any simple reduction of a gesture, symbol, or word, as they are presented to us in analysis, to a new sign invented by the subject in order to express in a unique language a meaningful intention, itself characterised by its particularity. Sign, symptom, and symbol are sustained not only by the unconscious meaning to be discovered in them, but also by the immediate meaning which they first seem to express.

A dreamer tells us: 'I dreamed of Mrs. X. She wore a red scarf'. The red scarf quickly leads to the subject's mother. That person is my mother, he says. That's all. Don't we realise that he has simply led us to a dead end, to a point of stagnation which he will be able to get out of by understanding why he dreamed of his mother in the guise of Mrs. X and by means of the red scarf? If the manifest sign, in fact, expresses only a single meaning, we will not be able to escape from the following alternative:

1. Either the subject is saying: 'I want to sleep with my mother', which means he wants to sleep with his mother, and we are in the realm of psychosis.

2. Or the subject, in order to express the fact that he wants to sleep with his mother, creates an absolutely new sign, a perfect neologism—but then the path by which we, or he, could accede to the latent meaning is totally inconceivable.

The objection also holds if we consider Politzer's reduction of the latent content to a 'meaning'.[3]

To put it briefly, since we shall have occasion to come back to it later, notions such as conflict, compromise formation, etc. . . . *are untenable in a structure whose two sole dimensions are those of a letter*—the manifest content—*and a meaning*, which would occupy the place of the unconscious. Who will be able to tell us on what stage the encounter between these two characters can take place: the one, as in a farce, always leaving the stage when the other comes on? To take up a comparison made by Politzer, if the unconscious should not be taken more realistically that the law scientists construct in order to explain certain facts in physics, who would be able to describe the conflict between ´gt^2 and the fall of an apple?

Between a single letter and a single meaning, a letter so particularly adapted to its meaning that 'conventional dialectics' 'are unsuited' to interpret it, how could we conceive of any other relation than one of adequation? How could we understand, moreover, Freud's account of the existence, in exceptional cases, of a co-operation between the unconscious and the preconscious which, when it occurs, gives to the resulting action a quality that cannot be mistaken: there occurs a particularly perfect action, free of any contradiction (of the type found in obsessional symptoms) (Freud 1915a: 194-5). The possibility of adding to each other the effects of the unconscious and those of the preconscious provides stunning proof that the latter is not simply the manifestation of the former.

(B) The Two Ways of Listening. Lacunae in Conscious Speech. The Notions of 'Formations of the Unconscious'

However schematic these considerations may be, they have nevertheless a direct echo in our day-to-day practice. In this connection, it would be particularly interesting to define the attitudes, the ways of listening that make up what each of us understands by 'free-floating attention'. In our view, one would find two very different types of listening, between which most individual cases would fall: we would be prepared to compare them under the rubrics: 'the attitude of simultaneous translation' and 'the attitude of attention to lacunary phenomena'.

Even if it does not follow directly from it, the attitude of simultaneous translation seems to us to correspond to the position of the unconscious as meaning, as Politzer has expounded it. The patient's speech (but also his other forms of production, such as his drawings) are taken here as raw material, for the interpretation of which the conscious intention of the patient does not have to be taken particularly into consideration. Free-floating attention, by not privileging any one bit of content, has the effect of privileging them all, of taking the whole of the discourse as a text capable of being translated into 'unconscious' language. But in this formulation one should really put the term 'language' in the plural, since the essential ambiguity of any material in regard to its meaning allows, for the same text, a totally coherent demarcation into 'oral', 'anal', and 'phallic', to take only the most classic idioms.[4]

More boldly, one could speak of the analyst's free associations, seeking support a bit hastily in the commonplace of a 'communication between unconsciouses'. We propose here the simple counterproof of a translation of the manifest content—of a dream, for example—not only into Freudian, but also into Jungian, existentialist or even (and this is not a gratuitous hypothesis) into Marxist. What else would we have done but project our object into different systems of co-ordinates, of which some are no doubt more convenient than others, but of which none has any claim to greater truth.

It is indeed because of the radical ambiguity of the letter, as we evoke it in this context, that any attitude of psychoanalytic listening seeks to be 'free-floating'. But whereas in the case we have just described, the egalitarian treatment of the material led to a sort of levelling in which all the contents are equally significant and charged with meaning, in another perspective, on the contrary, the evenness of the field of attention aims at bringing into relief the nodal points ('*Knotenpunkte*') in the patient's speech: points of intensity, of absence of intensity, lacunae, hollows.

We borrow this perspective from Freud himself who defines in precisely this way the presence of the unconscious in psychoanalytic experience. The data of consciousness are defective, 'lacunary' ('*lückenhaft*'); the unconscious is what allows us to re-establish a coherent sequence, an intelligible relation 'if we interpolate between them the unconscious acts which we have inferred' (Freud 1915a: 167). We see here how Freud can put forth a 'constructionist' thesis about the unconscious (the unconscious is 'inferred') while at the same time avoiding what we might call a Politzerian position: the unconscious is rigorously distinguished from the manifest text, and it is precisely for that reason that it can enter into relation with it:

(a) The unconscious is not coextensive to the manifest as its meaning: it must be interpolated in the lacunae of the manifest text.

(b) What is unconscious is in relation to the manifest not as a meaning to a letter, but on the same level of reality. It is what allows us to conceive of a dynamic relationship between the manifest text and what is absent from and must be interpolated in it: it is a fragment of discourse that must find its place in the discourse as a whole.

Let us conclude here by noting that the way of listening we are trying to define tends to bring to the fore the notion of a privileged manifestation, of a *formation*[5] proper to the unconscious: dreams, slips of the tongue, erroneous acts are the classic examples. Conversely, are we not also saying that not all of the patient's speech is interpretable, that there are utterances without unconscious correlates . . . most often, in the analytic context, empty chatter, but also, on occasion, 'full' speech [*parole 'pleine'*], the assumption of a hitherto unconscious meaning, for if analysis seeks to elucidate what it means to speak, it must also at times be the case that speech *means* . . . what it says.

(C) The Unconscious and the Problem of Consciousness

Before engaging the debate on the ontological status of the unconscious we believe it useful to recall what it is opposed to in psychoanalytic theory. Let us set it down as schematically as necessary: the unconscious, which is the specific domain of psychoanalysis, should be taken in the topographical sense. In this respect, it contrasts as much with the 'preconscious' (which is the unconscious only in the descriptive sense) as with consciousness.

This distinction, in fact, is found throughout all of Freud's work. From a purely descriptive, phenomenological point of view, the conscious, as a realm of consciousness situated (or situating itself) in time, may be contrasted with the totality of the contents it does not embrace at any given moment, and which are by definition unconscious. But the crucial separation, the one which coincides with the action of censorship, cuts across this 'unconscious' domain. The unconscious in the psychoanalytic sense is constituted by contents inaccessible to consciousness; the preconscious, on the other hand, is theoretically available to it; constituted by my non-activated memories, my knowledge, my stock of opinions, etc., it covers the whole area described, outside of psychoanalysis or prior to it, as 'unconscious' or 'subconscious'.

Freud designates this preconscious system distinctively by the name of 'conscious knowledge' (*bewusste Kenntniss*), which, of course, opposes it to consciousness *hic et nunc*, but even more to the system Ucs (Freud 1915a: 167).[6] The two terms here are entirely distinctive: 'knowledge' implies that the essential distinction lies in terms of systems, of a certain knowledge (or discourse) of self; the term 'conscious' insists on this same distinction since it serves to describe phenomena which are manifestly unconscious from the descriptive point of view but which are linked to the conscious from the topographical one.

This is Freud's constant position; it is radically and scandalously intolerant of any attempt at interpretation by the conceptual tools of a psychology of consciousness. We recognise in it the direct consequence of the experience of emergent 'insight', as it occurs in a psychoanalytic cure. In such cases it is rare, and even exceptional, for the discovery of the unconscious to occur as a phenomenon that can be situated within the time and field of a unified consciousness. Usually it takes a patient effort, proceeding from particular to particular, in which the reorganisation of perspectives is pursued through discontinuous, isolated moments of consciousness, often greatly separated from one another, none of which is characterised by that sudden re-conversion of the totality of meanings that could be called revelation.

Even more, if what may be called a 'moment of insight' in the narrow sense sometimes occurs—the resurgence of a forgotten memory, a sudden illumination—it may be said that this phenomenon, which is unquestionably conscious in the descriptive sense, does not allow us to decide whether it belongs topographically to the unconscious system. This was already the case, in the development of analytic technique, for the sudden and ephemeral flashes of memory under hypnosis. At a later stage, the energetical theory of the abreaction of a traumatic memory was in turn seen to be wanting when faced with remembrances which, even when accompanied by all the affective trappings apt to modify the structure of the field of consciousness, did not result in a stable restructuring of the subject. It is here that the theory of *Durcharbeiten* intervened: an interpretative elaboration or working-through whose role is to weave around a rememorated[7] element an entire network of meaningful relations that integrate it into the subject's explicit apprehension of himself, that is: into the Preconscious-Conscious system. In the passage from one system to the other, the moment of conscious insight [*prise de conscience*], in the descriptive sense, is only an ephemeral instant, all the emphasis being placed on the reorganising of the preconscious system.

Let us rapidly summarise our conclusions:

The problems posed by the Unconscious in the Freudian sense are a far cry from those posed by a psychology or a phenomenology of consciousness. The psychoanalytic unconscious is not, in fact, defined in relation to the intentional field in which the subject 'temporalises' himself, but in opposition to a system whose greater part is unconscious: the system Pcs-Cs.

If one wanted to find a philosophical correlate to such a system, one could do no better than to compare it to what Hegel describes under the term of 'consciousness' ('unhappy consciousness', the 'beautiful soul', etc.): an organised structure of self-apprehension which entails and includes a plurality of moments, an entire coherent discourse that is never actualised in its totality (a 'consciousness', a '*Bewusstein*').

Which is to say how far the contribution of psychoanalysis is from descriptions given in the realm of phenomenology. In Sartre, for instance, the critique of the psychoanalytic unconscious misconstrues the latter's radical heterogeneity by reducing unconscious contents to the misunderstood fringes and implications of present intention, or, in Freudian terms, to the limit between the conscious and the preconscious. The question thus posed (bad faith, conscious reticence, misunderstanding-pathology of the field of consciousness, etc.) do not lose their interest if we characterise them as marginal in relation to a domain which is properly psychoanalytic. They are situated rather at the level of that second censorship which Freud places at the boundary between the preconscious and consciousness, but which he hardly began to describe.[8]

II. *The Unconscious as a System in Freud. Orientation and Impasse of the Freudian Hypothesis*

Freud's text on 'The Unconscious' (Freud 1915a) throws into focus the subject it proposes with such rigour that we could profitably limit ourselves to following and commenting on all of its stages. Our intention here is somewhat different. We want to bring into relief, through reference to certain particularly difficult passages, the fundamental necessity which drives the author into the meanders of his metapsychological conceptions.

While we do not ourselves accept all of his topographical or economic concepts, we think it useful, nevertheless, to discuss them in some detail in order to show that Freud forges and reworks them in order to adapt them to the object he is pursuing: the unconscious system. *Thus the whole text is in search of a distinction which would found the real, topographical separation of the two systems*, a distinction which is sometimes sought in a qualitative difference (the theory of 'two inscriptions'), sometimes in an economic one (a 'cathectic energy' proper to each system).

(A) Necessity of a Second Structure

By its very strangeness, a first passage is very characteristic of the realistic imperative in Freud. This is the rather complicated reasoning by which he hopes to confirm the *legitimacy* of the hypothesis of the unconscious. Freud extends here to intrasubjective structures the reasoning by analogy which, according to him, allows us to move from our own consciousness to the existence of a psyche or consciousness in others.

Freud does not deny the weakness of this argument at the level of the *existence* of other minds, and he shows us right away that he is not wed to it by putting it into doubt as an example of the process of identification (Freud 1915a: 169-70). It is rather at the level of the *knowledge* of other minds that the argument is maintained, supported by the exemplary fact that the meaning of a bit of behaviour is often clearer in other than in ourselves (whereas our own existence would be more certain). Let us transfer this reasoning, at Freud's invitation, to the level of the individual psyche: here too we are faced with events and contents for which we cannot immediately account (the manifestations of the unconscious).

In a text such as this it would seem that a 'Politzerian' solution is called for: starting from a certain lived experience—our own drama—the 'unconscious' meaning of this experience must be inferred, constructed in the same way as it is for the experience of others.

Why then does Freud not avail himself of this category of meaning, which is, after all, not absolutely foreign to him? Why introduce the realistic hypothesis of a 'second consciousness' in us, a second consciousness that in fact has nothing in common with consciousness proper aside from a common degree of reality?

The only answer is that *Freud needs a radical division* between two domains situated at an identical level of reality; only this effective duality allows him to account for psychical conflict: in order for a meaning to be opposed to the experience of which it is the meaning, the experience itself must equally be meaning and the unconscious meaning must have in its turn the consistency of experience. Thus, says Freud: 'all the acts and manifestations which I notice in myself and do not know how to link up with the rest of my mental life must be judged as if they belonged to someone else' (Freud 1915a: 169). Once again, *lacunary* phenomena are posited at the origin of the hypothesis of the unconscious: but the latter does not consist in a more comprehensive meaning which allows these phenomena to be attached to the rest of the text, it is, on the contrary, a *second structure* in which these lacunary phenomena find their utility independently of the rest of the text.

(B) The Hypothesis of the Double Inscription

It is in Section II, 'Various Meanings of "the Unconscious"—the Topographical Point of View', that the notion of a systematic is introduced, symbolised by the abbreviations: *Ucs, Pcs, Cs.* The topographical point of view, Freud notes, removes us even further from a 'psychology of consciousness'(Freud 1915a: 173).

The question posed in the following pages (Freud 1915a: 173-6) will continue to appear throughout the rest of the text: what founds this topographical distinction? When an unconscious representation becomes conscious, is it the same one undergoing a change of state ('functional hypothesis')—the process being accomplished on the same material and in the same 'locality'—or is it a question of a second 'inscription' (*Niederschrift*), of a new 'fixation'?

Here Freud does not decide. The first viewpoint seems to him 'the more probable'; it is one we might call phenomenological: the same object, at the moment of insight, is subjected to different lighting. The second conception seems to him both 'cruder' and 'more convenient'.

In the discussion Freud pursues concerning the process of interpretation in therapy, we can see him oscillating between the two points of view. The question is here formulated in these terms: if the transition to the preconscious-conscious system entails a new inscription, can there be a coexistence of these two inscriptions—the preconscious-conscious and unconscious ones. This 'topographical' hypothesis seems confirmed by the fact that interpretation, while bringing a certain content to consciousness, does not at the same time abolish its unconscious effects. But Freud immediately questions his own example by indicating that in this case—that of an ineffective interpretation—it is probably not the same content in each of the two 'inscriptions'. Thus, nothing proves that when it really *is* the same content which becomes conscious, that content still remains inscribed at the unconscious level.

For ourselves, who would willingly decide in favour of the double inscription, the question would be to discover how to formulate the second point of view in a less 'crude' way, that is, by accounting for the modification produced in the unconscious, simultaneously with the second inscription in the preconscious-conscious.[9]

(C) The Economic Hypothesis

With Section IV of Freud's text, 'Topography and Dynamics of Repression', the theory of a double inscription is momentarily abandoned: the same term, the same representation can no longer be 'inscribed' simultaneously in the unconscious and in the preconscious systems: its arrival in one place abolishes its presence in the other.

Are we thus brought back to the hypothesis of a single, identical content which may or may not be illuminated by consciousness? Perhaps this is the case at the level of individual terms, but, at the level of systems of representation, the realistic distinction between the two domains subsists and is now based on a new economic concept, that of a 'cathectic energy' proper to each.

We cannot approve without reservation when Freud declares that 'the functional hypothesis has here easily driven out the topographical one'. We would say rather that if the transition of a term from the unconscious to the conscious, or vice versa, has become a functional one, it is at the cost of an even more clearly marked topographical distinction, supported by an economic one.

'Unconscious cathectic energy', 'preconscious cathectic energy': let us examine successively their point of application, the direction in which they act, and finally their true nature.

1. In the Freudian model, each of these energies is strictly specific to its system. There is no transformation of unconscious energy into conscious energy. This energy is applied to isolated terms, representations it cathects or decathects. The passage of an element from one system to another is produced by withdrawal of cathexis by the first and recathexis by the second.

2. Up to now things seem relatively simply: each system has a sort of cohesive force, an internal energy which, when applied to an isolated element, maintains it in the totality. But Freud does not always remain faithful to this scheme, especially in the case of unconscious energy. At times, the latter seems to exert a force of attraction on the representations: this is the case particularly in the theory of repression (Freud 1915c: 148) where the attraction by elements which are already repressed serves to collaborate with suppression by the superior system. But in other cases (or simply: according to another modality of Freud's thought), the unconscious cathexis would be, on the contrary, that which drives a representation to irrupt into the preconscious (Freud 1915a: 180-1).

In this way the essential question is presented—but we would have liked the contradiction to be more explicit—of knowing in which direction the unconscious acts: as a repetitive, attracting force for cohesion, opposed to conscious insight, or on the contrary, a force which would constantly tend to make its 'derivatives' emerge into consciousness and which would only be contained by the vigilance of censorship.

3. But perhaps this difficulty is tied to the major obscurity of Freud's economic hypothesis, which consists in purely and simply identifying this systemic 'cathectic energy' with libidinal energy, that is, with the energy of the sexual drives.

We should indeed recall that the libido as such cannot be specific to either one of the systems in question. For Freud, the drive is at first neither conscious nor unconscious, but organic. If it comes to be localised in a system, it is precisely only by linking itself to a representation, to an 'ideational representative'.

We see here the difficulty that then exists in assimilating the energy of the drive to the 'cathectic energy' of a system: while the latter must account for a representation's belonging to such and such a system, it is on the contrary the topographical position of a given representation that determines the topographical position of the libido that comes to be 'fixated' to it.

To press this assimilation to its conclusion would be to come to a notion that contradicts the general theory of the libido: that of a topographical and qualitatively irreducible opposition between an unconscious libido and a (pre-)conscious one, an opposition such that one could not be transformed into the other.

Let us conclude this study of Freud's text on the Unconscious: *Freud's aim is above all to establish the independence and the cohesion of the two systems.*

The most satisfactory explanation he gives is the economic hypothesis. But the only coherent interpretation we could present would have to distinguish in an absolute manner between the 'cathectic energies' involved and libidinal energy. We may for the moment give a *Gestaltist* model for this play of energies. The cathectic energy of a system would be comparable to the *Prägnanz* of a 'good shape'. But it is important to note at what level the passage from one system to another operates: it cannot be the global passage of the same structure from one mode of organisation to another, similar to the oscillatory effect at work in the perception of an equivocal image. What passes from one Gestalt to another is always an isolated equivocal element, capable of being captured by the *Prägnanz* of the unconscious or (pre-)conscious *Gestalt:* repression, as Freud emphasises, 'acts . . . in a *highly individual* manner. Each single derivative of the repressed may have its own special vicissitude' (Freud 1915c: 150).

A convenient example would be those puzzle-drawings in which a certain perceptual attitude suddenly makes Napoleon's hat appear in the branches of the tree that shades a family picnic. But if this hat is able to appear, it is because it can be related to an entirely different 'anecdote', which is not at all present in the rest of the drawing: the 'Napoleonic legend'.

In this model, what Freud calls *cathexis* is the relation of the detail in question (the hat) to the system which corresponds to it (the Napoleonic legend). The *anti-cathexis* is found in the same detail's relation to the term which evokes it in the other system (that is, the leaves of the tree); it is the *Prägnanz* of the 'conscious' system (the picnic) which keeps the tree and its leaves in existence and maintains the hat in a latent state.

III. *The 'Unconscious Text' of a Dream*

No one doubts any longer that the dream is truly 'the royal road to the unconscious'. In what respect? This is what we would now like to examine. In taking up the text of a dream analysis, we hope to find the desired explanations concerning the topographical question of unconscious inscriptions and the economic problem of the energy proper to the unconscious system.

(A) Analysis of a Dream[10]

Here then, as told by Philippe, a thirty-year-old obsessional neurotic, is a first dream, the 'unicorn dream':

> The deserted square [*place*] of a small town; it's odd, I'm looking for something. Liliane—whom I do not know—appears, barefoot, and says to me: it's been a long time since I've seen such fine sand. We are in the forest and the trees seem peculiarly coloured, with bright and simply shades. I think that there are a lot of animals in this forest and, just as I am about to say it, a unicorn (*licorne*) crosses our path; we walk, all three of us, toward a clearing that we suppose is down below.

It is a generally admitted hypothesis that the dream is the disguised expression of a wish-fulfilment. Let us say right away that what underlies this dream is *a wish, a desire to drink*, and we shall show how it can be clearly elicited from this story.

Nothing in the manifest text of the dream directly expresses a desire to drink; it is what Philippe says in the course of the session that first reveals it to us: namely, that he woke up a little later the same night afflicted with a rather strong thirst. But he does not mention any other dream directly preceding his awakening. In this regard, he indicates that he had dined the previous evening on salted 'Baltic herrings', which he especially likes. In the same way, we find in the narrative of the previous day's events the essential part of the dream material and other evocations of the desire to drink: Philippe had taken a walk in the woods with his niece Anne. As happened sometimes, they had stalked game and, above all, had noticed, near the bottom of a vale irrigated by a stream, numerous deer and does tracks, indicating one of the places animals came to drink. We shall anticipate here by remarking that it is very probable that at the moment the remembrance of the dream ends, they are accompanying the unicorn-doe, who is going to drink in the clearing.

The actual dream analysis leads us to three childhood memories.

The deserted square at the beginning of the dream presents something odd in that it lacks a monument or fountain; if we follow the dreamer's associations, the site would be the square of a small provincial town in which the 'unicorn fountain' is located. It is not only the quite remarkable depiction of the fabulous animal adorning the fountain that seems to have stayed in Philippe's memory; it is also, indistinctly at first, then gradually emerging from the story, the memory of a scene from a summer vacation he spent in that spot when he was about three years old: he tries to drink the water that springs from the fountain in the hollow of his cupped hands. We also find a correlate to this gesture, which is most important to the subject as a sign of an independence linked to an experience of motor mastery, in the second memory . . .

A walk in the mountains to which we are brought especially by the phrase: 'it's been a long time since I've seen . . . ' In fact, this is a daytime residue applied during the previous day's walk to the flaming brightness of particularly opulent heather (the same play of colours that amazes him in the dream, where it is transferred to the trees). The memory of this Swiss mountain site (the dazzling heather and the forest) is linked to a childhood attempt at imitating an older playmate, who was able to produce the noise of a siren by blowing into his two hands shaped like a conch shell. This call or signal reverberated particularly well in the forest.

It is a more precisely articulated call that we find in the third memory, that of a beach on the Atlantic, which we are led to by the herrings, by way of the Baltic, and by the unexpected ending of the sentence 'It's been a long time . . . such fine *sand*', as well as and above all by the name Liliane which does not correspond to anyone Philippe can identify. He then breaks down the name: 'Anne' is indeed his niece; is it then a question of 'Lili'? Lili is a person quite close to his circle, a cousin of his mother's, who was with him on the Atlantic beach when he was barely three years old (most probably at the beginning of the same vacation that brought him to the town of the unicorn). The memory that marks this stay particularly is one of being teased by Lili: since, in that dazzling July, Philippe never stopped repeating to her at every moment, with a grave and insistent (should we say seductive?) air: 'I'm thirsty'. Lili eventually ended up by asking him each time they met: 'Well, Philippe, I'm thirsty?' This affectionate mockery became in the following years a sort of formula, almost a sign of recognition between them, spoken in the same grave and falsely despairing tone (connivance, assurance of satisfaction): 'Philippe, I'm thirsty'.

Thus we find briefly sketched out in the evocation of these three memories a first approximate interpretation of the dream.

By way of a thirst clearly motivated by the consumption of herring, on the occasion of this need to drink, we might say, arises a dream which, for a time at least, calms to a certain extent the desire to drink and puts off the moment of awakening.

But we should immediately emphasise that the temporary satisfaction that the dream brings does not concern the need to drink, that is, the bodily state of hyperchloruration to which the dream brings no remedy: the dream seems to respond to something else, which is the *desire* to drink, Philippe's thirst, and it is that which we should investigate. The dream beings us back to Philippe's fundamental declaration: 'I'm thirsty' and to two consequences of that proposition: on the one hand, he drinks on his own, showing a certain motor co-ordination; on the other hand, he places himself before Lili as he who calls, speaks his thirst: he finds himself in this way pinpointed by the ironic and affectionate formula, 'Philippe, I'm thirsty'.

Of course, we still have to pursue the dream analysis we began and principally the study of this wish to drink. Why does he appear bound in this way to the call and the attempt at mastery? Why is it precisely under the sign of the unicorn that the memory of a gesture, performed no doubt for neither the first nor the last time, is engraved? Where, finally, do the other fragmentary memories of a burning summer lead us? For the moment, let us leave these questions in abeyance.

This thirst appears clearly as the very wish which is answered by the production of the dream. But what we see above all, already at this stage, is the *double force* that underlies the dream: on the one hand, the need to drink, a contingent, actual, unavoidable thirst (whose secondary effect will be to bring about his awakening), and on the other hand, the thirst, the wish to drink, which receives a measure of satisfaction from the very fact of the dream production. This double force comes together, without merging however, in the word *thirst*.

(B) From Need to Wish. The Problem of Drives

A dream, writes Freud, in the famous title of the third chapter of the *Traumdeutung*, is the fulfilment of a wish. Which is to say, an (unsatisfied) desire constitutes the energy necessary to the constitution of a dream. But what exactly is this desire whose effects we see before us? It seems to us quite insufficient to reduce it to a need to drink after the consumption of herring, to an organic necessity. And yet who would deny the link between the 'need to drink' and the 'wish or desire to drink'?

How to move from need, an organic energy, to desire, the active principle of unconscious processes—this is how we might formulate the problem to which we must address ourselves presently.

Between the purely organic 'need' which marks the outer limit of our psychoanalytic field and the 'desire' which orders its essential centre, Freud introduces the concept of drive (*pulsion, Trieb*).

A drive, Freud tells us, is a constant force of a biological nature, emanating from organic sources, that always has as its aim its own satisfaction through the elimination of the state of tension which operates at the source of the drive itself (Freud 1915b: 118-22).

As for desire, he tells us, it is in that direction of the psychical apparatus oriented according to the perception of pleasure and unpleasure; desire alone can set the apparatus in motion (Freud 1900: 598). Desire, as opposed to drive, appears, then, as a properly psychical force. Both the one and the other account for a movement, for a modification having as its goal the elimination of a state of tension; but this in no way justifies confusing the two.

The first thing we ask ourselves about is the *actual nature of the drive*. In Philippe's dream it immediately occurs to us to call it oral; but in introducing this element what exactly have we done, other than relate it to a privileged erotogenic zone, the mouth, of which we know that that it is the first to be distinguished in post-natal development. Philippe had been an easy feed, as they say, and no restraint had been applied in doing so—in conformity with the domestic maxim that it is better to be envied than pitied. But how then can we imagine, in a child so well provided for, a need bearing witness to some lack to be drunk? And yet, the fact remains: Philippe was thirsty. It is here that we begin to distinguish brute need, on the one hand, and drive on the other, in that the drive introduces into the sphere of need an erotic quality: libido will be substituted for need—and it is with the former that we must come to terms in psychoanalysis.

Here then, we might think, a first force has been recognised, one which tends to reduce the state of organic tension—libido: the oral drive, this 'drive energy' that we find in Philippe, would then be an anachronistic manifestation of a force which drives him to satisfy any physiological need, whatever it might be, by means of the oral libidinal zone.

We would certainly be tempted to simplify the investigation of the nature of the drive and thus of the enigmatic 'drive energy' if Freud from one end of his work to the other had not maintained the almost dogmatic requirement of a *dualism of drives*:

> Our views have from the very first been *dualistic*, and today they are even more definitely dualistic than before—now that we describe the opposition as being, not between ego drives and sexual drives but between life instincts and death instincts. (Freud 1920: 53, translation modified)[11]

Thus it is not possible for us to limit the study of the energy of drives, one of the energies that animate the dream, to the libido that is manifest in it in an oral context.

But how then are we to understand this other aspect of drive-energy, the ego-drives, the death-drives, which must also play a part, even in the production of this dream?

It is not perhaps without interest to recall here another expression which commonly served to designate Philippe: he belonged to that category of children often called 'Me-I' [*Moi-je*] because most of what they say begins with that ritual formula. But when he was called Mr. 'Me-I' it was not, we may be sure, in the same sympathetic context in which Lili returned to him that sign of complicity: 'Philippe—I'm-thirsty'. Here he showed that hateful egotism, the kind said to be so natural to children insofar as they do not have the added impudence to formulate it politely, the way 'grown-ups' do; thus this *ego* (me) that rubs shoulders with the *I* appears quite simply indecent—in short, insufferable.

Let us remark that with this 'me' there appears that which indeed one should never exhibit in good company: the word that sustains the void of the death-drive (ego-drive in the first terminology).[12]

If it is easy, on the whole, to represent the domain of the sexual drive energy—in other words the libido—it is surely not the case for the realm subject to the death drive.

We would like in this regard to report a second dream of Philippe's, of considerably later date than that of the unicorn.

> Someone (a boy of about twelve years old, it seems) has just slipped with one leg into a hole. He is lying on his side and shouts very loudly as if he were seriously injured. People (I am one of them) rush to see where the wound is: but nothing shows, either on his knee or his leg; all they find is a slight scratch on his foot, on the side of the heel, resembling a long, large comma, and which doesn't even bleed. He must, then, have hurt himself on an object hidden in the hole: people look for it, thinking of a rusty nail; actually it looks more like a bill-hook [*une serpe*].

Since the castratory context of this dream is clear, we will dispense with a general commentary in order to concentrate impartially on the principal themes its narration leads to. In other words, if it is clear that it is the 'desire for castration' that motivates the dream, what can we say more precisely about this paradoxical desire, so alien, it would seem, to any 'need'?

A fragment of an analysis of the bill-hook dream will allows us to locate the existence of the death drive in its function as matrix of desire and as essential support of the castration complex.

The first idea that comes to our patient following this story is that of a facial scar such as is mentioned on his identification card under the category of 'identifying marks'. Thus the wound has become a scar and a mark, now masked, we might say, by this trace. The dream unmasks the wound which, along the thread of his discourse, rises from the heel to the thigh, rear side, front side, and finally finds its place between them: flower, wound, cave or sanctuary.

The hidden wound constitutes the pivot of the dream. In its evocation, its importance is revealed by the very instantaneity of its occurrence, smooth and lightning-quick as a razor cut; the pain comes only after the moment of the wound and it seems that the catastrophic howl is linked less to the suffering which develops only gradually, than to the shock of the accident.[13]

We see with Philippe in this schematic portrayal of a threat to the integrity of the tegument a radical questioning of his unity as living body, a rupture, effraction, sudden disorder, fatal intrusion; in the chain of associations that the hook-cut of the dream gives way to in our patient, the themes of amputation, deadly tetanus, and decapitation emerge: it is the all-important theme of the end or the beginning that appears here in its catastrophic instantaneity. We should not as well that here it marks the origin of a state of tension—pain—linked to the subject's surviving that injury. But with pain we take leave of the indescribably, ungraspable fact of the death-drive: we are already entering into the field of a libidinal economy, here in its negative form as displeasure, as unresolved tension.

More commonly, but in a reverse order, we find the experience of a resolvent, almost ecstatic instantaneousness in the moment of orgasm which concludes—and gives meaning to—the increasing pleasure of amorous union.

The death-drive is that radical force, usually fixed and fixating, which surfaces in a catastrophic or ecstatic instant, at the point where the organic coherence of the subject in his body appears for what it is, unnameable or inexpressible, swoon or ecstasy, shouting its appeal for a word to veil and sustain it.[14]

Thus the death-drive surfaces without ever being seen. But we already perceive, though we cannot insist on it here, that it constitutes the 'bedrock' (Freud 1937b: 252), the foundation of the castration complex, that it allows—as indescribable and strictly unquantifiable limit—the development and the organisation of the sexual drives, and that finally—and we shall return to this—it imperiously gives rise to the development and structuring of language.

We could hardly have considered the energy sources of the dream without having asked the question of the *nature* of drives. Freud's affirmation concerning their dualism compelled us to take this long, circuitous path. It remains for us now to consider another aspect of the problem of drives, that of their *representations* in mental life.

It is emphasised that the drive, properly speaking, has no place in mental life (Freud 1915a: 177). Repression does not bear on it, it is neither conscious nor unconscious and it enters into the circuit of mental life only through the mediation of the '(*Vorstellungs-*)*Repräsentanz*' (or '[ideational] representative') (Freud 1915c: 148). This is a rather unusual term of which it must immediately be said that in Freud's usage, it is often found in divided form as one of its two components. We will translate this composite expression by 'ideational representative' and we shall inquire into the nature of this mediation, through which the drive enters into (one could even say 'is captured by') mental life.

It is on the ideational representative, it is said, that the primal repression constitutive of the unconscious operates (as we will show in detail further on); in the same way it is to representations that the derivatives of the biologically grounded drive energy will be bound.[15]

What exactly is this domain of 'representation' through which drives enter into mental life?

If we take the example of the unicorn dream, it is only in the context of its associations that we find the terms representing the oral drive, and we will underline two of them. The first is the memory of a gesture engraved like an image: Philippe, in recounting the memory, imitates the gesture of the couch, and it is this, moreover, that brings him, as we have mentioned before, to the evocation of the same cupped hands to produce the sound of a siren. We can say that for Philippe, this gesture will remain linked, in whatever circumstances, to the evocation of an oral drive: and if it should happen that he joins his palms thus to pick up some snow to cool his face, the gesture will retain on that occasion all its power to evoke the thirst quenched at the unicorn fountain. Assuredly, if this motor-representation thus remains electively tied to his thirst, it is also because such a gesture evokes in everyone, long before Philippe had 'rediscovered' it, that of the supplicant awaiting alms; the gesture of invocation, the 'sumbolon' at last realised in this mime. It is also, more concretely but t no less deeply, the complementary form—inverted in its concavity waiting to be filled—of the felicitous and full convexity of the breast.

The second term representative of the drive in the dream-association is the formula 'I'm thirsty'. Even more clearly than the gesture, it signifies the orality of the drive—fixates it, we might say—and we have already indicated one of the specific ways in which it was fixated and embodied in Philippe's history; he used to say 'I'm thirsty' (*j'ai soif*) or rather, it is reported (*'j'ai 'choif'*), virtually flaunting that declaration—often motivated in that burning summer—as a sort of insignia of himself ('me'!), Philippe, lost as he was on the immense beach. But this representative formula was fixated most of all through the agency of Lili, to the extent that the phrase 'I'm thirsty' has become a sort of password when Lili, in order to address him or talk to him, said: 'Philippe-I'm-thirsty'.

Inasmuch as we are thus able, through a fragment of analysis, to grasp what the 'ideational representatives' of the drive are, we may say that this gesture and this phrase are included among them. It is they, image and word, that will pursue their adventures in Philippe's psychic life; 'representatives' henceforth indifferent to or at least detached from the bodily disturbance underlying biological thirst, they drag along with them, always and in every circumstance, a small measure of basic avidity, of the anxious demand of this oral libido and of the fundamental levelling of the death-drive.

Having thus attempted to locate the specific level of drives, and having attempted to distinguish them from simple 'need', it remains for us to characterise what is called, strictly speaking, the *desire* of the dream,—that specific force which alone, according to Freud, can set the mental apparatus in motion.

How then is this essential motor-force present in the analysis of the unicorn dream? It is easy to see that what appears beyond the provisional formulation 'the desire to drink' is another desire, modelled less on the drive, forged essentially from these representations and their derivatives. It is around Lili, to whom the representative 'I'm thirsty' is addressed, that the essence of Philippe's desire is articulated. We are led there by more than one path: first of all the facile and ambiguous play on words which leads us from 'lili' to '*lolo*' in the latter's double meaning: the infantile one (milk) and the vulgar one (breast). Thus there emerges more clearly that 'desire for Lili' of which we are only beginning to see the implications. For what Philippe also tells us is that the nickname Lili seemed to be reserved for the exclusive use of her husband (and of himself, Philippe). We should finally emphasise the very special importance of the phoneme 'li' which we find again in the text of the dream, in *li*-corne [unicorn]; we pause here only to recall another facile pun mentioned by Philippe in this regard; Lili's *lit* [bed], evoking for him the happy couple formed by Lili and her husband, in contrast to the more difficult relationship between his own parents.

Thus we come by a laborious detour to that which, for an analytical ear, marks the crux of the dream and the soul of its desire—the unicorn: a fabulous composite animal, half-deer, half-horse, obvious symbol of exposed virility. But, as we shall see, it is not by chance that it should be the unicorn that arises in Philippe's dream: all the tracks, so to speak, led to it, just as it, in turn, leads on to the drinking spot, to the *moment of drinking* in which desire culminates and fades away.

Why then does this simplistic combination of Lili and horn [*corne*] come to impose itself on Philippe as an enigmatic symbol; why does this horn (horny, calloused feet) shift from feet to head (we will see this shortly in relation to the analysis of a symptom) just as in the dream of the bill-hook the scar had been displaced from forehead to heel? We will come back to this and be satisfied for the moment with indicating what precisely the analysis of Philippe's desire reveals to us: for him it is precisely a wish to establish a link, to forge a connection, to hide a gap, to defend against the catastrophe of a wound, to hold off at any price what might suggest castration in any way. In this sense the unicorn appears as the very realisation of that mythical unification, the fabulous animal which, in place of a third eye, carries the invulnerable and victorious appendage. The most widespread of legends has it that the unicorn is an animal difficult for the hunter to capture; he can succeed only by beguiling the animal with the help of a young virgin, for after placing his horn in her lap, the unicorn falls asleep.

The level of desire and its force is precisely this: the imaginary realm of myth and delusion, inasmuch as they take on the essential and natural function of concealing that radical force which is the death-drive.

To sum up—perhaps more enigmatically—we will say for the moment that the *unicorn* (*licorne*) appears in the dream-analysis as the *metonymy of Philippe's desire*.

(C) Remarks on the Mechanisms of the Dream and of its Interpretation. The 'Primary Process'. Metaphor and Metonymy

Thus there gradually appears, to the precise extent that we are able to deepen our analytical investigation, the outline of a text whose coherence is foreign to those procedures commonly recognised as logical.

Philippe's dream expresses and fulfils a wish to drink, which, upon analysis, is seen tot be complex, and composed for the moment of heterogeneous representations: Lili, foot, sand, horn, wound, trace, bill-hook, and finally the unicorn that seems to rise above and summarise this incongruous edifice, the fantasy-monument of Philippe's desire.

It is the specific coherence of this discourse (the interpretation of the dream) that we must now consider.

As opposed to logically-oriented speech, which unfolds in a clearly defined time and place, we observe that the unconscious text neglects these limits, that the *square* [*place*] of the fountain is a *beach* [*plage*], that this does not exclude the presence of a particular mountain, and that the summer of 195- is at the same time the summer of 193-. Upon closer examination, we see above all that the text includes rather peculiar articulations: not sequences punctuated by conjunctions present like signposts indicating the right direction, but, more simply: 'switch-words'. Thus the word sand, by simultaneously replacing and suggesting the heather, leads us not only to the sand which bears the footprints (tracks) of the does, but to the sand on the Atlantic beach as well; this word then appears in the text as containing (condensing) within itself meanings which are precise but which relate to another temporal and spatial context.

Finally, we could also emphasise another aspect of the particular coherence of unconscious discourse; which is that, in a certain sense, nothing is lost in it; thus the vivid colours of the heather are found again shifted onto the peaks of the trees, just as the unicorn in effigy on the central fountain which has disappeared from the square is seen again as companion and guide in the forest. It is obvious that these displacements are not merely accidental, and consequently the displacement of the flamboyant colours of the flowers onto the tree trunks must have a precise meaning, a 'shift of lightning' from the flower-wound onto a proud phallic symbol.

Timelessness, absence of negation and contradiction, condensation, displacement, these are indeed the specific characteristics 'which we may expect to find in processes belonging to the system *Ucs.*' (Freud 1915a: 187). Within the framework of the characteristics specific to this system, Freud goes on: 'I have proposed to regard these two processes [condensation and displacement] as distinguishing marks of the so-called *primary psychical process*' (Freud 1915a: 186).

It is here that we might in passing pinpoint this play of meaning and letter with an example: it is clear that in order to interpret the manifest text, we must first of all perform a rigorously 'literal' reading. From them on, we take into consideration the patient's 'chains of associations', that is, a more ordered discourse; these associations unfold roughly along two paths; on the one hand the purely literal level of the 'signifier'[16] (for example, the disentangling of Anne and Lili from Liliane) and, on the other hand, the level of meaning or 'significance' (for example, the fine sand leads to the beach).

We see, finally, that the chains of associations and the dream's manifest text coincide, as we have already mentioned, in a few 'switch-words', which are precious for our investigation; it is these terms that must be considered as the constitutive elements of the unconscious text. Thus the terms Lili, beach, sand, unicorn—occurring in the manifest text or the associations around the first dream—no doubt constitute already the elements of the unconscious chain that we are to discover.

We would not want to conclude these comments on the texture of the dream and the correlative process of our interpretation without returning to the question of the 'primary process', and insisting on what J. Lacan has already often emphasised—that is, the perfectly feasible identification in scientific linguistic terms of the two mechanisms of displacement and condensation (Lacan 1977a).

The mechanism of *condensation* (*Verdichtung*), which consists in the substitution of one signifier for another, is to be seen in terms of that of *metaphor*. Thus, in the dream-text, the signifier 'square' [*place*] seems to have replaced the signifier 'beach' [*plage*]. The metaphor square thus points to and masks the scene in question in the dream—the beach. But it is clear that this substitution underscores precisely the 'forefront' position, the 'publicity' given in the dream to the original beach scene. We shall return at length to the mechanism of metaphor, precisely to the extent that it is linked to repression.

Displacement, or *Verschiebung*, corresponds to *metonymy*. The unicorn appears in the dream as a marvellous metonymy, harking back to the fountain, but also to its own legend and, indeed, to a whole circuit whose structure still remains to be determined in detail. Technically, metonymy is precisely the figure that emphasises the connection between one signifier and another, thus sustaining the whole elementary mechanism of language, which dreams exploit without limit.

But what must be emphasised here is that the metonymic connection establishes a bridge between two (or more) signifiers whose relationship, in form or content, is much less obvious (much more arbitrary and singular) than in the case of metaphor: between '*place*' and '*plage*' the link may be apparent; but only the unicorn can rise above and bind together the incongruous medley of fantasies which sustain Philippe's desire.

The unicorn is a metonymy in the sense that everything in it, in the effigy as in the word, indicates not only condensation, of course, but also the *displacement* and the *interval* that separates the terms it joins. From the *li(t)* [*lit*=bed] in Lili to the horny callous [*corne*] that Philippe would like to have on his feet, the *licorne* [unicorn] maintains in the interval between its first two syllables the intermediate elements of the unconscious chain. On another level, it refers more simply to the fountain it overlooks, to the water that springs from it, to the very instant of drinking; finally, from feet to head, just like the scar in the bill-hook dream, it displaces the horn by transforming it from hard outer skin into a spike.

When we speak of the metonymic function of the unicorn (*licorne*), it is precisely to the extent that this signifier refers back, not to an object which would quench the thirst in question, but on the contrary, to the fact that it is itself, as metonymy and bearer of the phallic symbol, that which designates, covers or masks the gaping abyss of the subject or, if one prefers, his 'original castration'. Thus metonymy, like the scar, by its inexhaustible power of displacement, is made precisely to mark and mask the gap through which desire originates and into which it perpetually plunges, on the bedrock of the death-drive.

It is at one of these limit points in which the death-drive surfaces that we may mythically situate, according to Freud, the 'birth of the unconscious'—as we will show later on.

IV. *The Unconscious is the Precondition of Language. Interdependence of the Preconscious and Unconscious System*

(A) Situating the Problem: Language and the Primary Process

The preceding analysis leads us, as J. Lacan has shown, to identify what Freud calls the primary process—the free flow of libidinal energy along paths of displacement and condensation—with the fundamental laws of linguistics.

Were we to stop at this all too simple conception, however, we would run up against the most serious objections, and it is in Freud himself that we find them set out the most clearly (Freud 1915a: 196-204). Freud, in fact, did speak explicitly of language, but what he relates it to is essentially the preconscious system and the process that characterises: the secondary process, which opposes its barriers and detours to the free play of libidinal energy.

There is, of course, we read in Freud, a language which functions according to the primary process, but it is a very special language, not language itself: it is the language of psychosis. Let us go further; what differentiates this language from others is what makes it less of a language than they, for it treats words not as words, but as things, or as images in a dream:

> In schizophrenia *words* are subject to the same process as that which makes dream-images out of latent dream-thoughts—to what we have called the primary mental process. They undergo condensation, and by means of displacement transfer their cathexes to one another in their entirety. The process may go so far that a single word, if it is specially suitable on account of its numerous connections, takes over the representation of a whole train of thought. [Freud adds in a note:] The dream-work, too, ocaasionally treats words like things, and so creates very similar 'schizophrenic' utterances or neologisms. (Freud 1915a: 199)

How can we get out of this contradiction? For Freud, it is clear that something more has to be introduced into the primary process, a certain regulation, in order for language in the strict, or at least in the common sense of the term to be established. Let us indicate at once the idea which will govern the rest of our discussion: this ballast which removes languages from the exclusive domination of the primary process . . . is precisely the existence of the unconscious chain.

(B) The Fiction of Language in a Reduced State

The theoretical, deductive character of this section should be forgiven: it can be taken, if one wishes, as a myth—the myth of a language that would unfold on only one level, that is, without an unconscious.

On a single level? But we would rather say in a single discourse, for we should recall here the symbolism that modern linguistics, followed by J. Lacan, has taught us to use: the formula $\frac{S}{s}$, where the S symbolises the signifier, that is, language taken in its most literal, material texture.[17] As for the signified, s, the question is already much less simple, since we cannot be content with the purely 'mental' reality, the 'concept' it is said to connote by Saussure. As for the bar that separates them, it is there, in our opinion, that the essence of the problem lies, for if the very possibility of this formalisation implies the bar's resistance to any crossing over from one level to another, it must, however, lend itself to what we have to call effects of meaning, that is, it must account for what, in the final analysis, appears to phenomenological analysis as the openness of language to the world of meanings. We say, 'in the final analysis', for at the outset we must maintain that this intentionality is absolutely irreducible to the link between a thing and a signal, such as the theory of conditioned reflexes sought to introduce at the origin of human language. It could easily be shown that what is conceived of as such, as designation—the word table learned by gesture—is conceivable—in the child, for instance—only within an already constituted language in which he is immersed, and in a universe itself constituted by language.

In order to construct our myth, however, let us take things at their origin, as if language, for the individual in his primitive infantile state, came to be connected little by little, a pure neo-language and not the assumption of a pre-existing linguistic world. We will be pardoned for offering for consideration the example which has been much bandied about recently because of its very richness: the so-called *'fort-da'* example (Freud 1920: 11ff). If, by allowing him to master them, the opposite pair of phonemes A-O comes to symbolise for the child the presence and absence of his mother, is it not by this same movement that presence and absence are themselves constituted as the two categories into which the child's whole universe is divided, whereas previously (to the extent that one can speak of a prior time) it was wholly and without mediation satiety or void. The banality of what we are saying joins up with the universality of the myth of *Genesis*: in a single motion, the separation and the naming of heaven and earth occur.

In this example, reduced to the simplicity of its four terms—presence and absence which are signified, the O and the A as signifiers—the co-extension of the two systems (signifier and signified) appears in all its clarity, as does the essential fact that A refers to presence only to the extent that it refers to its phonemic opposite, O.

If we now suppose that the system is enriched through differentiation, by the introduction of those successive dichotomies which, from Plato to modern linguistics, characterise the moment of 'definition', the structural characteristics will remain the same: if the signifier refers to the signified, it is only through the mediation of the entire system of signifiers—there is no signifier that does not refer to the absence of the others and that is not itself defined by its position in the system. And the only correspondence between the signifier and the signified is the correspondence of the totality of signifiers to the totality of the signified, which correspondence is a perfect one, without any overlap.

If we stop at this point, the system thus obtained resembles schizophrenic language in more than one respect, and it is with a touch of malice which is not without a certain profundity that Freud compares the latter to abstract philosophical thought (Freud 1915a: 204). We can sense this by referring to the dizzying effect of a dictionary: each word, definition by definition, refers to the others by a series of equivalents; every synonymous substitution is authorised (as Freud indicated in the case of the schizophrenic), but language ends up in tautology, without at any moment having been able to hook onto the least 'signified'. Here is indeed the origin of that constant sliding of the signifier over the sea of the signified, as J. Lacan has described it. But we are faced here with a truly demented sliding without any limit, the model of a language subject only to the primary process.[18]

It is here that J. Lacan introduces his theory of so-called 'capping points' [*points de caption*] by which, at certain privileged points, the chain of signifiers comes to be fixed onto the signified.[19] It would be wrong to see in this a surreptitious return to a nominalistic theory, in which the function of cutting short the circular dash of language is assigned to a link with some 'real' object, to that link of habit that a certain type of modern experimentation designates as 'conditioning'.[20]

If we return to the example of the dictionary, we may say that what prevents one terms from sliding—endlessly—into another is not its empirical relation to a thing, but the fact that it is not univocal and includes several definitions, that it is the whole group of meanings *b*, *c*, etc. which prevents word x from flying out the door opened by meaning *a*. We see that our fiction of 'language in a reduced state' joins that of a language without equivocation, and that this unequivocal language would be, paradoxically, one in which no stable meaning could exist.

(C) Metaphor as Constitutive of the Unconscious, and Primal Repression

> Between the two chains . . . those of the signifiers as opposed to all the ambulatory signified that circulate because they are always in the process of sliding—the pinning-down or capping point I speak of is mythical, for never has anyone been able to pin a meaning to a signifier; but on the other hand, what one can do is pin a signifier to a signifier and see what happens. But in that case, something new always results . . . namely, the appearance of a new meaning . . . [21]

It is in the 'thesaurus' of various definitions that fall into place for a given word that we must look for the path to that which limits the primary process. A thesaurus of metonymies, according to J. Lacan, to the extent that the signifier thus finds itself included in a number of chains.

But at the same time, we would say, a thesaurus of past metaphors, for it is always a metaphor, a substitution of signifiers that is found at the root of the creation of new meanings.

Let us recall here the diagram that Lacan gives of metaphor in its linguistic symbolisation:

It consists in the substitution, in the relation of signifier to signified ($\frac{S}{s}$), of a new signifier S′: used as a signifier of the original signifier S, which, by virtue of that fact, falls to the rank of signified. Thus, according to the algebraic formula:[22]

$$\frac{S'}{S} \times \frac{S}{s} \longrightarrow S' \times \frac{1}{s}$$

Formula (I)

What has happened is apparently something quite simple, a change of name: the signified s that I first named S, is now connoted by S′.

But we also see, and this is what interests us, that something has fallen below, has been 'simplified out' in the algebraic sense of that term—the original signifier. *It is to the extent that the fate of this signifier S is distinct from a pure and simple suppression* that metaphors offer poetical resources creative of meaning, as opposed to mere 'nominal definitions': 'Metaphor must be defined as the implantation, into a chain of signifiers, of another signifier, by dint of which the one it replaces falls to the rank of signified, and, as latent signifier, perpetuates the interval onto which another chain of signifiers can be grafted'.[23]

What happened to the signifier S′? It has fallen to the rank of signified, but at the same time, to the rank of latent signifier; so that we are prepared to write the formula of this process as follows:[24]

$$\frac{S'}{S} \times \frac{S}{s} \longrightarrow \frac{\;\frac{S'}{s}\;}{\;\frac{S}{S}\;}$$

Formula (II)

What we see in formula (II) is nothing other than the *very diagram of repression*, in which what had apparently been 'simplified out' in preconscious speech has been preserved on another line.

This formula is able to account for a certain number of essential characteristics not only of repression, but also of the relation between the repressed unconscious and the preconscious, and of the structure of the unconscious chain.

1. Let us insist, first of all, on the *layered structure*—the four layers—of the formula. A certain ambiguity is essential to it, since the two lower layers, which constitute the unconscious chain, are themselves in the position of signified in relation to the preconscious chain, but at the same time they are themselves split—at least potentially—into a letter and a meaning, exactly like the preconscious chain. We thus find symbolised what we sought to show in our critique of Politzer's position as well as in the imperative, running throughout Freud's text, of maintaining in their autonomy as systems—in correlation, of course, but even more, independent of each other—the preconscious and the unconscious.

2. In what respect does this formula, which is originally that of metaphor in all its generality—poetic, conscious metaphor—seem to us particularly suited for symbolising *repression*?

To tell the truth, the question of deciding whether purely conscious metaphors exist does not seem easily resolved. In any case, leaving this question aside for the moment, we will try, rather, to apply our formula to different types of repression, and more precisely to the two main categories distinguished by Freud: after-expulsion (*Nachdrängen*) and primal repression (*Urverdrängung*).

In the case of after-expulsion, Freud tells us, the representation is repressed by a double action: first, a repulsion on the part of the upper preconscious system, then an attraction on the part of what has been previously repressed. Freud differentiates this first action (repulsion) into a decathexis—a breaking of the connection that existed in the upper chain, and an anti-cathexis—a replacement, in the upper chain, of the repressed term by another. We see that this description coincides in essence with the mechanism of metaphor.

But, Freud tells us, there would be no repression if the repressed term did not connect up with elements of the unconscious that were already there and which exert on it a real attraction. What does this mean, if not that the term of the lower chain, $\frac{S}{s}$, finds itself absorbed, as it were, by the signifying connections it contracts at the unconscious level, that is, by what we have already encountered as unconscious cathexis or 'unconscious systemic *Prägnanz*'.

But for this attraction to operate, there must already be an unconscious system, and that is why Freud has recourse to a concept which we believe essential to his theory, and in particular to the domain of psychosis: primal repression.

> We have reason to assume that there is a *primal repression*, a first phase of repression, which consists in the psychical (ideational) representative of the drive being denied entrance into the conscious. With this a *fixation* is established; the representative in question persists unaltered from then onward and the instinct remains attached to it. (Freud, 1915c: 148, translation modified)

We shall comment on certain expressions: 'the psychical (ideational) representative of the drive being denied entrance into the conscious . . . ' That is: the object of primal repression was never conscious; but since, on the other hand, it was not unconscious either before being repressed, at least in the sense of the dynamic unconscious, we have to admit a sort of mythical primitive state in which the differentiation of the preconscious and unconscious systems does not yet exist, and in our opinion, this myth is directly parallel to the previously presented myth of a unilinear language.

'With this a *fixation* is established.' Fixation is here to be taken in the broadest sense. It is, of course, fixation in the classic psychoanalytic sense, but at the same time and inseparably from it, it is, on the one hand, a fixation in the unconscious, what Freud in another passage we have quoted calls indifferently fixation or inscription, that is, the insertion into an unconscious chain; on the other hand, it is the fixation of the drive to this mental representation, a process by which, and by which alone, the drive is introduced into and present in the unconscious.

> It is this [the anticathexis] which represents the permanent expenditure [of energy] of a primal repression, and which also guarantees the permanence of that repression. Anticathexis is the sole mechanism of primal repression; in the case of repression proper ('after-pressure') there is in addition withdrawal of the *Pcs.* cathexis. (Freud 1915a: 181)

We see that all the energy found at the beginning of the constitution of the unconscious resides in the anti-cathexis; here there can obviously be no question of an unconscious attraction, since the latter does not yet exist; on the other hand, a withdrawal of preconscious cathexis is out of the question, since we may say that the preconscious does not yet exist as a system. We may think of things in the following way: all the energy of both the preconscious and unconscious systems comes from this kind of original cleavage, as one can imagine that a negatively charged particle of electricity and a positive one could be formed by splitting from a void of energy. But the creative gesture, for Freud, springs, despite all this, from a certain energy he calls anti-cathexis. In the formula for metaphor, it is necessary here to conceive of the existence of certain *'key-signifiers'* placed in a metaphorising position, and to which is assigned, because of their special weight, the property of ordering the whole system of human language. It can be seen here that we allude in particular to what J. Lacan has called the paternal metaphor.

3. Another point should surprise us and hold our attention: it is the identity of the two terms which, in the unconscious chain, are found in the position of signifier and signified: $\frac{S}{s}$.

Here we will take a detour through Freud. Our point of departure above was his reflections on psychosis. It is in order to account for the different between the phenomena encountered in psychosis and in neurosis that Freud comes to posit an essential distinction, that between thing-representations (*Sachvorstellungen*) and word-representations (*Wortvorstellungen*). Note immediately that both of these must be taken in all rigor for what they are: elements of language, signifiers. Thing-representations, Freud says, characterise the unconscious; it is these that constitute the language of dreams, concerning which we know that 'topographical' regression is accompanied by a requirement of expression in a language of images (*Rücksicht auf Darstellbarkeit*).[25] Word-representations, words taken in their most material sense as acoustic traces, characterise the preconscious system. Now, Freud returns here to the question that haunts his entire endeavour: the question of double inscription:

> We now seem to know all at once what the difference is between a conscious and an unconscious presentation. The two are not, as we supposed, different registrations of the same content in different psychical localities, nor yet different functional states of cathexis in the same locality; but the conscious presentation comprises the presentation of the thing plus the representation of the

word belonging to it, while the unconscious presentation is the presentation of the thing alone. (Freud 1915a: 201).

Our formula illustrates this passage in a striking manner: at the level of preconscious language, the distinction between signifier (words) and signified ('images') exists. At the level of unconscious language, there are only images, serving simultaneously and inseparably as signifier and signified. In a sense, it may be said that the unconscious chain is pure meaning, but one can say as well that it is pure signifier, pure non-meaning, or open to all meanings.

It is indissolubly because of the existence of this unconscious signifying chain that preconscious language possesses a certain fixity of meanings, the stability [*capitonnage*] that characterises the secondary process—and because of the existence of a preconscious chain with the characteristics familiar to us that the unconscious chain has taken over, so to speak, the characteristics of the primary process, such as we have mythically presented them 'in the beginning', as characteristics of the signifying chain reduced to a single dimension. We must, however, distinguish between the primary process's mode of operation in our 'primal fiction' and in the case of the unconscious chain: in the first case there was, after all, a distinction between the level of signifiers and the level of the signified, and an uncontrollable sliding of one over the other; in the second instance, the possibility of 'any meaning' arises from a real identity of signifier and signified. Is this to say that here there is no more possibility of sliding? On the contrary; but let us say that what slides here, what is displaced, is the drive energy in its pure, unspecified state.

Let us conclude this chapter of theoretical elaboration. The *origin* of the unconscious must be sought in the process that introduces the subject into a symbolic universe. One could describe, abstractly, two stages in this process. At a first level of symbolisation, the network or web of significant oppositions is cast onto the subjective universe; but no particular signified is caught in any *single* mesh. What is simply introduced, along with this system coextensive to experience, is pure difference, scansion, the bar: in the 'fort-da' gesture, the edge of the bed. This is, need we repeat it, a purely mythical stage, but the prenomena of psychotic language show that it can reappear 'secondarily', in 'regression', in the form of the uncontrollable oscillation of a pair of differential elements.

The second level of symbolisation is that which, following Freud, we called primal repression,[26] and, following Lacan, metaphor. It is this which really creates the unconscious, by introducing that ballast which will always be missing in a unilinear language, and which is lacking—to a greater or a lesser extent—in the symbolic world of the schizophrenic. The signified is from then on caught in specific meshes, at certain privileged points: the indefinite oscillation of + and -, O and A, 'good' and 'bad', right and left, comes to a halt. To borrow a term used by Merleau-Ponty in relation to perception, this second stage is one of an *anchoring* (*ancrage*) in the symbolic world.

As to the *ontological status* of the unconscious thus constituted, need we recall that, if that system is linguistic, such a language can by no means be assimilated to our 'verbal' language?

The 'words' that compose it are elements drawn from the realm of the imaginary—notably from visual imagination—but promoted to the dignity of signifiers. The term *imago*, somewhat fallen into disuse, corresponds fairly well, if taken in a broad sense, to these elementary terms of unconscious discourse.

By virtue of the very fact that they *remain* images, we do not find any distinction in these terms between a signifier and a signified; the signifying image refers to nothing but itself as signified. It is closed—as well as open—to every meaning.

The 'sentences' that are found in this discourse are short sequences, most often fragmentary, circular and repetitive. It is these that we discover as *unconscious fantasies*, or, more, inclusively, as *complexes*.

Imago, unconscious fantasy, complex—these three levels of the organisation of unconscious contents present the two following, seemingly contradictory characteristics: the fixity or even the rigidity of their formulation and their structure, and the interchangeability of the elements they may come to incorporate in the actual existence of the subject. The most striking example of this is given to us in analysis, when all the characters of a real situation occupy successively, as in a circular permutation, all the slots in the structure of the complex.

These are the different data which we have tried to account for by the formula of the repressive metaphor.

V. *Clinical Study of Some Fundamental Mechanisms of the Unconscious*

Thus there emerges more and more clearly the perspective of an *unconscious* structured like a certain type of primal language and which is a necessary *correlate* of *language* in the strict sense. We think we have shown sufficiently in the preceding pages that such a conclusion could not but impose itself upon the analyst.

We must now show how this conception offers improved possibilities of approach to the treatment of neurotic symptoms.

(A) Secondary Repression and Primal Repression.

Before illustrating our theory clinically, perhaps we may visualise things temporarily (and, of course, somewhat imprecisely) in a diagram which is useful not only for simply picturing the two systems and their inter-relations, but for situating as well the level of a question left partly in abeyance: that of the *specific energy* permitting the anti-cathexis necessary to *primal repression*.

Thus our (summarising) diagram shows on the right side the 'clinical' level of the problems, reserving in a sense the left part for the 'mythical' level of the 'creation of the unconscious'.

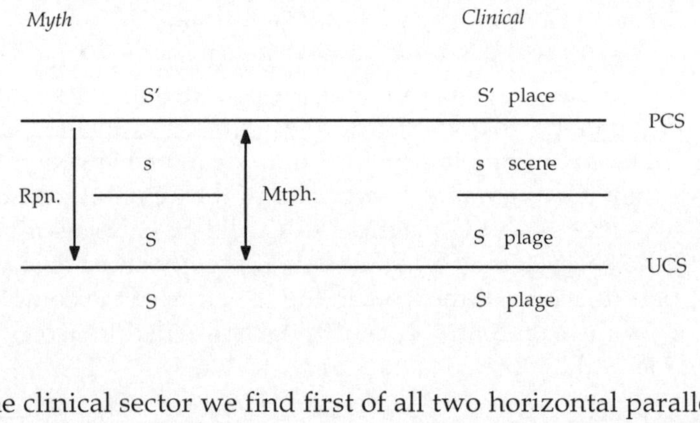

In the clinical sector we find first of all two horizontal parallel lines portraying the two systems, chains or discourses of which we have at great length demonstrated the implied necessity in any Freudian perspective. The upper chain is that of the Pcs. or Cs. system, the lower is the Ucs. Their structures are in correlation. Following J. Lacan, we indicate the element of preconscious discourse by the conventional formula $\frac{S'}{s}$. As for the element of unconscious discourse, the result of repression and the necessary correlate of conscious discourse, it is characterised by the relation between two signifiers $\frac{S}{S}$. We have seen, above all, and hope to have clearly shown, that the two formulas are linked by the metaphorical process of repression; we thus indicate the metaphorical link by a vertical line pointing in both directions, while the vertical line parallel to it, which points only downward, indicates repression. We should note that, in this instance, our point of departure is a past act of repression, thus, so to speak, the following formula:

$$\frac{\frac{S'}{s}}{\frac{S}{S}}$$

If *'place'* is the signifier S', we can say that it has been metaphorically substituted for the signifier *'plage'*, that is, S, which is repressed. We thus have in the upper chain (the manifest discourse) the signifier *'place'* which is there joined to the signified 'scene' or 'place of action'. The signified, s, is thus indeed the 'scene' where the action takes place. If we reversed the direction of repression we would again find the original sign $\frac{S}{s}$, that is, the beach [*plage*] as the scene of action $\frac{\text{plage}}{\text{scene}}$. Let us note in passing the selective nature of the repression which in this case (if we adopt the 'literal' viewpoint to which Freud has accustomed us) is applied to the *'ge'*, homologous in the context of the unconscious chain to the *'je'* [I] of 'I'm thirsty' or 'Me-I'.

Such then is the process of (secondary) repression properly speaking, simply illustrated, in conformity with the perspectives of our diagram. It will now be easy for us to pose the unresolved problem of primal repression (the mythical sector, at the left of our diagram).

Freud says quite explicitly, as we recalled, that there could be no secondary repression if the repressed term did not enter into connection with unconscious elements that were already there, and which exert upon it a real attraction. What does this mean, if not that the term of the lower chain, $\frac{S}{S}$, or $\frac{\text{plage}}{\text{plage}}$, finds itself absorbed, as it were, by the connections of signifiers through which it enters the level of the unconscious, in this case by the 'je', homologous to the 'ge' we remarked on just now.

Now, and we can repeat ourselves here, for this 'unconscious systematic *Prägnanz*' to become manifest, for this attraction to act, there must *already* be an unconscious system, the one 'created' by primal repression.

We shall try, still with the help of the same example, to illustrate this 'creation', concerning which we recall that it must also be considered as a myth.

If we return to our diagram and move towards the left of our lower chain, we arrive in the mythic sector where primal repression, in 'creating' a first unconscious chain with the help of the drive's ideational representatives, virtually makes possible access to real language. Let us then move to the left $\frac{\text{S}}{\text{S}}$, or $\frac{\text{plage}}{\text{plage}}$, or even better, $\frac{\text{ge}}{\text{ge}}$ which gives us by metonymic displacement $\frac{\text{Thirst}}{\text{Thirst}}$. Here we come to the repressed signifier-relationship concerning thirst. We had already indicated in our dream analysis to what extent the formula 'I'm thirsty' constituted one of the fundamental unconscious themes of the dream. But the real question even then was to know how to articulate what appeared there as the *desire* to drink with the oral drive and *need* to drink.

How can we move from '*drive energy*', which we presuppose, to '*desire*' as we have elaborated it: a composite fantasy symbolised by the metonymy of the unicorn [*licorne*]?

The dream analysis shows us insistently that the mediation between the drive energy and the desire is in this case electively assumed by the formula 'I'm thirsty', which becomes the 'ideational representative': that which, according to Freud, introduces the drive into mental life. It is, as we have recalled, through the process of its 'fixation' (inscription) to a representative, that the drive is introduced into and present in the unconscious.

It is, then, in the energy necessary for the maintenance of this anticathexis that everything that can be considered as energy creative of the unconscious lies.

As a suggestive illustration, we can, in this case, reconstitute the original myth of Philippe's thirst, if not with certainty—who could?—at least with maximum probability.

When Philippe as a child was still in that state of dependence his mother likes to remind him of—and which is universally invoked as an all too convenient explanation—her certainly felt a longing to drink in that unmediated, unnuanced was we evoked in the words: plenitude and void. Whether he was permitted to drink or not probably made little difference to the insistence of an ever-renewed need, until the day when (we can speak retrospectively in this way, as in a fairy tale)—was it Lili or another?—someone articulated clearly: 'Philippe is always thirsty' and called him 'Philippe-I'm-thirsty'.

To recognise and say that Philippe was thirsty was to introduce, despite the benign appearance of the remark, an entirely new dimension. being thirsty no longer drowned Philippe in the depths of a blind drive, it became for him at most a passion . . . he continues to cultivate; for being thirsty was not only gaping and shouting, it was from then on being recognised as being subject to a *drive defined* by the word *thirst*; it was above all, and this is the essential part, to introduce through the signifier 'thirst' the basic dimension of *Lili's* thirst—for Lili used to say, in referring to herself—his memory is definite on this point -: 'Philippe, I'm thirsty'. (In truth, as may be realised, the memory is ambiguous, and it is this which gives it its value. Lili spoke this way 'as a joke', but we know what 'a joke' means. For everything indicates that Philippe had understood the joke literally and, beyond that, with all its resonances.)

That this is a relatively recent memory of the age of three years takes away nothing of its value as a retrospective illustration of an experience that marked Philippe in a fundamental way, for we are not naïve enough to believe that this privileged memory constitutes and delimits our subject's experience.

We are now able to give a first formula which will summarise the myth of the birth of the unconscious: *it results from the capture of drive energy in the web of the signifier*.

Let us then complete the mythic sector of our diagram by indicating *undifferentiated drive energy* as a horizontal arrow; similarly, we will add the incidental fragment of Lili's manifest chain of signifiers, enclosed in a 'balloon': 'Philippe, I'm thirsty'.

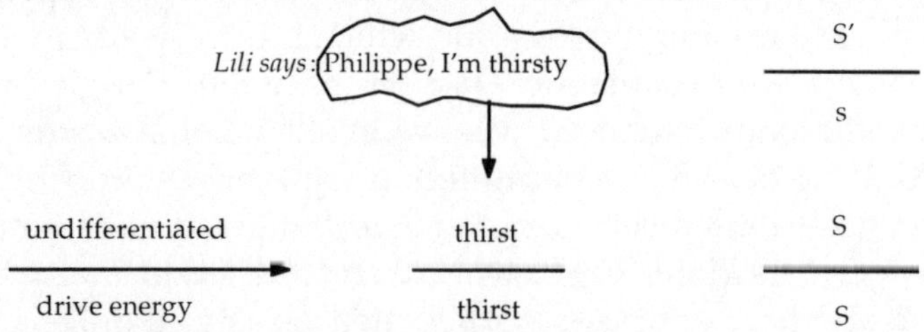

It is this 'I'm thirsty' that will constitute one of the original kernels of the unconscious chain.

Of course, we may still inquire as to why it was precisely this signifier that was repressed in order to constitute one of the basic terms of this primordial unconscious. Without wanting to pursue the development of this analysis too far, we think that it is nevertheless opportune to develop one aspect of it.

We have already seen, in the course of our previous analysis, that by means of the new-formed name Liliane, Lili took on a special weight at the level of the dominant unconscious formations of Philippe's mental life. Besides the already noticed fact of the easy passage from *lolo* to Lili, concerning the drinking question, and the phonemic opposition lo-li . . . (!) that we will not develop here, we should recall that Lili was not the name of the person in question, but only the diminutive used exclusively by her husband . . . and himself.

It thus appears fairly clearly, as we have already shown, that beyond the *desire to drink*, by which we have summarised the wish that formed the dream, there appear one after the other, Philippe's desire for Lili, Lili's desire to drink, and finally, above all, *Lili's desire for her husband*.

We can then say that if the incident 'Lili says: Philippe, I'm thirsty' takes on the function of a catalyst creating the unconscious, it is to the extent that the signifier THIRST arises there like a representative intersection, a crossing of paths that leads not only to a dual situation of dependence on the mother, but to an Oedipal one as well, in the direction of Lili's thirst.

Thus we have shown by a first reconstitution of the fantasy of Philippe's thirst the myth of the birth of the unconscious, to the extent that the latter 'results from the capture of drive energy in the web of the signifier'.

But we must now focus more rigorously on the mythical location of the encounter between drive and signifier.

In the unicorn dream it is at the very moment of drinking, when all tension disappears in a flash; the moment when 'Me-I'm thirsty' is realised and abolished, that the death-drive, as we said earlier, emerges at the surface. For the nurseling it is the instant in which, literally sated, he dozes off, just as the unicorn of the legend drops off to sleep and loses himself after yielding to the hunter's ruse: it seems, for an instant, that with the plenitude there opens up the fascinating call of a void: of bliss or catastrophe. But for Philippe today it is no longer drinking that satisfies or moves him thus; what remains is sometimes, granted, the anxiety of finding himself in a place which might lack water, but mostly what survives today is precisely the 'me-I'm-thirsty', a veritable magic formula that opens and shrouds abysses for him, from above or below, and which he cannot express otherwise. he becomes uneasy on hearing it, just as in a dream a chasm or light vaguely perceived suspends the dream in a *scream* or a laugh.

Doubtless we are able to understand that from the day 'I'm thirsty' (*j'ai soif*) or simply 'Choif' could replace this inarticulate scream, Philippe began to master something in the order of the ineffable. At the same time as he took on in this way a fragment of language, his primary unconscious was born together with this first masking of the death drive.

This appears to us more clearly in the bill-hook dream, where the scream is a part of the dream itself, evocative of the 'kiai' (that sacred cry in Zen Buddhism) which is capable of killing or bringing back to life: now in this dream, what comes, instead of death, to fill up the gaping wound, is a scar, a 'trace'. And we shall see that this trace is far from indifferent, that it is even revealed to be the signifier *par excellence*.

This red trace on his heel, the only apparent injury caused by the hidden castrating hook in the dream, refers us back, as we have seen, to a scar that Philippe in fact bears on his forehead. It is the trace of a relatively serious childhood accident: in the context of a struggle for recognition with a boy considerably older than himself there occurs a wound, which is experienced as catastrophic and which brings him back to a regressive situation of satisfaction as his mother's coddled child. Today, this sign, this identifying mark, remains in some sense the sign of the favourite, even the elected one. As symbol of preferential distinction, and as signifying above all this wound and, beyond it, many others, the scar also refers directly to the dominant mark of ritual circumcision. Through the dream analysis the meaning of the foot bearing a wound is revealed as correlative to the circumcised penis and the present versions of his desire. To have been the favourite is in fact to have been an object of his mother's desire.

For our subject nothing indicates security and unshakeable shelter (consolation, fortress, and impasse) better than the scar, the trace of a mother who received him with love; but even more than security, the scar signifies today that he was loved with a passion. Thus this mark remains the symbol of an unmediated, sterile and imprisoning consolation; above all, it stigmatises and freezes the subject into the fantasmatic but aberrant position of signifier of desire.

Just as the mark of his circumcision virtually founds the instrument of his virility and fertility in a wound and a consecration, the mark on his face seems in a similar way to have dedicated him entirely to his mother: the scar is there to signify that his body in its entirety remains the sterile privilege of his mother's desire.

The unicorn's horn indicates the very location of this scar: it is as though in Philippe's unconscious the horn originated in it.

In regard to the question we asked: what is the specific energy allowing the anti-cathexis necessary to primal repression, the true 'creator of the unconscious', we can do no better for the moment than to answer through the analysis of Philippe's case which we have just elaborated. The specific energy is the fact of the death-drive precisely in so far as it is manifest as a radical and immobile force, or, better yet, as the opposite of a force, a void, for example, which is only related to libidinal drives in the sense that it founds them. We should like to be more precise and say that the representative of the drive is above all a representative of the death-drive: thirst or scar (trace, mark, hook); it is these primordial representatives that constitute the *primal unconscious*, that which exists only in the *state of primal repression*. As it appears in our fragment of analysis, it is from these primal unconscious representatives that what is called the subject's desire may (with varying degrees of success)develop: it is from this primordial text, inseparably bound to the surfacing of the death-drive, that representatives of libidinal drives appear and what can indeed be called '*desire*' is structured. It is from the signifier *thirst* that the libidinal complex 'thirst of (for) Lili' develops. It is from the trace (scar) that the libidinal complex of the 'favourite' derives.

More generally, we can say that language, like the unconscious, is primarily and indissolubly linked to the surfacing of the death-drive in so far as the latter remains precisely that foundation of the world of desire, which, alive, we can neither see nor name. We believe it useful to insist on this specific dimension of the 'primal' unconscious; if it escapes us, it becomes very hard to work effectively with the 'psychotic' unconscious, as well as in the domain of the neurotic unconscious—which is an effect of the secondary repression whose mechanism we have set out in detail.

For Philippe, then, the signifiers *thirst* and *trace* seem constitutive of the primordial unconscious. Thirst and trace are and accomplish primal repression, that is, the 'fixation' of the ineffable or catastrophic surfacing of the death-drive.

It is on the basis of this primal unconscious, whose mythical genesis in this instance we have tried to describe, that the unicorn will be able to evolve as the metonymy *par excellence* of Philippe's desire.

(B) The Formation of the Neurotic Symptom

We would like to consider further, in regard to Philippe's case, the mechanism of an apparently minor symptom called up by the dream associations. It might be referred to as the symptom of the 'grain of sand'.

It did not take Philippe long to tell us that he did not like the beach—but in such a fashion that it was easy for us to suspect the existence of some more fundamental difficulty. More memories, and very clear ones, of the summer on the Atlantic emerged, details related to experiences of cutaneous sensitivity: the contact of hot sand on the whole surface of his skin; of cool and humid sand when, in a game, he was buried in it; sand burning against the soles of his feet; and most of all, a major detail, contact with a plate of zinc heated by the sun.

To be on a beach for him now means to have sand everywhere, in his hair, in his teeth and ears; whether a little or a lot, some sand always remains, all the more annoying when there's hardly any. The height of irritation is occasioned by the *single grain* of sand that remains malignly hidden after a careful cleaning; the one that swells against the skin—but also by the wrong fold, the badly sewn seam, the little pebble in his shoe. All in all a very common irritation, but which assumes for Philippe the proportions of an obsessive preoccupation (is there not a crumb in the fresh sheets? a hidden pebble that will reappear in a carefully inspected shoe?), a more or less mastered obsession which can on certain occasions lead him to the brink of anxiety or throw him into a state of considerable irritation against others, himself, and the incriminated objects. This is how the symptom of the grain of sand appears.

What we would like to bring into relief in this instance is the specific constitution of the *unconscious chain* correlative to the secondary repression emergent here in the symptom.

Thus, through a cutaneous excitation, something unconscious arises and imposes itself to the point of leading the subject to the brink of anxiety or anger.

In this particular case, thanks to the work done on the dream, it seems to us almost possible to determine the constitution of that unconscious 'something'. If we consider the signifier *sand*, which appears as a grain at the centre of the symptom, we can develop on the lower chain the following sequence: on the one hand, the signifiers 'beach', then 'Lili', the major term of the chain. On the other, the important terms in the associative chain linked to the symptom: 'skin' and the 'foot' which was already alluded to in the manifest text by Liliane's 'bare feet', and by the associations recalling the attention paid to tracks.

Here a complementary indication is necessary in order to arrive at the ultimate term of the unconscious chain manifest in the symptom. It is the fact that Philippe distinguishes a privileged zone of the surface of his body—the soles of his feet—inasmuch as it fulfils one of his typically obsessional fantasies: having an insensitive and almost invulnerable skin, resistant and 'hard as *horn* (*corne*)'; (note, by the way, that in that expression the reference is to horses' hooves). He remembered only the pleasure he was to have later in walking barefoot, not only on sand, but also in the beds of dried-up torrents, and even, a far more singular fact, in the scree of glacier-hewn slopes: he was proud of the horny calluses developed in this way.

We shall not elaborate further the question of cutaneous erotisation except to say that Philippe manifested a whole series of symptoms related to his skin, of which the grain of sand was only a relatively simple example. We should add, however, a necessary remark: Philippe, who had very diverse attitudes toward different parts of his body, had particularly cathected his feet, and in a similar fashion, his head.

Let us return now to the unconscious chain thus completed by 'horn' insofar as it is precisely this 'horn' which will bridge the gap between feet and head, in conformity with its metonymic function. We can spell it out entirely and write:

LILI—beach—sand—skin—foot—HORN (CORNE), as it appears to us after an attempt at analysing that indefinable thing which intrudes by means of a small cutaneous irritation to form a grain of sand.

It will suffice now, in order to summarise this chain, to condense its extremities; the *LI-CORNE* (unicorn) will be sketched out. *It is in this way, in the final analysis, that the unconscious is discovered.*

It seems to us that if a formation may be identified by the term *complex,* it is indeed something like *this sequence frozen by the illusion of its grotesque discourse into the effigy of the UNICORN.*

We will not resume here an analysis of the unicorn, which would in some sense be a repetition of what we have already elaborated concerning Lili. It would show us again that *what gives it its irresistible force* is its relation to a major element, *the phallus, the signifier par excellence of desire.*

We will pause rather to pursue a little further the dream of the billhook. We have already emphasises that this dream (occurring after the unicorn dream) led us more directly that the earlier one to the primal repression constitutive of the primordial unconscious.

The moment of drinking and the signifier *thirst* appeared to us in the unicorn dream as the surfacing and concealment of the death-drive; the catastrophic *scream* and the signifier *trace* appear to us in this hook dream even more clearly as the emergence and the fixation (primal repression) of the same radical force constitutive of the primordial unconscious.

At the level of the clinical analysis of the second dream, that of the bringing to light of the unconscious properly speaking (the fruit of secondary repression), we find certain constants of Philippe's unconscious, such as the foot. Instead of being the one who 'leaves a trace', he bears it on his heel in the form of a red scratch on the very spot where the horny callous is usually hardest. Similarly, this trace refers us to the forehead, to the precise spot in which the mythical animal's horn is planted; if we then consider, as the analysis leads us to, the themes of castration in this dream, the phallus appears as marked by the wound, or better, as being fixated to the wound itself. Philippe seems to be marked in his totality by the sign of this castration; he appears, one could say, as one huge scar or a single marked phallus, which makes it difficult for him to become the bearer of a phallus, except through the metonymic intermediary of the unicorn. And we may inquire here, in comparing this analysis with those of other obsessionals (such as the case of Philon, which we have developed elsewhere), whether this particular position with regard to the castration complex is not specific to obsessional neurosis.[27] It is as if for Philippe the theme of castration were never separated from that primal repression in which the signifier comes to mask the surfacing of the void of the death-drive; he remains, as is said, in the breach, constantly occupied, it seems, in mastering the primordial unconscious without ever really succeeding—or if so, at what a price . . .

The analysis of the bill-hook dream should allow us to reintroduce dialectically, at the level of secondary repression, the scar of the real wound and to decathect it of maternal passion; it should lead us above all to free Philippe somewhat from the breach he feels compelled to fill like an omnipresent phallus. Thus he will be able to have (and no longer be) a phallus by founding it precisely on this mark, and to open the field of his desire by assuming castration instead of fending off or denying it.

If the unicorn dream leads us principally to the Oedipal—i.e., libidinal—context of Philippe's unconscious, the bill-hook dream opens more directly to us the path of the castration complex and the energy specific to the death-drive.

Both of these forces are found in the constitution of the neurotic symptom of the grain of sand: the unconscious chain of the bill-hook dream—foot-sand-trace-head—coincides with and confirms the unicorn dream, as we see, in more than one aspect.

We can now say that the grain of 'sand which-bears-and-loses-the-trace', by irritating Philippe's skin and foot, leaves in its turn a trace there; it quickens the edges of that imaginary wound, crevice or gap, trace or thirst; it summarises and reminds Philippe, in its malign way, of the difficult assumption of his desire.

Postscript (Jean Laplanche)

My contribution to this essay—chapters I, II, and IV—is a transcript of a presentation offered for discussion at the Colloquium of Bonneval in October 1960. Its publication today leads me to underscore what seems to me most worthy of attention among the problems raised.

1. Two of Freud's fundamental discoveries overlap in Lacan's maxim, according to which 'the unconscious is structured like a language': (a) the discovery of meaning, even in those phenomena previously considered the dross and refuse of human activity—formations of the Unconscious; (b) the discovery that this 'unconscious' meaning always occurs implicated in a conflict, bearing wishes, undergoing,

through compromise or substitution, the *marks* of that struggle. In our first two chapters, we attempted to shown that the data of analytic experience imply that the Unconscious has a *reality* which has a hold on that conflict and is electively available to it.

2. To attribute to the Unconscious a reality of the *same type* as that of the letter of a text is to satisfy in a specific theoretical model this double requirement. But from that point on all the ambiguities of the phrase '*like* a language' appear.

Should we attempt to elucidate the reality of the Unconscious by that of language (the object of linguistics), we would have a hard job avoiding two dangers: either reducing the specificity of the Freudian Unconscious and forgetting the fundamental difference between the interplay and nature of representations on the unconscious level, on the one hand, and the preconscious-conscious one on the other; or, through a subversion of linguistic concepts, specifically those of metaphor and metonymy, furnishing custom-made a certain notion of language, in order subsequently to show easily enough that the Unconscious functions no differently.

No doubt a dialectical confrontation would not leave psychoanalytic and linguistic concepts unchanged. But for that to occur, the dialectic, in each of its stages, must be observed and the concepts reformulated. To proclaim hastily that Freudian displacement *is* metonymy and condensation metaphor is to choose to ignore much information and many developments for which we are indebted to Freud as well as to the linguists, to skip (to say the least) numerous mediations.

It will be noticed that in our text, the linguistic model of metaphor is used not in order to assimilate it to the unconscious process of condensation, but to illustrate the mechanism of repression as it functions *between* Unconscious and Preconscious, *between* primary and secondary processes.

3. A step further. The Freudian unconscious and the language of the linguists are in such radical *opposition* to each other that a term for term transposition of their properties and laws may properly be regarded as a paradoxical undertaking. So that the confrontation between psychoanalysis and linguistics seemed possible to us only through a splitting of each of their domains. A splitting of the psychoanalytic domain into an unconscious area governed by the primary process and a preconscious area governed by the secondary process: this is a familiar theme. But a splitting of the linguistic domain as well, issuing in a language which is none other than the one thanks to which we communicate,

and it is this 'fiction of language in a reduced state' that we have attempted to sketch.

Thus the comparison occurs among four terms: the 'language' of the Unconscious, if it does indeed possess the essential characteristic of being a circulation of *Vorstellungen*, is *comparable* only to that vertiginous layer of language which certain poets occasionally allow us to glimpse.

4. From then on, our inquiry posed a certain number of questions, opened up more hazardous paths.

What is the relation among those languages which are at once aberrant and primary: the language of the Unconscious, schizophrenic language, poetic language, and finally, our fiction of a 'language in a reduced state'? For if this last example, in our myth, was supposed to exist alone before the separation of heaven and earth, the other languages mentioned here are languages from after the separation, bearing within them the vestiges of an origin . . . which never existed.

What are the conditions of the transition from the primary process to the secondary process? This is the classical problem in psychoanalysis of 'binding': binding of psychical energy, binding of representations, binding of meaning, finally, which confers on it a certain stability. Pressing our line of thought to the limit, we attempted to show binding at work in the process of *primal repression* conceived of on the model of metaphor. Which leads us to this surprising proposition: what conditions the transition from the primary process to the secondary process is precisely the constitution and maintenance of the Unconscious as a separate domain. *The Unconscious,* we said, rather than a language, *is the very condition of language*.

5. This brings us to 1959. We are aware, however, that the problem of binding is too complex to be reduced to the simple mechanism of signifiers established through metaphor. What is the relationship of this binding of meanings—in which the law of castration, 'of the father' is preponderant—with that binding by the 'ego' which psychoanalytic thought since the *Project for a Scientific Psychology* has never stopped affirming? How are they opposed and articulated in their effects, in the psychotic effect of their failure as well? Such is one of the prolongations of this text we should be tempted to undertake.

1965

NOTES

Foreword

1 They were first published in the *Bulletin de Psychologie*, then, from the year 1974-1975, in the periodical *Psychanalyse à l'Université.*

Part One—Reference to the Unconscious

1 In this series entitled *Problematics.*

2 [*Translator's note*: The *Diplìme d'êtudes Approfondies* is a postgraduate qualification comprising a year-long course of lectures and seminars, followed by a research-based thesis. It is roughly equivalent to an M.A. in the British university system.]

3 Three courses had been announced within the framework of the DEA 1977-1978. These were: J. Gagey, *Ideology and Theory;* M. Dayan, *Fantasy and the Event*; and the one published here.

4 [*Translator's Note*: An English translation of this paper appeared in vol. 48 of *Yale French Studies* in 1972, and is reproduced in full, in the present volume, beginning on p. 232, below.]

5 The entire Freudian analysis of mourning shows that it is *not* what it seems to be, that is to say, a 'sadness of loss'.

6 Here, of course, I am quoting the passages which serve me best: the letter should be read in its entirety . . . an 'entirety' which has been truncated by the 'editors', who must have considered uninteresting the passages they did not understand.

7 In German, we must remember, *Angst* signifies both fear and anxiety. It is sometimes *Angst* taken in its absolute meaning, but at other times *Angst vor*—in other words, 'anxiety about'. Cf. my course on 'Anxiety, Pain, Unpleasure', published in *Problématiques I*, 1st part, under the title 'Angst in Neurosis'.

8 [*Translator's note*: 'Investment' is used here to translate the French term *'investissement'*. Throughout the present translation, 'investment' is used in preference to Strachey's 'cathexis', and is held to be a more accurate rendition of Freud's original term—*'Besetzung'*. See Laplanche & Pontalis 1988: 65, note a.]

9 [*Translator's note*: Laplanche's translation of Freud's title is *'La reconnaissance de l'inconscient'*, which suggests: 'the "surveying" or "recognition" of the unconscious'.]

10 Freud sometimes uses the term 'the other' (*das Andere*), which is not another person, but *das,* the neuter form. This is not the other (with either O or o) in the Lacanian sense, but 'the other thing', in the psychical sense.

11 [*Translator's note*: This article is reproduced, in full, beginning on page 232. All susbsequent references by Laplanche to this article refer to the present volume.]

12 See Colloque de Bonneval 1966: 170-177.

13 Cf. Lacan 1977a.

14 We are familiar with the entire history of these terms. Lacan had spoken of 'representative of the representation', and Freud of something that can be translated by 'representative-representation'.

15 [*Translator's note*: Interpolations in square brackets, in this and in other quotations throughout the volume, are comments made by J.Laplanche.]

16 [*Translator's Note*: The Latin tag can be translated as 'following that, therefore on account of that'. Laplanche's reference to Hume at this point relates to Hume's definition of 'causation' as 'regular succession'.]

[17] I am thinking particularly of the in-depth work by Didier Anzieu (1986).

[18] Laplanche & Leclaire 1972.

[19] *Sic*. Any attempt to proclaim the'illusion of interiority' or the imaginary dimension of the 'depths' should take into account that it is first and foremost Freud with whom it has to *contend*, rather than lean on. Cf., further on, 'the dimension of depth of the mind'.

[20] [*Translator's note*: See footnote 8, above.]

[21] Cf. the correspondence between Freud and Groddeck, in Groddeck 1977a.

[22] In principle, I have nothing against a theory which awards a place to genesis, but I refuse to reduce genesis to factors of differentiation, development or maturation.

[23] Alongside the biological models, Freud also provided geological or geologico-archaeological metaphors. On this theme, there is an article in a recent issue of *Études philosophiques*, by Monique Schneider (1977), which begins to unravel the issue. There are other geological schemas in Freud, such as the notion of successive layers, each of which is covered over by the next.

[24] We should add that in German composite nouns, the intermediate 's', which may be present or absent according to rules of euphony alone, absolutely does not indicate a genitive. Witness the fact that it is appended to feminine nouns which do not take an 's' in the genitive case: *Vorstellung* does not have *Vorstellungs* as its genitive, and *Vorstellungsrepräsentant* is not 'representative of the representation'.

[25] There is an element in this text which is ambiguous, not to say contradictory. Here is the complete sentence: 'These instinctual impulses are co-ordinate with one another, exist side by side without being influenced by one another, and are exempt from mutual contradiction.' Obviously it is hard to reconcile 'being co-ordinate' and 'existing side by side without being influenced by one another'. At the risk of failing to show due respect for the sacrosanct 'text', I would gladly see 'co-ordinate' as a slip, and re-establish it as 'unco-ordinate'. I would even venture to leave open the interpretation of this being an error of typography and/or of Freud's. What follows, in any case, is clear on the question of this lack or co-ordination.

[26] See Laplanche & Pontalis 1988: 171-3. Entry on 'Free Energy/Bound Energy'.

[27] Since Lacan, reference has been made to 'the Saussurean algorithm', so that one is left with the impression that 'algorithm' designates an elementary cell; I myself have used the term algorithm in this sense. Well, an 'algorithm' (for which any Greek etymology would be pure whimsy, since the term comes from the name of an Arab mathematician Al Kawarizmi . . .), in its precise meaning, does not in any sense signify an elementary cell, but, on the contrary, the *system* that regulates the rules which bear on the operation of these elementary cells. Speaking of the Saussurean algorithm thus constitutes a form of displacement, since Saussure himself never developed any sort of 'calculation' on the basis of this formula S/s. When he takes an interest in the relations between these cells, it is in a purely static relation: this S/s is of interest only because it is inserted into a structure, alongside all the other possible S/s cells. What is called the 'value' is exactly this differential between one of these cells and all the others which exist in the language. So that by speaking of the algorithm in a rather inexact way, Lacan focuses our attention on something that is different from the cell itself, on what was already the interesting element of rhetoric—that is to say, the transformations which operate on these cells and which, indeed, go so far as to modify them, and to produce, according to Lacan's terminology, effects of meaning. In yet other terms, Saussure is interested essentially in what he calls language—that is, a structure, and analysis, like rhetoric, but in a different way—interested in transformations which modify, which 'work', in the Hegelian or Freudian sense, these fundamental cells

[28] It is with Chomsky that the opposition becomes pertinent, by subsuming under 'competence' not only the elements of the code, but everything which is within the province of the 'syntactical structures'.

[29] I am returning here to the analyses of J.F. Lyotard, in *Discours, figure* (Lyotard 1971: 260 n.54). It is doubtless important to affirm that the unconscious is not made up of 'verbal' language. However, what is essential is that this is not 'language of communication'—even if this were 'non-verbal'—and, inversely, that 'in verbal language itself there are figures which block communication, and which are rejects of the unconscious.'

[30] Cf. Laplanche 1976: 38-47.

[31] For the concept of 'afterwardsness' see 'Notes on Afterwardsness' in Laplanche 1999.

[32] I refer you once again to the work of J.F. Lyotard, *Discours, figure* (1971).

[33] I would refer anyone who wishes to explore this question of the diversity of difference, in regard to the question of the difference between the sexes, to Laplanche 1980b: 2nd part, 'Symbolisations'.

[34] I am using a 'vulgar' phonological transcription, which will broadly suffice for my argument.

[35] For a summary of this way of proceeding in etymology, cf. Todorov 1982: 248-54, on the history of the symbol.

[36] [*Translator's Note*: Laplanche's point here depends on the double meaning of *voler*: 'to steal' and 'to fly'.]

[37] I would refer you here to the famous and remarkable analysis, by Lacan, of 'his sheaf was neither miserly nor spiteful' (see Lacan 1977a). The fertility of this sheaf, *like all 'fertility'*, stems precisely from the fact that it is not just a question of metaphor, nor simply of metonymy, but of a complex and reciprocal interplay of 'metabolas', which is where I situate 'true' symbolisation.

Part Two—The Problematic of the Id

[1] [*Translator's Note*: This paper is reproduced in full, below, beginning on page 232.]

[2] You can refer to the passage which this student chose for his argument—the paragraph entitled 'The Unconscious and the Id'.

[3] Let us recall how Groddeck, speaking frankly, evaluated this so-called borrowing: '*The Ego and the Id* is fine, but it is absolutely without any impact for me. Fundamentally, it is written in order to be able to get hold of ideas borrowed from Stekel and myself. What is more, his id is only of limited value for the neuroses. The step into the organic is made secretly, with the assistance of a drive of death or destruction taken from Stekel and from Spielrein. He leaves aside the constructive aspect of my It, probably so that he can bring it in fraudulently the next time. There are a few agreeable things in the paper' (Groddeck 1977b: 147-8, LT's translation).

[4] Freud 1923a.

[5] The notion of a 'second censorship' (between the Cs. and the Pcs.) is nothing but a trick to make things easier, if one does not conceive of it as the echo, the reflection of the first censorship—that of repression.

[6] Here I adhere to a schematism which Freud himself never made his own, even at the beginning.

[7] 'You can clearly see what I'm like, I always function like this, whatever the circumstances . . . ' The response from the analyst to this obsessional discourse (the Rat Man's), is simply: 'for example?'. As Freud recalls, after Hegel: 'the example is the thing itself'.

[8] What is gained by replacing what is pre-established by instinct, with what is pre-established by 'structure', if not an increased rigidity?

[9] [*Translator's Note*: See Laplanche & Pontalis 1988: 130-143.]

[10] Cf. my course on 'Moral Anxiety' in Laplanche 1980a: third part.

[11] There are two passages where the term 'unknown' returns in *The Ego and the Id*, which Rosolato used in describing what he termed 'the unknown relation'.

[12] [*Translator's Note*: Texts by Groddeck available in English, are Groddeck 1949 (articles), 1950, 1951 (lectures and articles), 1977a (articles and correspondence with Freud). For an introduction to Groddeck's work, see Lore Schacht's introduction to Groddeck 1977a.]

[13] 'Soul' does not take a 'spiritualist' sense in Freud's work, and the adjective needed to translate *seelisch* would be 'animistic', unless we were to bring back into usage the old Cartesian term 'animal'.

[14] Groddeck is the true precursor of contemporary developments on the theme of 'a child is being killed'. [*Translator's Note*: Laplanche is referring here to an essay by Serge Leclaire, entitled 'On tue un enfant'. See Leclaire 1998. Its title plays on the French translation of Freud's essay 'A Child is Being Beaten' (1919).]

[15] See also, in Groddeck 1950, the story of a broken arm, where Groddeck finds sexual, phallic symbolism in the very circumstances of the accident.

[16] Cf. Laplanche 1980c: 'Pour situer la sublimation'.

[17] For the basics on the question of affect, I would refer you to André Green's essential work—*Le discours vivant* (1973).

[18] Cf. The correspondence between Georg Groddeck and Sigmund Freud, in Groddeck 1977a: 31-107.

[19] I am using this term 'projection' in a sense which is more geometrical than psychoanalytic.

[20] [*Translator's Note*: Strachey's translation has been modified here, in accordance with Laplanche's argument. Freud's '*Trieb*' has been translated as 'drive'. It should be noted that the phrase 'instinctual satisfaction' is derived from the same term.]

[21] Cf., among others, my course on sublimation in Laplanche 1980c.

[22] The third account of the death drive is the one we propose ourselves, through a methodical and structural interpretation of Freudianism . . .

[23] Certainly in a more profound way than the rather formalistic article by Paula Heimann in the same collection (Heimann 1952).

[24] See Laplanche & Pontalis 1988: 187-189.

[25] When it is said that we have no idea of death, or that there is no idea of death in the unconscious, it could just as easily be shown that there is no idea of birth. In other words, birth in the true sense of the word—not just as a physical process, but as the entry into being—is as unthinkable as death.

Part Three—The Unconscious: a Psychoanalytic Study

[1] [This essay was originally delivered at a colloquium on the unconscious at Bonneval (Colloque de Bonneval 1966). Chapters I, II, and IV were written by J. Laplanche; chapters III and V by S. Leclaire. The present translation is by Patrick Coleman, and first appeared in *Yale French Studies*, vol. 48 (1972). Our thanks are due to *Yale French Studies*, for permission to reprint the article. The system of references has been amended, so that the current edition of this article makes use of translations of Freud and Lacan which are more familiar and more easily available to readers of English. It should be noted, however, that the translator's choice of English terms for certain Freudian concepts—for instance: 'cathexis', 'after-expulsion' and 'instinct'—differs from those adopted in the preceding sections of this book. For clarification see footnote 8 on Part One, and footnote 20 on Part Two, above.—Ed.]

[2] [Throughout this section, references to and quotations from Politzer are according to the French edition, Politzer 1968, with translations by Patrick Coleman.—Ed.]

3 Let us recall his argument: 'In short, we are faced with two hypotheses. One, the Freudian hypothesis, considers the dream as a veritable transposition of an original text that the dream distorts; for the other, on the contrary, the dream is the result of the operation of an individual dialectic. The essential difference between these two conceptions arises from the fact that in the first, the dream is something which is derivative, and that in the second, it is the primary phenomenon and is self-sufficient. In the latter case, the dream does not have, strictly speaking, two contents: a latent and a manifest one. It can only have a manifest content, in fact, if we try to interpret it in terms of conventional dialectics. Now it is just these dialectics that are powerless in the case of dreams: the dream is not their product since it can be explained only by a personal dialectic. The dream, therefore, has only one content, the one Freud calls the latent content. But the dream has this content immediately, and not *after being disguised*'.

Although Politzer pretends to answer in this way the theory of the 'dynamic' unconscious, we can affirm that it is on this point that the Freudian theory remains 'irrefutable' (Freud 1923a: 14): when it founds the autonomous existence of the unconscious (autonomous—that is, not purely correlative to conscious expression) on the phenomenon of repression, resistance, and, in the last analysis, on the notion of conflict, the dialectic which Politzer invokes here, but in vain, since he has eliminated the distinction of levels that would allow it to function.

4 Doubtless the notion of over-determination will be invoked to justify these multiple decodings; but to our mind, it is an abuse of language to apply homogeneously to the whole of a psychological text a phenomenon that takes on all its meaning at the level of individual elements of speech, in a special way for each of these elements, determinable in the very structure of the element in question. Limited in its extension, as we see, in relation to the whole of the psychological text ('its surface'), over-determination is no less limited 'in depth'. It is as 'double signification' that it is introduced by Freud: 'a hysterical symptom develops only where the fulfilments of two opposing wishes, arising each from a different psychical system, are able to converge in a single expression' (Freud 1900: 569). Nothing here authorises the confused manner in which this central notion of Freudianism is recurred to in order to declare all possible interpretations compatible without showing how they are articulated among themselves. It would seem that Freud, at least, did not discover such an 'interminability' of the unconscious in his own experience. We would never have done with denouncing the (easily determined) error and the (infinite) *pathos* which prevail on the subject of 'interminable' analysis. One would have to have limited oneself to the title of Freud's article on the question not to understand that, according to him, analysis is 'interminable' only because it runs up against a very well-determined obstacle: the castration complex.

5 According to the term put forth by J. Lacan.

6 Of course, Freud, impelled by apologetic necessity, brings up the unquestionable existence of the preconscious (memories, etc.) as an argument for defending the possibility of an unconscious mind in general. For a moment in this text, the 'descriptive' distinction (Cs/Pcs, Ucs)—and not the 'topographic' one (Cs, Pcs/Ucs)—seems to be in the forefront. In fact, the essential systemic distinction is quickly rediscovered since, at the end of the section (in the passage beginning 'The stubborn denial . . . ' [Freud 1915a: 168]), Freud indicates that the question of the unconscious is in essence posed only by the facts discovered by psychoanalysis, and that outside the latter one need only 'neglect certain enigmas of the psychology of consciousness to spare oneself the hypothesis of unconscious psychical activity'.

7 [With the insistence that the Freudian experience of 'memory' has less to do with the recollection of an 'event' than with the repetition of a structure has come the use of the verb *se remémorer* to designate the analytic phenomenon.—Ed.]

8 The example that Sartre, in his refutation of the Freudian unconscious takes over from Stekel: the frigid woman who would 'in reality' have pleasure, but does not want to recognise it, plays at this boundary and not at that of the Ucs. This is the process of misperception

or disguising of an affect, suppression (*Unterdrückung*), which psychoanalysis distinguishes from repression (*Verdrängung*).

9 What fate does Freud assign to the theory of double inscription in the rest of the text? We will see below that the introduction of the economic point of view allows his apparently to eliminate the 'topographical' hypothesis in favour of the 'functional' one. In point of fact, the topographical hypothesis of 'double inscription' reappears again later (Freud 1915a: 188-9) when Freud indicates that two different inscriptions for preconscious and unconscious memories probably have to be admitted. Freud indicates here that what he rejected earlier (Freud 1915a: 180) was in fact only the double inscription 'for the relation between conscious and unconscious representations'. But if we refer to the preceding passage, we see that it is indeed regarding the relation between the preconscious and unconscious systems that the 'topographical' hypothesis was abandoned. What does this mean? Freud seems to be more than supplementing what he said before; this is a real correction, which should end up, in his opinion, 'putting an end to our oscillations in regard to the naming of the higher system—which we have spoken of indifferently, sometimes as the *Pcs.* and sometimes as the *Cs.*' (Freud 1915a: 189). Does this solution not point in the following direction: the passage from the Ucs to the Pcs would happen necessarily through the Cs, and this without a new inscription, but the subsequent passage to the preconscious would imply a new inscription, which could be diagrammed as follows:

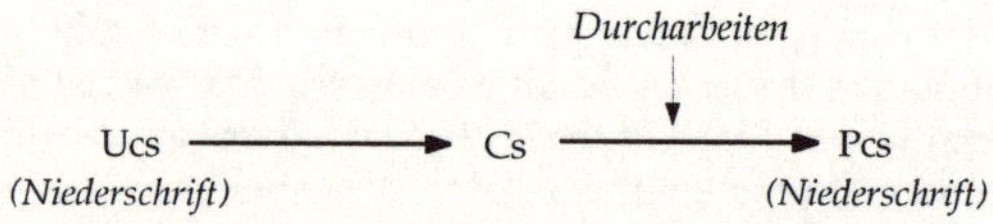

10 [The following dream analysis is pursued further in Leclaire 1968.—Ed.]

11 [Because the analysis is dependent on it, we have translated *pulsion de mort (Todestrieb)* as 'death-drive'. See Laplanche's more recent work—*Life and Death in Psychoanalysis* (1976)—in which much importance is attached to respecting the latent diacritical distinction in Freud's texts between instinct (*Instinkt*) and drive (*Trieb*).—Ed.]

12 [See Laplanche 1976 for his later thinking on the latent structure of Freud's theory of drives. It will result in a divergence from the present formulation: the 'death-drives' will 'repeat' the 'sex-drives', and Eros—the bound and binding sexuality of the later theory—will reveal its complicity with what had earlier been described as narcissism (and, consequently, the 'ego drives').—Ed.]

13 As another memory of noisy panic caused by no real injury bears witness.

14 Let us emphasise here that the death-drive, thus conceived, is to be clearly distinguished from the negative libidinal manifestations usually grouped under the term aggressiveness.

15 Let us mention in passing that, starting from these 'representations', Freud provides a very simple framework for the (so confusedly debated) question of affect: '[ideational representatives] are cathexes—basically of memory-traces—whilst affects and emotions correspond to processes of discharge, the final manifestations of which are perceived as feelings' (Freud 1915a: 178).

16 The 'signifier' is the literal, formal element which constitutes the sign.

17 *La Psychanalyse*, Vol. 3, 67-68

18 In a paranoid schizophrenic we have treated, language seemed totally subjected to pairs of opposite terms, of which the most striking was the pair left-right: 'You say the right sleeve and it's the left sleeve . . . '; 'When we talk and you say my right I will think my left, when you say my left I will think my right . . . ' etc. The analyst's naïveté is to direct himself to the signified, to the 'content' (a felicitous naïveté, by the way, and one that has produced many discoveries). But here one would quickly discover that the whole of the meanings could not

be classified on either side of the alternative. There was indeed a 'left alliance', but also, alas! a 'right alliance'. 'Right' was not only 'the maladjusted', but also 'getting along well with my family', etc. A banal example of intellectual ambivalence founded on an affective one? Of course; but even more radically, we find here a 'linguistic ambivalence' which we try to outline in our fiction of a 'reduced-state language'.

19 [The *point de capiton* is literally one of the attachments that hold upholstery down.—Ed.]

20 What is the determining element, the *primum movens* in the experience of conditioning? The signifier or the signified? This reminds us of a good professor's quip that in Pavlov's experiment, a dog had taught his master to play the trumpet each time he, the dog, salivated. If we are not granted *a priori* the human semiological system, the question remains insoluble.

21 J. Lacan, *Séminaire* of 22-1-58, p. 33 (mimeographed copy of the S.F.P. Archives)currently (1999) available in French as *Séminaire V Les formations de l'inconscient.*

22 We use here one of the formulas given by J. Lacan, in his article on psychosis (Lacan 1977b).

23 J. Lacan, *La Psychanalyse*, vol. V, p.12.

24 We thus use the possibility of transformation written in the following general way:

$$\frac{A}{B} \times \frac{C}{D} = \frac{\frac{A}{D}}{\frac{B}{C}}$$

25 Cf. in this regard 'A Metapsychological Supplement to the Theory of Dreams' (Freud 1917b: 227-8), where the subjection of the dream to the primary process is represented as the consequence of this regression to the level of representations of things.

26 It is that this precise point that our research diverges. J. Laplanche wants to maintain the distinction between two types of metaphorisation, which he relates to the two stages of repression according to Freud. S. Leclaire is concerned with the prior logical moment, that is, the first level of symbolisation, whose constitution is necessary so that metaphor may 'function'. This divergence of interest explains why for J. Laplanche, what is 'primal' is the whole of the two levels of symbolisation, of which the second would be primal repression (or metaphor), while for S. Leclaire what is 'primal' is the very constitution of the first level of symbolisation (myth of the meeting of the biological and the signifier, the problem of the 'fixation' of the death-drive). (J.L. and S.L.).

27 *Evolution Psychiatrique*, 1959, III, 383.

Bibliography

Anzieu, D. (1986) *Freud's Self-Analysis and the Discovery of Psychoanalysis*, trans. P. Graham, London: Hogarth Press and the Institute of Psychoanalysis.

Colloque de Bonneval (1966) *L'inconscient*, Paris: Desclée de Brouwer.

Dayan, M. (1977) 'Madame K. interpréta', *Topique* 19: 17-116.

Fontanier, P. (1977) *Les figures du discours*, Paris: Flammarion.

Foucault, M. (1970) *The Order of Things*, London: Tavistock.

Freud, S. (1894) 'The Neuro-Psychoses of Defence', S.E. III: 41-68.

Freud, S. (1895) *Studies in Hysteria*, S.E. III

Freud, S. (1899) 'Screen Memories', S.E. III: 301-322.

Freud, S. (1900) *The Interpretation of Dreams*, S.E. IV-V.

Freud, S. (1901) *The Psychopathology of Everyday Life*, S.E. VI.

Freud, S. (1905) *Three Essays on the Theory of Sexuality*, S.E. VII

Freud, S. (1909) *Analysis of a Phobia in a Five-Year-Old Boy* ('Little Hans'), S.E. X: 1-149.

Freud, S. (1911) 'Formulations on the Two Principles of Mental Functioning', S.E. XII: 213-226.

Freud, S. (1913a) 'The Claims of Psycho-Analysis to Scientific Interest', S.E. XIII: 165-191.

Freud, S. (1913b) 'The Theme of the Three Caskets', S.E. XII: 289-301.

Freud, S. (1914) 'On Narcissism: An Introduction', S.E. XIV: 67-102.

Freud, S. (1915a) 'The Unconscious', S.E. XIV: 159-215.

Freud, S. (1915b) 'Instincts and their Vicissitudes', S.E. XIV: 109-140.

Freud, S. (1915c) 'Repression', S.E. XIV: 141-158.

Freud, S. (1917a) 'Mourning and Melancholia', S.E. XIV: 237-258.

Freud, S. (1917b) 'A Metapsychological Supplement to the Theory of Dreams', S.E. XIV: 217-235.

Freud, S. (1919) 'A Child is Being Beaten', S.E. XVII: 175-204.

Freud, S. (1920) *Beyond the Pleasure Principle*, S.E. XVIII: 1-64.

Freud, S. (1923a) *The Ego and the Id*, S.E. XIX: 1-66.

Freud, S. (1923b) 'Remarks on the Theory and Practice of Dream-Interpretation', S.E. XIX: 107-121.

Freud, S. (1925) 'Negation' S.E. XIX

Freud, S. (1926) *Inhibitions, Symptoms and Anxiety*, S.E. XX: 75-175.

Freud, S. (1932) 'The Acquisition and Control of Fire', S.E. XXII: 183-193.

Freud, S. (1933) *New Introductory Lectures on Psychoanalysis*, S.E. XXII: 1-182.

Freud, S. (1937a) 'Constructions in Analysis', S.E. XXIII: 255-269.
Freud, S. (1937b) 'Analysis Terminable and Interminable', S.E. XXIII: 209-253.
Freud, S. (1940) *An Outline of Psychoanalysis*, S.E. XXIII: 139-207.
Freud, S. (1950) 'Project for a Scientific Psychology', S.E. I: 281-397.
Green, A. (1973) *Le discours vivant*, Paris: PUF.
Groddeck, G. (1949) *Exploring the Unconscious*, trans. V. Collins, London: Vision Press.
Groddeck, G. (1950) *The Book of the It*, trans. V. Collins, London: Vision Press.
Groddeck, G. (1951) *The Unknown Self*, trans. V. Collins, London: Vision Press.
Groddeck, G. (1969) *La maladie, l'art et le symbole*, Paris: Gallimard.
Groddeck, G. (1973a) *Le livre du ça*, Paris: Gallimard.
Groddeck, G. (1973b) 'Le double sexe de l'être humain', *Nouvelle Revue de Psychanalyse* 7, Spring: 193-198.
Groddeck, G. (1977a) *The Meaning of Illness*, trans. G. Mander, London: Hogarth Press.
Groddeck, G. (1977b) *Ça et moi*, Paris: Gallimard.
Hartmann, H. (1958) *Ego Psychology and the Problem of Adaptation*, trans. D. Rapaport, New York: International Universities Press.
Heimann, P. (1952) 'Notes on the Theory of the Life and Death Instincts', in Klein et al. 1952.
Hjelmslev, J. (1966) *Le Langage*, Paris: Editions de Minuit.
Jakobson, R. (1963) *Essais de linguistique générale*, Paris: Editions de Minuit.
Jones, E. (1957) *Sigmund Freud: Life and Work*, vol. III, London: Hogarth Press.
Klein, M. (1932) *The Psychoanalysis of Children*, London: Hogarth Press.
Klein, M. (1952a)[1948] 'On the Theory of Anxiety and Guilt', in Klein et al. 1952.
Klein, M. (1952b)[1952] 'On Observing the Behaviour of Young Infants', in Klein et al. 1952.
Klein, M. (1975)[1935] 'A Contribution to the Psychogenesis of Manic Depressive States', in *Love, Guilt and Reparation*, London: Virago Press.
Klein, M. *et al.* (1952) *Developments in Psychoanalysis*, London: Hogarth Press.

Lacan, J. (1977a) 'The agency of the letter in the unconscious or reason since Freud', in *Écrits: A Selection*, trans. A.Sheridan, London: Tavistock.

Lacan, J. (1977b) 'On a question preliminary to any possible treatment of psychosis', in *Écrits: A Selection*, trans. A.Sheridan, London: Tavistock.

Laplanche, J. (1976) *Life and Death in Psychoanalysis*, trans. J. Mehlman, Baltimore: Johns Hopkins.

Laplanche, J. (1980a) *Problématiques I: L'angoisse (1970-3)*, Paris: PUF.

Laplanche, J. (1980b) *Problématiques II: Castration-symbolisations (1973-5)*, Paris: PUF.

Laplanche, J. (1980c) *Problématiques III: La sublimation (1975-7)*, Paris: PUF.

Laplanche, J. (1993) *Le fourvoiement biologisant de la sexualité chez Freud*, Paris: Synthélabo.

Laplanche, J. (1999) *Essays on Otherness*, ed. J. Fletcher, London: Routledge.

Laplanche, J., & Pontalis, J.-B. (1988) *The Language of Psychoanalysis*, trans. D. Nicholson-Smith, London: Karnac Books and the Institute of Psychoanalysis.

Laplanche, J., & Leclaire, S. (1972) 'The unconscious: a psychoanalytic study', *Yale French Studies* 48: 118-178.

Leclaire, S. (1968) *Psychanalyser*, Paris: Seuil.

Leclaire, S. (1998) *A Child is Being Killed: On Primary Narcissism and the Death Drive*, trans. M.-C. Hayes, Stanford: Stanford University Press.

Lyotard, J.F. (1971) *Discours, figure*, Paris: Klincksiek.

Martinet, A. (1960) *Elements de linguistique générale*, Paris: A. Colin.

Masson, J. (1985) *The Complete Letters of Sigmund Freud to Wilhelm Fliess 1887-1904*, Cambridge MA: Belknap Press of Harvard University.

Nacht, S. (1966) *De la pratique à la théorie analytique*, Paris: PUF.

Nacht, S. (1971a) *Le masochisme*, Paris: Payot.

Nacht, S. (1971b) 'Indications et contre-indications de la psychanalyse ("analysabilité")', in *Guérir avec Freud*, Paris: Payot.

Pasche, F., & Renard, M. (1956) 'Realité de l'objet et point de vue économique', *Revue Français de Psychanalyse* XX, 4: 517-524.

Politzer, G. (1968) *Critique des fondements de la psychologie*, Paris: Presses Universitaires de France

Politzer, G. (1994) *A Critique of the Foundations of Psychology*, Pittsburgh: Duquesne University.

Ricoeur, P. (1970) *Freud and Philosophy,: An Essay on Interpretation*, New Haven: Yale University Press.

Rosolato, G. (1969) *Essais sur le symbolique*, Paris: Gallimard.

Rosolato, G. (1978) *La relation d'inconnu*, Paris: Gallimard.

Roustang, F. (1982) *Dire Mastery: Discipleship from Freud to Lacan*, trans. N. Lukacher, Baltimore: Johns Hopkins University Press.

Schneider, M. (1977) 'Metaphores geologiques et figurations du psychisme', in *Études philosophiqes* 1.

Schur, M. (1976) *Freud: Living and Dying*, New York: International Universities Press.

Swain, G. (1978) *Le sujet de la folie*, Paris: Privat.

Todorov, T. (1982) *Theories of the Symbol*, trans. C. Porter, New York: Cornell University Press.

Winnicott, D. (1989) 'Fear of Breakdown', in *Psycho-Analytic Explorations*, ed. C. Winnicott, R. Shepherd & M. Davis, London: Karnac.

Index